1980

ri and Paul begin a conversation about ow ann arbor could se a traditional ewish deli like the nes they grew up vith in detroit (Paul) nd chicago (ari).

november 1981

Paul notices that the building on the corner of kingsley and detroit is available. he calls ari to see if he's ready to ~~~ deli that th~~

march 15, 1982

zingerman's opens its doors for the first time. ari and Paul are behind the counter making ~~~dwiches and cutting ~~d and cheeses

1986

the 700-square-foot addition to the original zingerman's building is completed. the pie-shaped wedge houses the sandwich line and provides expanded room for dry goods.

1988

zingerman's magic brownies are baked for the first time. the recipe was developed courtesy of ms. connie prigg, a zingerman's staff member at the time who now lives in baltimore.

zingerman's begins a food rescue program to feed the hungry in our community. food gatherers collects nutritious food from shops, restaurants & hotels and quickly delivers it to the people in need in our community.

one of the country's top ten places to buy "...a genuine jewish nosh." "usa today"

1996

zingerman's catering, famous for extraordinary deli trays and for bringing "the zingerman's experience" beyond the deli's doors and into southeast michigan, is launched.

1997

the new bread bag from zingerman's bakehouse earns national design recognition from "Print" magazine. zing artists become "Print" favorites, receiving similar recognition the next three years in a row for four other zingerman's design projects.

1998

food gatherers delivers over 2,000,000 pounds of food to help feed those in need in washtenaw county. after three years of outstanding effort, jude walton and maurice (mo) frechette make the jump to full-fledged managing Partners of zingerman's mail order.

D1534913

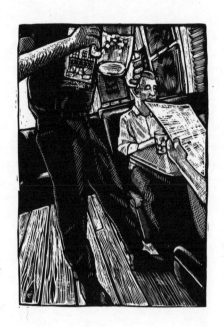

Zingerman's®

Guide to Good Leading, Part 2

A Lapsed Anarchist's Approach to

BEING A BETTER
LEADER

Ari Weinzweig

Zingerman's
PRESS
Ann Arbor
2012

Published in the United States of America by Zingerman's Press
Manufactured in Michigan, United States of America

First Edition, second printing

2016   2015   2014   2013   4 3 2

Cover illustration: Ryan Stiner
Cover design: Nicole Robichaud
Interior illustrations: Ian Nagy and Ryan Stiner
Text design: Raul Peña
Text font: Adobe Caslon Pro

ISBN: 978–0-964-89569-0

www.zingermanspress.com

Printed, bound, and warehoused locally in southeastern Michigan.

Printed on FSC certified paper with a recycled content of 100 percent post-consumer waste.

A FEW FRIENDLY WORDS OF WARNING

It's about a year ago now that we were working through the final page proofs of Part 1 *of this series. We were doing all the sorts of stuff that one does in the final days before a book goes to print—looking for those inevitable, impossible-to-see typos that have escaped the eyes of the eight different, detail-oriented proofers; watching for repetition; making tiny adjustments to layout; moving a small bit of a footnote from one page to another. I like to show the proofs to smart people, figuring they might spot some issue that everyone else has missed. As always, folks found missing commas, unattached asterisks, and a few less-than-perfectly-conveyed concepts. In the process, several readers whom I know and respect started to ask questions about issues that . . . well, they were things that I'd already been worrying about, at times even slightly obsessed over, but eventually decided to go with my gut and leave in the book anyway.*

Still, hearing aloud all the questions that had already been argued out and answered at length in my own mind sent me back, again, to a small cycle of worrying and wondering. Anyone who's sent anything out to print, or even served dinner to a dozen highly esteemed guests, likely knows that feeling—"Should I, seriously, let all this stuff (imperfect as it is) go out into the world? Or would it be better to wait, keep working at it, and make it just another small bit better?" The voice of safety in my head almost certainly says to pull back. But . . . of course, you can't wait forever; there are flaws and faults in everything, and at some point, I've learned, you need to swallow hard, take a deep breath, exhale slowly, and take the plunge. Which is why, about a week before we went to print with Part 1, *I decided to take the same advice I give everyone else struggling with similar self-doubt—give it your best shot and be up front with people, acknowledge their questions, give honest answers, and then get on with it. After all, as early 20th-century Romanian anarchist Eugen Relgis wrote, "There is no such thing as perfection—there is only a tendency toward perfection."*

A few days before we went to print, I decided to put down on paper exactly what it was I was worrying about, stick it in the front of the book as a friendly warning to readers, take a deep breath, and let the book go out into the world. I'm glad I overcame my concerns. Part 1 *has drawn a lot of really positive praise, for which I'm deeply appreciative. And, while I hardly think that the 600 or so words of warning I snuck into the front of the book at the last minute were the key to its success, they certainly didn't hurt. Everything we do at Zingerman's, and really everything that I've written about in this book, is about being real, about laying out* our beliefs, thoughts, concerns, and considerations so that employees, customers, and the community can make up their minds about how they want to work with what we have to offer.

The warning in Part 1 worked well, so, as we take off with Part 2, here are a few more words of caution to convey before we formally begin the actual book. For openers, I'll tell you up front that the ideas and approaches that follow reflect what's in my mind right now, somewhere in the summer of 2011. At the moment, sales are good, the Deli renovation is well underway, the sun is shining, and Part 1 is selling well. By the time you actually read this, it's safe to say that, maybe five minutes after I make the decision to let this book go to the printer, I'll think of some other angle or identify a new nugget of an idea that I'd so far failed to understand. Apologies in advance if I should have some slight change of heart, direction, or emphasis when you and I meet at some point down the intellectual line.

Second, I ask for your patience about repetition, and at the same time, the lack thereof. As Relgis said, striking that perfect balance is, I've realized, pretty much impossible. Inevitably this book, as the second in a series (with more parts still to come), will err in both directions, probably simultaneously and in the same paragraph. Many of you who already know our work will find the background explanations unnecessary and repetitive. At almost exactly the same instant, somewhere else in the world, another reader who's new to what we do will be wondering why I failed to give more in-depth historical detail. C'est la vie. As with Part 1, the point is to allow you to read and roam freely—you can skip the intro and start with the epilogue, pop back to the preface, then, if you like, shoot straight to Secret 26 (The Entrepreneurial Approach to Management). Wherever you want to begin reading, the book should still all, pretty much, make sense.

Should I have shorted you some essential piece of background information . . . well, the "answers" are all easily available. A lot of info, of course, can be found in Part 1, A Lapsed Anarchist's Approach to Building a Great Business, but if you're stuck in the airport in San Antonio and can't wait to learn more about the "Twelve Natural Laws of Business" or the background on the way we do visioning, just email me at ari@zingermans.com, and I'll do my best to explain as quickly as I can.

Last, please understand that what follows here is only my own personal sense of what we're about here at Zingerman's. While most everyone who works here will have heard most or all of these approaches in one form or another, these essays have not been formally vetted or fretted about by every person in the organization. To the contrary, being the free-thinking independent individuals that they are, the reality is that nearly everyone here will have his or her own, slightly different, but *still strongly held, take on these subjects. Which is actually the point of our entire approach—everyone here has his or her own creative way to work.*

Because I've referenced him so regularly in the book, it seems fitting to quote Robert Greenleaf, from his work, Servant Leadership, *on the subject. "As I look through my particular window on the world, I realize that I do not see all. Rather, I see only what the filter of my biases and attitudes of the moment permits me to see. Therefore, if in the course of this essay, I make a declaration without appending 'it seems to me,' please assume such a qualification on everything I say."*

I should say that I've had a few friends who've said that what we do here at Zingerman's seems almost too good to be true. I assure you that we are both real and also really far from perfect. We're certainly working hard but we never get all this stuff exactly right either. And, strange as we may seem, we really do exist. To quote from one of my favorite books, Why the Bee is Busy, and Other Rumanian Fairy Tales *by Idella Purnell and John Weatherwax, "Once upon a time what happened did happen, and if it had not happened, you would not be hearing this story."*

Thanks, in advance, for reading and reflecting. I look forward to sharing thoughts together somewhere down the line.

the view from the back table next door at the deli

CONTENTS

Good Leadership, Tango Dancing, Hog Farming, and the Brain Weight of Wisconsin Anarchists

I guess that's quite a heading. It's actually topped, though, by a line from C. L. James, a quote I'm confident hardly anyone around these parts will have heard and, I'm pretty sure, has never been seen in a modern-day business book. In fact, this could mark its debut in the world of entrepreneurial writing. Obscurity aside, this little line from the 19th-century Wisconsin anarchist author still makes me smile every time I read it: "The real strength of Anarchism," James asserted, "is . . . not in count of heads, but weight of brains." The quote comes from his book *Origin of Anarchism*, which I'm *very* sure will not be showing up on Amazon's top 200 list this year. Regardless of your views on the world, you've gotta grin at least a little—life is short, and I'm all about finding the fun as often as I can. Although it's not the main theme of this book, and I've yet to write an essay about it, I'm pretty sure that humor is the single most underutilized management tool out there. Just because we're in leadership doesn't mean we can't laugh a lot. I'm confident we can be successful in business without being excessively serious all the time. Besides which, if you were looking for a mainstream approach to leadership you most likely wouldn't be holding this book in your hands in the first place, would you?

Laughing is also what I do every time I watch *Ride That Pig to Glory*, the short film by cinematographer Joe York on sustainable hog farmer Emile DeFelice. Joe makes truly remarkable, utterly unique, food-oriented documentary films for Southern Foodways Alliance—a great nonprofit that preserves, protects, and keeps alive old-time Southern foods and the traditions that surround them. Emile raises heirloom hogs in a sustainable way at Caw Caw Creek Farm down in the central part of South Carolina. You can see the film—and about two dozen of Joe's other films—at southernfoodways.org. It's subtitled "A meditation on pastured pigs and tango dancing," which reminds me to tell you that Joe manages to work in a good bit of footage of Emile and his girlfriend, Eme, doing a terrific tango in their local dance studio. He interviews Emile at length, gathering insights into his views on life, his way of working, and, of course, plenty of shots of the prizewinning Caw Caw Creek pigs. Like C. L. James, he's surely not the wealthiest man in his state, but I'm fairly certain that he's having far more fun than your average 21st-century American farmer. He's definitely smart, he's creative, and he's most certainly very successful on his own terms.

In all of those senses, I'd say that Emile's approach is a good model for the kind of sustainable, slightly strange, but exceptionally successful in its own weird way business that I'd like us to emulate here at Zingerman's. By mainstream standards, the way Emile operates would likely be considered close to crazy; he probably breaks most every rule of modern, mass-market agriculture. In fact, more than one mainstream farmer I've met in the area has smiled, rolled his eyes a bit, and actually made a comment to that effect. Unfortunately for those who choose to critique his approach, the quality of Emile's work is generally acknowledged to be exceptional. Caw Caw Creek pork tastes great, his hogs are happy, and so, best I can tell, is Emile. As you can see in the film, his pigs roam freely and productively in the pasture. Emile's energy does much the same, running 'round the intellectual fields of the universe to arrive at his unique, highly effective approach to agriculture. The region's top chefs line up to order his prizewinning pork. Many have called Emile an inspiration. C. L. James, I'm quite certain, would have asked him to join the anarchist cause—Caw Caw Creek won't win if you score only on standard metrics like herd size or annual sales, but if you're going by James's "weight of brains," wit, worldview, and pork quality, Emile probably comes out ahead on all counts.

Since I've opened up here by referencing an obscure Eau Claire, Wisconsin anarchist and a tango-dancing hog farmer from central South Carolina, I should probably circle back to modern-day business reality. Let me be clear here, before I drift too far from my field, 19th-century anarchists and eccentric hog farmers aside: *What follows is all about business.* And, I should add, is also all about life, because everything in this book will, I'm pretty confident, positively impact what you do outside of work as well as in it. What follows is all exceedingly practical and eminently doable; we've been using the "secrets" here at Zingerman's with a high degree of success for nearly thirty years now. While our approaches do draw on a lot of less-than-well-known bits of knowledge and some slightly obscure authors, they're all about applicable, down-to-earth, hands-on, practical, learnable, usable techniques you can put to work in any industry. While they may not be mainstream, we use them with great success on the floor, with real food, real finance, real problems, and real people. They aren't perfect, but they are most definitely effective. I (and a lot of others) would say they're a very good way to have some fun while you're doing "serious" working, too.

Anyway, as I was watching and loving Joe's film, one line in particular really got me laughing so much that I still smile about it now, the way I do about C. L. James's assessment of anarchist brain activity. "If I ever have a question about what I'm supposed to be doing here," Emile explains, "all I have to do is look at the agriculture industry, and then do the opposite." When I heard him say it—with a pretty straight face—I really did laugh out loud. I think it's hilarious. Like all good humor, though, there's actually a lot of truth beneath the surface-level silliness. And, in many ways, the insight is equally true for us here at Zingerman's. Although our respective realities aren't anywhere near as reactive as Emile makes them sound, his tongue-in-cheek contention isn't all that far off base. Just being different isn't really what drives us to do what we do, but Emile's outlook is right on—the way we work here is definitely a path that's a lot less traveled than the one that most everyone else around us is heading down.

Another Way to Work

I don't know if the approaches in the *Zingerman's Guide to Good Leading* series are the full-on opposite of what they teach in business school, or at IBM, GM, or Walmart, but what I do know is that they're pretty different from what most of the folks at that end of the work world are doing. I've never lived in the world of big business, but I've heard from enough others who have to know that the visioning, values, and appreciative organizational stuff I wrote about in *Part 1* are hardly the way work is done in most places. One of the best comments I got on the first book was when a young woman, who was having dinner at the Roadhouse, bought a copy of it for her mother's birthday. As I was inscribing it, I had the chance to read what she'd already written inside the cover: "Mom, you'll love this. It's the anti-business business book." I wish I'd asked her name so I could give her full credit for the quote.

The idea of doing the opposite of what everyone else already does is also applicable to almost every aspect of the actual book as well. Reflecting on Emile's insight, I realized with ever greater clarity that the actual volumes that make up the *Zingerman's Guide to Good Leading* series (like the one you've got in your hands right now) break most of the rules the experts told me apply when producing a popular business book. In spite of suggestions from book-selling specialists, the volumes in the series are all long, well over the 100-page limit supposedly dictated by the wisdom of the marketplace. "If they're too long no one will read them," I was told more than once. "No one reads any more" is another that is frequently offered—though I don't believe it. Similarly, and again contrary to the advice of those "in the know," the essays inside are far above the 4th-grade reading level I was advised to adhere to. The books in the series are also allegedly unworthy of your attention because each is constructed as a collection of essays, even though almost everyone in the industry warned me that "no one will ever buy a book like that." We also went ahead and put recipes in as well, which I don't think is generally done with business books—if you need a break from reading you can always head for the kitchen and cook. Which I suppose is my modern-day adaptation of Emma Goldman's 100-year old saying: "When things are bad, scrub floors." When I'm having a bad day, I adapt Emma's excellent exhortation and head home to my kitchen to start cooking.

In spite of the fact that we've brooked all that expert advice, the books somehow seem to be selling—*Part 1* made *Inc.* magazine's "best business books of the year" list a few months after it came out. Although in the short term our sales totals are almost certainly lower than they would have been if we'd worked within the mainstream model, we went to a second printing six months after we picked up the first run from the printer. We've mindfully chosen to stay out of the mass-market distribution system, and the books aren't (at least by our doing) available on Amazon. Instead we're selling them in savvy small bookstores, free-thinking food shops, independently minded retailers of all sorts, and to clued-in customers who come to the Deli, Roadhouse, Bakehouse, or, of course, ZingTrain. I should also say that we printed the books here in Ann Arbor instead of abroad. Contrary to the cost-consciousness that seems to dominate the industry, we decided to go with nicer, 100 percent recycled paper, which, of course, costs more and means we charge more than your average, less substantive tome. It also makes for a much nicer book—the look and feel, the heft of it in your hand, and the texture of the paper as you turn the pages are all enjoyable. Flip through and you'll find the black-and-white scratchboard drawings of Ian Nagy and Ryan Stiner—I'm pretty sure they, too, will add a bit of beauty to your otherwise business-like day.

By the way, people also advised me not to put out books as a series because it's not easy to assemble a collection that holds together, and also allows each book to stand solidly on its own. Oddly though, I realized as I was writing this preface, that same independent, yet integrated, infrastructure actually occurs *inside* each book as well. Each essay, I think, can be read by itself, without having to go in order. Or if that feels too chaotic, you can, of course, just read straight through from start to finish. As with most everything else in the book, there's really no required right way to read this. I also realized in writing this intro that the model—in which each element is able to stand independently and productively on its own, yet still come together to create an entity that's greater than the sum of the individual parts—is *(of course!)* a really marvelous metaphor for our entire organization. The Zingerman's Community of Businesses is basically mirrored in the construct of each book; the "secrets" form their own little synergistic community right here between the covers. Now that I have the metaphor in mind, I really believe that kind of crazy congruity of context between book and business is itself a pretty good model for most all of the management stuff that follows—the more that intentions, ideas, energy, and implementation are in alignment, the more effective all of it is sure to be. As Hugh MacLeod alluded in his excellent book of the same name, sometimes you have to just *ignore everybody*.

Old Anarchist Ideas and a New Approach to Business

In case you didn't read *Part 1* (which you of course aren't obligated to do), it was all about business building. It's got Secrets 1–18 behind the successful organizational food-service stagecraft that we know as Zingerman's. The book shares our history, as well as my own experiences working here and out in the world. It tells you most of what we know and have learned about visioning, mission statements, guiding principles, culture building, appreciation, and all sorts of other stuff that has helped us create the Zingerman's Community of Businesses. It also includes insights about anarchism and business, and how I one day realized that the work of late 19th- and early 20th-century anarchists like Emma Goldman, Alexander Berkman, Voltairine de Cleyre, Gustav

Landauer, and others was, almost unwittingly, woven into the fabric of the organizational philosophy we'd carefully constructed over the years. I talked about how the anarchists' approaches to free thinking, free choice, initiative taking, collaboration, creativity, caring, and going for group greatness are shockingly in synch with what progressive business people now advocate in our own era. And how, in writing the introduction to *Part 1*, I was suddenly struck by the idea that what we were doing here at Zingerman's was, in essence, what one—or really just *I*—might call "Anarcho-Capitalism." The book also contains comments from staff, ten Zingerman's recipes for use in your kitchen, some of our organizational recipes, a goodly assemblage of quotes from obscure anarchists and modern-day business writers, and two and a half dozen of Ryan and Ian's scratchboard images.

Obviously I'm not going to reproduce the first volume here, but if you happen to pick up *Part 2* before its predecessor I want you to have some idea of what "we've already discussed." Anarchistic soul that I am, I actually encourage you to get out of order—read what you want, when you want, have some fun, and adapt it all to what you do in any way you feel is right for you. More than anything, I hope the books will accomplish something akin to what Freda Diamond said of Emma Goldman: "She opened your mind and made you think about things you never thought about before." With Freda's spiritual support, I hope this series, in all its parts, will incite you to any number of exceptional insights of your own.

Getting back to the book that's in your hands, what follows is the second set—Secrets 19–29. This time it's all about ideas that you, I, and anyone else who's looking for more productive, respectful, sustainable ways to lead might want to explore in an effort to improve our leadership effectiveness. It's definitely not the *only* way, but it is *our* way and it is kind of working— we've successfully gotten through the recent years of economic insanity in pretty good shape; sales are approaching $40,000,000 a year. We've got eight Zingerman's businesses (all in Ann Arbor and each with its own unique specialty). We have well over 500 people working here year round, and we hire another three hundred or so temporarily at the holidays. Thousands of people every year either come to ZingTrain seminars in Ann Arbor or attend versions of them that we put on for clients around the country. Not all that bad for having started with just 1300 square feet, two employees, twenty-nine seats, and $22,000 in loans back in 1982. While you can certainly dismiss all of this as silly, or even stupid (and I'm sure some will), I know that what follows has, for us and others who've studied it, been truly transformative. As Emile DeFelice pointed out, it is pretty much the opposite of the way they do it in most of the mainstream work world. But it is our way, and we kind of like it.

Adapting, Not Adopting

Back when we opened the Deli in 1982, my partner, Paul Saginaw, pointed out, accurately I think, that there really isn't all that much in the food world that's truly new. It's really about new combinations and different configurations; it's what we sell, the spirit behind our service, and the way we bring it all together that makes a restaurant or retail shop special. Totally true then, and, I'd say, equally true today. We don't claim to have invented corned beef, croissants, candy bars, cream cheese, extra virgin olive oil, or macaroni and cheese; we just put them together here in our own, full-flavored, traditionalist, unique-to-Zingerman's way. To take this supposition a step further, about ten years after Paul made his point, Stas' Kazmierski, one of the managing partners at ZingTrain, taught me the phrase "Adapt, not adopt." Stas's saying is simple and pretty darned superb. The most successful people in any field, in my experience, never just take something from someone else lock, stock, and barrel. To the contrary, being mindful of their own environment, they process what they've learned, adjust it a bit, sink roots in their own particular "terroir," and then put it to work in a way that works for them in their own space. Which is surely what we recommend—before you just plant a Zingerman's "secret" in the soil of your organization, we always advise that you take Stas's suggestion and put your own special spin on our stuff before you start selling it to your partners, staff, colleagues, and customers.

Going further with Paul's comments about the food world, we've similarly taken all sorts of techniques, tips, and insights that we've gleaned from around the intellectual world, and adapted them to our own little organic garden of an organization here in Ann Arbor. We've learned *a lot* from the work of Robert Greenleaf, Peter Block, Anese Cavanaugh, Peter Koestenbaum, and all the others that I've referenced in the "secrets" that follow. Assess, adapt, add in a bit of old anarchist ideology, adjust a bit more, and, in our case, fold in a lot of good food and a slew of smart, creative people, and I guess it's not all that shocking that we were able to grow something that both Emile DeFelice and Emma Goldman would at least be intrigued to come to lunch to learn about.

Most particularly, and almost certainly most obscurely, the work that follows is annotated with references to the writings of a whole array of "old" anarchists. Although I read a lot of their work while I was getting my history degree here in Ann Arbor, it's really the *re*reading I've done in recent years that's had the most overt impact on my approach. I guess it's another example of the old Buddhist adage, "When the student is ready, the teacher will appear." I just wasn't quite ready back in my school days. But I definitely am now. More to the point, the anarchists had a lot of interesting stuff to say back in their day, most of which fell on fairly deaf ears and, more often than not, got them into a lot of trouble. They definitely were not getting the sort of speaking engagements at business conferences, business schools, or graduation ceremonies at major universities that are coming my way with ever increasing frequency. The anarchists were devilishly right on, though, and interestingly insightful. In fact, I cite them here, a century after most of them spoke or wrote their words, with the hope that this modern reframing of their beliefs will incite you to reconsider your approach to your business, leadership, and, in fact, life as a whole. It's all serious stuff, but it's also a lot more fun. As Emma Goldman said so succinctly, anarchism "is the spirit of youth against outworn traditions." I say, "You go, girl!"

Back in their day, the anarchists' ideas were seen by the mainstream business world as the ultimate evil. At best, these individuals were mostly ignored; at worst, they were arrested, exiled, or in a few extreme cases, executed. Interestingly, they foretold their own intellectual fate. To quote Gustav Landauer, in the early 1900s, "In the era of individualism, geniuses precede events. Their work often remains ineffective for an extended period, appearing to be dead. It remains alive, however, waiting for others to apply it practically." A hundred years down the road, I think we're realizing Landauer's forecast. Most of the American work world calls what we do "progressive management"; I call it our version of Anarcho-Capitalism in action.

While the themes that follow are in synch with what the anarchists advocated in their day, the framing is pretty much flipped on its head from a hundred years ago. Ideas that were once considered outrageous are now a model for outstanding business success. After a talk I gave on this subject at the University of Michigan library last year, I was standing in front of the stage with some of the folks who'd stayed after to ask questions. One of them was Travis Schuster, who did a six-week stint in our Mail Order business during the holidays and happily stayed on to become a long-term part of the ZCoB (Zingerman's Community of Businesses). True to what I know to be his inquisitive nature, Travis had swung by to hear me share thoughts on

Anarcho-Capitalism and then hung around to talk things through a bit. One woman asked me where she might learn more about Emma Goldman, Gustav Landauer, et al. I shared some sources, then reiterated what I'd said from the stage—as inspiring as all the anarchist quotes I'd read during the talk might be to me and others in the room, it was kind of wild to keep in mind that most of the men and women I was quoting were put in jail, kicked out of the country, or even killed for what they were saying. When I paused after making my point, Travis laughed. "Yeah," he added, "and when I do it, *I* get a raise."

Point taken. There's something to be said for going, as Emile DeFelice does, the other way. Our road may be less traveled but, I think, it's a lot more fun and a lot more effective at that. So here's to good tango, weighty brains, good business building, good learning, a good bit of laughing, and ever better leadership to come.

driving up for coffee at the roadshow,
the 1952 spartan aircraft trailer alongside the roadhouse

In Pursuit of the Dangerously Possible

As I sit, poised to write this foreword, I glance at the calendar on my computer: June 27, 2011. It is my Great-Aunt Emma Goldman's birthday, and I am reminded of the legacy and lessons of all who have gone before me. If she were still alive, she would be 142. I'm sorry that she's not here to hold this book in her hands and to read, reflect, and I'm sure creatively challenge the challenging and creative ideas inside it.

My father followed a very different path from my great aunt. Emma, the anarchist, was often in jail and almost always pushing the envelope of what mainstream society could handle. While she was at the height of her ability to wreak havoc, my father was climbing the ladder of American success to become the CEO of a major corporation. He wanted me, his youngest daughter, to get married at eighteen, give him three and a half grandsons, and then take care of him in his old age. Emma, on the other hand, believed in the independence of women, their right to earn their own living, to live for themselves, and to love whom they pleased. She believed in everyone's right to beautiful, radiant things. She was very definitely a free thinker, and she was anything but mainstream.

Were my father still alive, he would have a fit if he knew I was writing about Emma. She was the relative we just didn't talk about. Both my father and great aunt came out of a Lithuanian tradition that championed the pursuit of universal justice and free speech, so those words should not have caused my father to want to strangle her (and later muzzle me for saying similar things in my own way). But his life took form in the 1930s, a time when people were being deported for speaking or writing words like that; my Great-Aunt Emma actually had been forcibly sent out of the country in 1919 for what she said. In the 1940s, many of my father's relatives died in the concentration camp at Buchenwald, simply because of who they were. And then, in the 1950s, he and I watched Senator Joseph McCarthy on our tiny television screen aggressively investigate, humiliate, and imprison thousands of Americans for espousing ideas of individual freedom, the sort of freedom that Emma had so passionately advocated.

What you are holding in your hands is a book written by a man who is still seeking Emma's truth, yet, like my father, is also a CEO and a leader in business. Ari Weinzweig is one of a handful of modern servant leaders persevering earnestly to embody truths about leadership and business that my father would have said were possibly dangerous. Emma would probably have said they were "dangerously possible."

In my four-decade career as a consultant, I myself have worked with, and served, many senior leaders and CEOs. I call myself a "professional thinking partner." Though I studied cognitive psychology and neuroscience in graduate school, the tide of the river has pulled me to partner with leaders of large organizations as they think their way through such questions as, How can the leaders of this organization foster innovation? How can I serve these people most effectively when the board and shareholders only care about the numbers? What can the people in my organization make possible together? In my experience, most of today's leaders have been trained for a world that no longer exists. They face tomorrow's challenges with yesterday's thinking.

You might better understand why this is so, and why there was so much resistance to my Great-Aunt Emma's ideas, by trying a little experiment. I first learned it from a physicist and black-belt judoist named Moshe Feldenkrais:

- Fold your hands by interlacing the fingers as you have done habitually since you were a well-behaved young child.
- Now bring your attention to the way you are doing this. Is the right thumb in front of left or vice versa?
- Next, unfold your fingers and refold them in the opposite, non-habitual way (i.e., if right was on top of left, put left on top of right or vice versa).
- Go back and forth between the two ways while asking yourself, Which feels most comfortable? Which feels most awkward? Which feels most secure? Which one helps you be the most aware of the spaces between your fingers? Which helps your hands feel the most alive to you?

Most of us feel safer and more comfortable with what is habitual. Most of us are thus surprised to learn that it is the awkward, new, and *non-habitual* way that leads us to feel most alive. The way most of us are trained to think is that we have to do "it" all on our own. This is the idea that is comfortable to modern-day leaders. We face the world alone. In this way, the world becomes a series of unending needs that we silently tell ourselves we have no ability to meet. We yearn for the freedom to connect, yet most of us work in isolation and alone. I frequently hear high-level people in organizations say that they feel they are "at the end of their rope." To me this means that they aren't able to handle alone all of what has been asked of them. They have run out of resources. They struggle, but fail, to find answers that they don't have. But it doesn't have to be that way—in today's complex world, the true task of a leader is not to be a problem solver; it is, as Emma did, to encourage the pursuit of the dangerously possible.

The book you are holding in your hands has emerged from the space between "either" and "or." It's a different way to look at the world, drawing on ideas from my Great-Aunt Emma and others who found their own paths in the world. Emma wrote that, "The ultimate success of a truth depends not on the many, but the perseverance and earnestness of the few." This book fills that bill. It offers rarely seen ideas and practices that foster two aspects of thinking that are critical to our future growth—collaboration and innovation. In a world where leaders like my father were trained to command and control those "below" them in order to win the largest share of the market in a way that would be secure and predictable, collaboration and innovation are non-habitual, uncomfortable, and, for some, actually scary. Yet, in my opinion, they are essential to leading us to the more positive, connected, and successful places we seek.

Those days of market-share dominance, the way that my father ran his company, are numbered. In the divided—and divisive—world in which my father worked, leaders guarded what they had closely. If you had two things and I had one thing, it meant that you controlled the market. Today, though, we live in an age of *mind share,* an era where the free exchange of ideas will be the most critical currency. In this connected world, it's all about abundance. If you have an idea and I have an idea, and we both decide to share them, we each walk away wealthier than before we met; we leave better armed to interpret and implement our ideas, and to serve the needs of positive and sustainable businesses.

My experience tells me people are ready for radically different leaders who work in a way that brings out the best in everyone involved, a way that is more rewarding, caring, and collaborative and also more productive. What we were taught about leadership, even a decade ago, is now dangerously out of date. The leaders of the future focus on far more than just profits for a select few who happen to be at the top of the corporate ladder. Instead of dividing, they inspire, empower, and enable, then edit and meld the diverse intellectual assets of an organization into models of success that others aspire to emulate. They innovate from the bottom up because all of the people together are smarter than any of us are as individuals alone. We don't need isolated leadership teams—we need holistic systems that can recognize, connect, and capitalize on the intellectual diversity of an organization to develop passion and curiosity at every level.

None of that is possible if we rely solely on the old models of leadership most of us were taught. As a people, we have lost trust in leadership. Trust is one thing we are not born with. It is created, destroyed, and re-created by our actions and by how we receive one another. It is a verb, not a noun, threading us together, strand by strand, mind to mind, and yes, heart to heart.

This book is like a kaleidoscope formed by many tiny jewels. In all its facets it will push you to ask over and over again, How can I best serve the organization I am part of? Reading it, your thinking will turn, and what will be revealed is a new pattern of possibility.

I encourage you to read on because, as people said of my Great-Aunt Emma, this beautiful, radiant book will open your mind and make you think as you never have before. You will discover how some remarkable leaders serve visions and hope, along with pastrami on rye and cold, juicy, kosher dill pickles, in a small college town in southeastern Michigan.

INTRODUCTION

Leading towards a New Way to Work

A Short Bit of Zingerman's History

Although Zingerman's has grown to about $40,000,000 in annual sales, I still teach our new-staff orientation class a couple times a month. When I don't, my partner, Paul Saginaw, does. The class—called, simply, Welcome to Zingerman's—is an interactive and, I hope, instructive two hours of me getting to know the people who've chosen to come to work with us, and of them getting up to speed on our history, our vision of the future, our values, and our approaches to each of our three bottom lines (food, service, and finance). As much as we've grown over the years, both Paul and I agree that teaching that class is one of the most important things we do. We are, honestly, honored that anyone opts to come to work with us, and properly and personally welcoming them is the least we can do.

Paul and I have always operated with the outlook that we, as owners and leaders, need the people who work here far more than they need us. If no one had ever chosen to work here, and then decided to do great work once they came on board, we'd probably still be struggling to keep a small, twenty-nine-seat sandwich business going in a hard-to-find-building in a not-very-good neighborhood. But clearly a lot of good things have happened over the last thirty years, and really all of it only because a lot of smart, hard-working people have given us the chance to lead. Despite the illusions (or is it delusions?) of some people who sit at the top of corporate org charts, the reality is that no leader will accomplish anything productive without colleagues who willingly choose to go wherever their (singular *and* plural) vision says they're going. And if our new staff members are kind, caring, and intrigued enough to entrust their futures to us, we both believe we'd better take the time to meet them, hear their hopes and history, and then, in turn, share our story, our dreams, expectations, and passions with them in a productive, and very personal, way. Leaders without followers are most definitely destined to fail; they usually end up being nothing more than barely-heard-of historical footnotes.

Similarly, books without readers are also destined to fail, collecting dust on store shelves, serving as paperweights, stacked up in bargain bins, or pulped for their value as recycled paper. Given that there's about 9,000,000 times more information out there than any of us are ever going to get to in our lives, I'm honored that you've even picked this book up to begin with. What you're holding is, truly, an expression of the hard work, insight, and experience of thousands of people who've contributed to making Zingerman's what it is over the last thirty years. As I would with any new member of the Zingerman's community, I hope this is the beginning of a long, mutually rewarding relationship.

For those of you who know nothing about us, but somehow stumbled onto this book anyway, here's the very long story in a very short seven sentences. My partner, Paul, and I opened Zingerman's Delicatessen in March of 1982. We started in a small, 1300-square-foot space near the Ann Arbor Farmer's Market, with two employees, a twenty-five-sandwich menu, twenty-nine seats, and a modest selection of specialty foods. Three decades later, the Zingerman's Community of Businesses includes eight businesses and counting, each with its own unique specialty, each led by managing partners who actually own part of their business (eighteen at last count) but operate as one, collaborative, synergistic, quality-, service-, and community-conscious organization. We make sandwiches, bake bread and pastry, make cheese and gelato, sell specialty foods from all over the world, smoke (over real wood) traditional Southern barbecue, fry chicken, roast coffee, and craft handmade candy bars. After we've done all that, we turn around and ship a lot of it to food lovers all over the country. And we also have our own little training business too. Most all of what we sell and serve is full-flavored, traditionally made food, with the exception of ZingTrain, which its co-managing partner Maggie Bayless likes to describe as "full-flavored training." Phew . . . that's thirty years in under three hundred words. To state the obvious, there's a lot more to it than that, but see the extra stuff at the back of the book, our websites, or someone who knows us if you're not already up to speed on the Zingerman's story.

The End of the Old Model?

With all that organizational orientation out of the way, let me get to the real point of this publication: *what we (and other like-minded folks around the country) are doing is creating a new, more constructive, sustainable way to work.*

The more I work, learn, listen to others, write, and reflect, the more passionate I've become about it all. In my dreams at least, many people in the world are now ready to find that sort of better way to work. I *want* to believe that the economic crisis of 2008 and 2009 served as a warning, a sort of Hurricane Katrina for the country's socioeconomic existence, a naturally occurring crisis that shows us in extreme form that our system isn't working. My hope is that the crisis got people paying attention and opened their minds to a more positive, more sustainable approach to business, leadership, and organizational life in general. I'm probably overly optimistic on that front— most people fall quickly back into what they were used to as soon as the short-term crisis subsides. Change isn't easy for most folks—as Dawna Markova describes it in her book, "we become imprisoned in our own rigidities." But the change that I believe is happening is going to go forward nevertheless.

The books in the *Guide to Good Leading* series are, basically, how-to handbooks to help you make that new way to work a reality. This volume is all about learning ways to lead that bring out the best in everyone in an organization. It's about creating a workplace that is both rewarding to be part of *and* also more productive. It's about working in synch with the 12 Natural Laws of Business (see page 332 for the complete list of Natural Laws); crafting an organization that's focused on quality, care, and collaboration; building a community that benefits the greater good, a place that's more fun while still functioning effectively in the field of the free market.

To put this in context, I'll quote Winston Churchill, who was, I know, anything but an anarchist. "Now," he said as the British turned the tide of a very long war by defeating the Germans in Egypt in 1942, "this is not the end. It is not even the beginning of the end. But it is, perhaps, the end of the beginning." He was talking about World War II, not the way we work, but the point is the same. I'm not here to prophesy anything apocalyptic; the complete collapse of the work world probably isn't nigh, nor do I think the country's going to come apart in the next two weeks. I don't have any illusion that what I'm saying or what we're doing here at Zingerman's will stop the average American executive in his or her tracks and get them to see the wisdom in Emile DeFelice's efforts at doing the opposite of what the mass market is currently about. One can ignore nature's warnings (heart attacks, hurricanes, and the like), or one can take them seriously and set out to correct the course and live in more effective ways. My hope is that the latter is the course we'll choose. *I believe that a new era of business is dawning.*

The old model of work, the one I, and almost everyone else reading this, grew up with, was that work was something . . . you did. Some people were into it. Most didn't mind it. A whole lot more didn't like it at all, but tolerated it in the very understandable interest of supporting their families and making their mortgage payment. People who felt that way worked only as long as they had to. Five o'clock meant you could head home for the evening. TGIF was a free pass to see your family, go for a run, party, or sleep in for two days straight (three when there's a legal holiday and you don't have small children). People put up with it until they retired, at which point they could go off and do what they had really wanted to do all those years when they were punching the clock.

Putting passion into work in that old model was reserved only for a few isolated extremists—high-powered CEOs, sports phenoms, musical prodigies, or the like. Most people, though, weren't wired like that; they worked to get through, toeing the line for fear of being fired, taking home a check at the end of the week, then paying the bills that had arrived in the interim. Most people who worked long hours were belittled for not having work-life balance. At best, they were seen as unhappy workaholics who usually forced their addiction onto their subordinates, who, in turn, were stuck working way too much as well. Looking back over those last few sentences, I see that I wrote that whole bit in the past tense as if it were history. But I realize in rereading it that, of course, what I've described is actually the way most people still relate to what they do every day for a living. I'm just not one of them.

I happen to like my work. A lot! And I happen to believe that work— when it's done well—can be really rewarding. In fact, I've found work to be uplifting, exciting, and downright self-actualizing.

Good Work versus Bad Work

Wendell Berry wrote, in a letter to the editor of *The Progressive* magazine in the fall of 2010, "It is true that the industrialization of virtually all forms of production and service has filled the world with 'jobs' that are meaningless, demeaning and boring—as well as inherently destructive. I don't think there is an argument for the existence of such work, and I wish for its elimination, but even its reduction calls for economic changes not yet defined, let alone advocated, by the 'left' or the 'right.'" I agree. So, too, I'm sure, would most of the anarchists that I quote in the essays that follow. Berry added, "The old and honorable idea of 'vocation' is simply that we each are called, by God, or by our gifts, or by our preference, to a kind of work for which we are particularly fitted." That, to a T, is how I feel, and I feel fortunate to feel that way.

"Implicit in this idea," Berry went on, with a bit of well-grounded cynicism and I'm sure a sparkle in his seventy-six-year-old, rooted-in-the-Kentucky-countryside eyes, "is the evidently startling possibility that we might work *willingly*, and that there is no necessary contradiction between work and happiness or satisfaction. Only in the absence of any viable idea of vocation, or good work, can one make the distinction implied in such phrases as 'less work, more life,' or 'work-life balance,' as if one commutes daily from life here to work there. But aren't we living even when we are most miserably and harmfully at work? And isn't that exactly why we object (when we do object) to bad work?"

The predominance of bad work has been building for a long time. The anarchists wanted to end it in a bad way. Back in 1911, Emma Goldman wrote: "If I were to give a summary of the tendency of our times, I would say, Quantity. The multitude, the mass spirit, dominates everywhere, destroying quality. Our entire life—production, politics, and education—rests on quantity, on numbers. The worker who once took pride in the thoroughness and quality of his work, has been replaced by brainless, incompetent automatons who turn out enormous quantities of things, valueless to themselves, and generally injurious to the rest of mankind. Thus quantity, instead of adding to life's comforts and peace, has merely increased man's burden."

Then there's this from her contemporary, Alexander Berkman: "It stands to reason that a person can give the best of himself only when his interest is in his work, when he feels a natural attraction to it, when he likes it. Then he will be industrious and efficient. The things the craftsman produced in the days before modern capitalism were objects of joy and beauty, because the artisan loved his work. Can you expect the modern drudge in the ugly huge factory to make beautiful things? He is part of the machine, a cog in the soulless industry, his labor mechanical, forced. Add to this his feeling that he is not working for himself but for the benefit of someone else, and that he hates his job or at best has no interest in it except that it secures his weekly wage. The result is shirking, inefficiency, laziness."

Skip forward to our own era where, unfortunately, bad work is still the norm. Poet David Whyte, in *Crossing the Unknown Sea: Work as a Pilgrimage of Identity*, quotes Brother David Steindl-Rast, telling him as he struggled to find his way in life that, "The antidote to exhaustion is not necessarily rest. The antidote to exhaustion is wholeheartedness. You are so tired through and through because a good half of what you do here in this organization has nothing to do with your true powers, or the place you have reached in your life. You are only half here, and half here will kill you after a while."

I think he gave David Whyte some pretty sound advice. Bad work is almost always exhausting; people finish it feeling physically and emotionally drained: doing *less* bad work is only *slightly less* exhausting than doing more. Bad work, to use a technical term, just plain sucks. I don't want to do it, and I don't want anyone else to have to do it either. Bad work is about people being treated as if they have nothing insightful to offer, as if they know next to nothing, or are "too stupid to understand upper-level activity." Bad work is about people being regularly managed in ways that are at best disrespectful and, at worst, downright abusive. It's about people going to work every day in settings that aren't in synch with their values—going "into the closet" when you go to work is a hard way to go. At best, bad work is tolerable but it's never, ever terrific.

Now, I know that just wanting bad work to come to an end isn't going to change the world overnight. But why not think big, right? I really believe that the approaches that we've learned and adapted and teach—taken from insightful, passionate people like Robert Greenleaf, Peter Block, Ron Lippett, Anese Cavanaugh, Emma Goldman, Gustav Landauer, and others—really can reconfigure the way the world thinks.

The Start of a New Era

Good work is life altering, fulfilling, and fun. Good work is about learning, laughing, growing, all the while earning enough money to make your dreams come true. It's about collaborating with people you care about and who share your values, contributing something positive to the people and the community around you. It's fun, not something you flee from. It's a place you want to be, even if you rightfully have other places you want to go. Good work is about positive energy—both feeling it and building it. Good work is about doing something you believe in, work that you care about in a workplace that cares about you. It's endlessly sustainable, not energy-sapping. While people might certainly, on any given day, go home tired after doing *good* work, they're rarely spiritually exhausted. When we're into what we're doing, giving it everything we've got, learning and laughing even under duress, the experience is likely to be energizing, even if, in the moment, physically tiring.

At its upper reaches, good work can be one of the most rewarding things one ever engages in. If we build our business in sustainable ways; if we treat everyone with respect regardless of title, background, race, religion, or resume; if we encourage people to be themselves and help them get there; if we work to bring out the best in everyone; if we convey to people how much difference their work actually makes and then simultaneously teach them how to make a difference in the way that their workplace is run; if we keep everyone learning and laughing; if we work the numbers so that everyone wins from a financial standpoint . . . then we create very good work. When we get good work right, we make a reality of Emma Goldman's once radical and, at the time, seemingly fantastical belief in "the freest possible expression of all the latent powers of the individual . . . [which is] only possible in a state of society where man is free to choose the mode of work, the conditions of work, and the freedom to work. One to whom the making of a table, the building of a house, or the tilling of the soil, is what the painting is to the artist and the discovery to the scientist— the result of inspiration, of intense longing, and deep interest in work as a creative force."

Peer to Peer, Not Parent-Child

To be clear, I'm not talking about a return to some supposedly long-lost way of working. "Polite and paternalistic" may sound better than "abusive and autocratic," but the old family-run business isn't what we're working towards either. Living Servant Leadership ("You want *me* to serve *them*?") and using Stewardship ("You're saying I should negotiate with new employees as if they were my peers, not treat them like replaceable machine parts?") were *not* the core concepts of the 18th- and 19th-century craft shop any more than they were of the big 20th-century auto plants. While I'm all about traditional food, and while the way we're working does probably have some connection to community life of days gone by, these ideas are as radical today as they were when Emma Goldman et al. were going at it a century or so ago and, for that matter, a hundred or a thousand years before that as well.

I'm giving the final word here to Brenda Ueland, author of *If You Want to Write: A Book about Art, Independence and Spirit.* Brenda did not, as far as I know, actively call herself an anarchist, but she reportedly went out with one for many years, and her writing certainly exudes the anarchist spirit. Although the book was published in 1938, it's as radical and relevant now as it ever was. I've probably read it twenty-nine times and I still gain new insights every time through. What follows is the advice she offered up to aspiring writers, but I think it's equally applicable to any of us who are learning to lead and live in this new way. In fact, it's so succinct that if you want to skip out on the rest of this book and go play in the sun, you can just read the next few lines, and then head straight out to the park:

> *You have talent, are original, and have something important to say.*
>
> *It is good to work. Work with love and like it when you do it.*
>
> *It is a privilege to get to do this.*
>
> *Be Bold, Be Free, Be Truthful.*

I hope that what follows here will help you develop your skills as a leader; I know that writing it has helped me develop mine. I hope, too, that you learn some ways to make what you do every day into "good work," and to help others around you do the same.

The "Secrets"

The essays that follow aren't really secrets but they are, in essence, the "secrets" that so many people have been asking us for. Secrets 1–18 were all in Zingerman's Guide to Good Leading, Part 1. *Secrets 19–29 follow here. Each is an important piece of what makes Zingerman's Zingerman's. Read and use each on its own, or adapt them all to your organization. Many thanks to all the insightful folks—both within our organization and without—who have contributed ideas, comments, stories, edits, and advice!*

aubree geller stocking bread at the deli

Fixing the Energy Crisis in the American Workplace

Why Ignoring the Natural Laws of Business Is a Recipe for Big Trouble

Most of what we do at Zingerman's is about appreciating what we have today while at the same time envisioning, imagining, believing in, and building a better tomorrow. That upbeat, proactive approach has certainly changed the way I look at the world; I wouldn't say that thinking positively comes totally naturally to me, but over the years I've definitely learned that the best way to get better at anything is to focus not on what's broken but on what's already working well. This first "secret" in the book is a bit of an exception to that positive approach. What follows is a look at what I believe has gone badly wrong. It's about how, by operating in violation of the Natural Laws of Business, we as a country have slowly but surely created a crisis, a crisis that's clearly apparent in the passive, unhelpful, low-energy effort we see in the vast majority of American workplaces today.

This essay is not upbeat—at least not at the start. Which I guess is all right in that it's worth spending a small bit of time getting clear on what's really going on in the world before we embark on all the ways we want to make it better. It helps (me at least) to accept just how horribly widespread the "bad work" that Wendell Berry wrote about (see page 28) is in the world. The descriptions of the employees in what follows are exactly what we don't want the energy to feel like when you walk into Zingerman's. It's more than a bit depressing to dwell in such dark places. They're not uplifting, but they are reality. If acceptance is the first step on the road to recovery, then understanding the energy crisis in the workplace gives us context to pursue what I believe is a very realistic, though radical to most folks, world filled mostly with good work.

Everyone in a leadership role can probably relate to this: Frustration builds, one's mind gets going, and it's hard to keep from sinking into the mental quicksand. The questions start coming and seem like they'll never stop:

- Why am I the only one who gets it?
- What's *wrong* with all those employees?
- Why don't they see what needs to be done?
- What's wrong with the economy?
- Why can't all these people get with it and start to innovate?
- What's keeping everyone from being more creative?

You know all the usual explanations—"employees just don't get it"; "most people aren't very innovative"; "creativity is being killed by texting and video games"; "young people's work ethic just isn't what it used to be." I really don't believe those are the issue. The problem, I will posit, is not *them*. It's a simple two-letter word that starts with *u* and ends with *s*: *US*. Not as in "United States." As in "us," you know, "you and me."

Whether it's the practice of good medicine, Six Sigma quality initiatives, the LEAN approach in automotive, or good old-fashioned problem solving, most everyone knows that it's never helpful to focus just on symptoms. To really address a problem, to fix it so that it doesn't come back a couple weeks after you thought you'd finished with it, you have to address the root cause.

Which is why, to my sense of things, there's nothing wrong with most employees. Despite those frequently asked, rather demeaning questions above, most frontline employees are more than capable of "getting it," and also of getting it done. Most employees, I think, are actually very innovative and they have been all along; pretty much all humans are born creative and are capable of using their creativity quite regularly. And even when the economy is not at its best, we have the power to pick up the pace right now, without waiting for Washington, the World Bank, or anyone else to help. The real problem, the root cause of the crisis, is not the employees.

The problem is that by operating in violation of the Natural Laws of Business, the country's workplaces are suffering a severe energy crisis.

I'm not talking about fossil fuels or gas prices. I'm talking about the way most people work. You don't need to be an expert to see what I'm talking about; the energy crisis is about as obvious as anything can be. Walk into most any mall, or call most any mail-order business, other than the really great ones, and it's not unlikely that you'll experience the energy crisis in all its glory. It'd be hard to miss. We all know that the odds are that the place is going to feel flat. People behind the counter or taking your calls seem bored. Energy is, at best, average; at worst, it's abysmal.

I've shared this image with hundreds of people (of all ages and all backgrounds) over the last few months, and they all get it, almost immediately. If you doubt my doom-and-gloom, energy-crisis assessment, take a look at this data from a Harris Poll cited in Dean Tucker's great book, *Using the Power of Purpose*. Of those employees surveyed,

- Only 37 percent clearly knew the company's goals.
- Only 20 percent were enthusiastic about those goals.
- Only 20 percent saw how they could support those goals.
- Only 15 percent felt enabled to work towards them.
- Only 20 percent fully trusted the company they worked for.

Pretty dismal, don't you think? But thanks to Dean, I realized it was actually worse than I thought. He had the deft wisdom and wit to translate that workplace data into what it would mean for a football team. Of the eleven players who get sent out onto the field:

- Only four actually know which goal they're going towards.
- Even more depressing, only two of them actually care.
- When they break the huddle, only two of the eleven know which position they're supposed to line up in.
- Only two guys on the team feel like their efforts on the field will actually make a difference.
- All but two players would be just as likely to be rooting for the other team as for their own.

Is that a %@&#** energy crisis or what? Awareness of this issue is actually starting to appear in the mainstream press. In a September 3, 2011, article entitled "Do Happier People Work Harder?" the *New York Times* reported that "The Gallup-Healthways Well-Being Index, which has been polling over 1000 adults every day since January 2008, shows that Americans now feel worse about their jobs—and work environments—than ever before. People of all ages, and across income levels, are unhappy with their supervisors, apathetic about their organizations and detached from what they do." And they added even more compelling data: "In a 2010 study, James K. Harter and colleagues found that lower job satisfaction foreshadowed poorer bottom-line performance. Gallup estimates the cost of America's disengagement crisis at a staggering $300 billion in lost productivity annually. When people don't care about their jobs or their employers, they don't show up consistently, they produce less, or their work quality suffers." It's hard to pin down an exact number for the current level of national debt, but no matter whose figure you use, if you start contributing $300 billion a year to paying it down, regardless of your politics, it's pretty clear we'd be in a lot better shape five years from now than we are today. The energy crisis in the workplace has reached a critical stage.

American business is paying people (often with lots of benefits) to work at somewhere between 15 and 37 percent of capacity.

Unlike hurricanes or tsunamis, the energy crisis in the workplace didn't spring up suddenly, and the country isn't going to come apart in a few months if we don't fix it immediately. The point isn't that some cataclysm is coming. The world will wake up tomorrow just as it always has, lots of companies will continue to make money, lots of others won't, politicians will still try to prove themselves right, and the weather in Michigan will still be weird.

The early anarchists were actually raising the alarm about it a century ago. They didn't call it an "energy crisis" and hardly anyone was listening. But check out this line from Romanian anarchist, author, and poet Eugen Relgis, who wrote, "The minds of the majority of mankind are in a lethargy. Let us arouse their latent possibilities, through free and positive education. The absolute humanity, which is within our hearts, will see more clearly and function better when it will be guided by the intelligence." Or Emma Goldman's statement: "Man is being robbed not merely of the products of his labor, but of the power of free initiative, of originality, and the interest in, or desire for, the things he is making."

A hundred years later, there's good news and bad news. While I stand by my statement that the sky isn't falling, the bad news is, honestly, it already fell. The energy crisis in the workplace isn't impending; it arrived a long time ago. We've just grown so accustomed to it that most Americans barely even take note of it. Here's the good news, though: budget deficits can't stop us from building strong businesses.

We can fix the energy crisis for free!

Let me back up a bit and share the story of how I realized, to borrow the late Vic Chesnutt's song title, the *gravity of the situation*. What made this all come clear to me wasn't anything I got from Emma Goldman; to the contrary, the idea came to me at one of the most prestigious capitalist conferences in the country, the annual Inc. 5000. It's a gathering of the country's quickest growing companies. Anarchism, I'm sure, has never been on the agenda, but by the time I'm done, maybe it will be. I've spoken there three or four times, and my revelation came at the 2010 conference, held in September of that year in Washington, D.C. The *Guide to Good Leading, Part 1* had just come out, and I'd been asked to speak about the lead essay, which is, as you may know, "Twelve Natural Laws of Building a Great Business." (See page 332 for the complete list.)

Before I went up to present, I had the chance to hear Gary Hirshberg, founder and CEO of Stonyfield Farm, give what I thought was a great keynote. He spoke at length about the impending environmental crisis, about how our ongoing violation of the natural laws of our planet is leading us, inexorably, towards exhaustion of limited resources. He talked about the cost all of this is having—and will continue to have—on the country, on companies, on health care, on people's personal lives. Gary followed all that by outlining the extensive and creative work that Stonyfield has done to turn things around in their corner of the world—within a matter of years they've successfully saved on resources *and* are making more money. He didn't just preach about environmentalism being the right thing to do. He actually showed how an effective, sustainable, ecologically sound business can deliver better bottom-line results.

The energy-crisis image clicked about three quarters of the way through Gary's presentation. I'd been thinking of our organization as an organic farm ever since I'd written it into Secret 15 on sustainable business in *Part 1*. The metaphor worked well. It became clear to me back then that although our organization didn't look as neat and polished as more mainstream businesses, we actually had a very healthy "ecosystem" in which each element—even those you might not normally notice—contributed positively back to the others. That as a result, the "soil" in which we were working was rich, energized, and vibrant. By contrast, I'd argued, the corporate world was much more like mono-cropping—everything was arranged in neat rows, but the soil was depleted and erosion high. As a result, that old model could function only with large amounts of artificial inputs. In the fields, that meant fertilizers and pesticides; in organizations, it meant big bonuses and stock options. Listening to Gary talk about the environment, I was shocked that I hadn't realized the parallel sooner. If, by operating in violation of nature, we had created a serious energy crisis in the environment, then the corporate world, by consistently violating the Natural Laws of Business, had created a comparable, equally critical, energy crisis in the workplace as well.

I'm guessing you know what I'm talking about. You can see, hear, and feel the lack of liveliness in the faces of all too many hard-working people all over the country. Their eyes are dull and their voices fall flat. While they do enough to get by, their work is neither exceptional nor overly inspiring. All too often, they're watching the clock more than they're watching the bottom line, getting by the way a bad team does when they're so far behind in the fourth quarter all they really hope for is that nothing worse will happen before the final buzzer sounds. You can decide for yourself whether or not you want to call that a crisis, but I don't think anyone's going to argue that it's a really great recipe for national success. And, no offense, but just calling "time out" or cutting (or not cutting) taxes isn't going to turn things around; it's pretty much impossible to get high output from very limited inputs.

It's that energy—the way employees feel, and the feeling we get from being around them—that came to my mind while Gary was PowerPointing his way deeper and deeper into the import of environmental issues. If the way to work our way back into the planet's good graces was, as Gary was saying, to live in harmony with nature, then the solution to the energy crisis in the workplace was simply, and similarly, to live in synch with the Natural Laws of Business. As organizations opt to live those laws, the frontline people who populate America's businesses will tune in and turn on, and their energy levels at work will quickly go up.

With increased energy will come the kind of innovation, creativity, and positive performance results that everyone is after.

I don't think this energy issue is about some small, statistically insignificant slice of the nation's economy. Seeing so many organizations suffer is painful. It's clear the problem is a big one, possibly the single biggest struggle we face in the nation today. I don't think that switching political parties, low-cost capital, or more manageable mortgage rates are the answer. All may have relevance, but they're neither the cause nor the solution. This problem is bipartisan. I can't see any correlation between workplace energy and political views, organizational size, for-profit, not-for-profit, geography, age groups, ethnic origin, product offering, or pay rates. The problems can pretty much play out anywhere. The energy crisis is endemic.

Just to back up this belief, I'll reference Peter Koestenbaum's book, *Leadership*, in which he states, "85 percent of organizational effectiveness and industrial competitiveness can be attributed to morale, spirit, and heart, and to the commitment and loyalty employees give their companies, to the inventiveness, imagination, and creativity they devote to their jobs." By contrast, he continues, "only 15 percent of organizational effectiveness and corporate competitive advantage can be attributed to the systems and the technologies designed to cope with current economic realities." So if over three-quarters of what counts most—the level of emotional engagement—is coming in far below capacity, then it's no wonder that so many companies (and countries) just aren't working.

The good news is that the solution is actually pretty simple.

A couple days after I came home from the Inc. 5000 gathering, my attachment to this concept got even stronger. I was presenting at a ZingTrain seminar here in Ann Arbor. At the end of each afternoon we bring in a panel of assorted frontline staff, managers, and partners to answer assorted questions from seminar attendees. The panel gave some great answers—across the board, their content was right on. I'd have given them an A+. But what blew me away more than the content of what they were saying was *the energy behind it.* When it came time to answer whatever question the audience threw at them, each of them would light up. You could see and feel it in a second. Their eyes opened wide, they smiled, they leaned in to get closer to the questioner.

Think about the context—these weren't the stars answering questions at a press conference before a nationally televised performance at Carnegie Hall or the Super Bowl. These were people whom the rest of the world would probably pay little attention to, playing supporting roles in the story that is Zingerman's, a successful but still almost-irrelevant-in-the-scheme-of-the-world small food business in a mid-sized town in the state that's had one of the worst economies in the United States for as long as I can remember. Most of them were probably pretty tired, and they surely had six or seven or seventy other things they would rather have been doing than sharing their thoughts with a little conclave of business people from around the country.

Yet, without fail, their enthusiasm was *enormous*. The answers these folks were giving clearly came from their heads, but there was a hugely positive level of emotional energy emerging from their hearts as well. The energy they put into the room was exceptional. Please note that nothing about the event was staged; this was just good, grounded, honest excitement about the work they were doing. You probably could have powered a couple of food carts on the emotional wattage they were putting out. That sealed the deal for me. It was clear that one of the biggest reasons that we—and other good organizations we knew—were surviving the economic nightmare so well was simply that positive energy.

By living the Natural Laws of Business, we were tapping the full energy of the people who work here and getting way better results in the process.

What I'm talking about here is not just some "soft stuff" to slough off onto your HR department to deal with. Energy is . . . nearly everything. It's how we feel, how we act, how we approach the world. It is, in essence, the emotional atmosphere in which we operate. Low, negative energy brings trouble. But positive energy brings everything we're after: innovation, creativity, caring, generosity of spirit, belief, big ideas, and all that extra effort that so often makes the difference between good and great. And that is, very truly, what I believe we're getting from most everyone who works here.

By contrast, most of the rest of the world is squandering massive amounts of available human energy every day. Pick your analogy—the way they're working is akin to filling a bucket that has a big hole in the bottom; like running the AC with the windows wide open; or like driving on the highway while you're still stuck in low gear. (No offense to anyone's political allegiance, but I can't figure out how raising or lowering tax rates would have any impact on this problem—it strikes me as being akin to arguing about whether or not to switch the fan from "Auto" to "On" while operating that dang AC with all the windows still wide open.)

By not living the Natural Laws of Business, companies are basically paying people *not* to contribute.

Mind you, Zingerman's is not the only company that's created a high-energy work environment. There are certainly others doing a similar, or even better, job than we are. While they're not the norm, they are out there, and, by dint of the fact that you're reading this, the odds are that you own, manage, or work in one. Or at least you'd like to. There are also high-energy *elements*—departments, divisions, districts, or whatever—doing good work inside of organizations that otherwise might not be at the high end of the energy range. Without knowing much about how those successful companies operate, I'll say the odds are extremely good that—knowingly or not—*they're living most all of those Twelve Natural Laws*. And as a result the energy in their organizations is almost always high.

You can usually see the impact of their harmonious relationship with the world just by looking into the eyes of their employees. The people who work there are excited. They look happy. Their heads and hearts are in the game. They're smiling, laughing, and learning. It's not like they don't have disagreements or shortfalls or screw-ups or snipe at each other. We're all human. But they are focused and they're definitely having fun. More often than not, when the energy feels that good, the results are either equally good, or the staff at least is on a path they believe is going to get them to success.

The other day a business reporter asked me if I believe that what we do here at Zingerman's was "almost unnaturally positive." I thought about it for a minute and then I realized it was actually the opposite. "What we're doing," I told him, "is probably the more natural way to work. It's in synch with the Natural Laws of Business. This is the way it's *supposed* to be. Look over the list of the laws—things work better when you share a clear vision of where you're going, when people believe in what they're doing, and when the leaders give great service to the staff." I paused for a minute to process the idea. "It's actually the *other* way of working, where people aren't having fun, they're not in a great organization, they don't have clear expectations of what they're supposed to do, and they don't know where the company is going," I said, thinking aloud, "that is the *unnatural* way to work."

People are actually *supposed* to like what they're doing.

Of course it's not black and white. None of us live the Natural Laws perfectly all the time. But it's increasingly clear to me just how consistently you can correlate a company's energy levels with how effectively an organization operates. Mind you, the correlation isn't one of size, nor does it have anything that would appear in a Dun and Bradstreet download. You have to be a bit of a rebel, a Hugh MacLeod (*Ignore Everybody*) kind of person to pull it off. Most people persist in sticking to the status quo, even when "the way we've always done it" violates the Natural Laws of Business and does nothing but bring down their energy.

It's a situation that helps no one. Instead of going into making great companies, people's passions are "outsourced"—the energy they don't expend at work emerges later, after they punch out, in the form of hobbies, families, sports, music, kids, or community work. Not that that's a bad thing. Some people, I'm sure, are perfectly at peace with it, and there are a lot of great things that happen with hobbies, families, sports, and donating time to nonprofits. Most folks probably consider this to be perfectly fine—their work, it's true, isn't exactly exhilarating, but hey, it's work, so it's not really supposed to be, right? Or it can be much worse. Being so-so—let's say it's a 7 out of 10 on the energy scale—is a success compared to what's going on in much of the corporate world. A huge segment of society is operating at about a 4 or a 5. In those settings work becomes an unwanted burden that people put up with only in order to get by; they shut down in order to survive.

The millions of victims of the energy crisis in the workplace are, in essence, the "working dead."

This image came to me very clearly when I was teaching one of our new-staff orientation classes. Usually, I teach to a diverse group. More often than not, the class is a mix of managers, servers, dishwashers, bakers, busboys, or bartenders. Ages are mixed, too; some are seventeen and others are forty-seven. Some have college degrees, others dropped out of high school. You get the idea—we've got people coming to the class with very different levels of experience in life and in our organization. Most of them, however, have been here at least a few days, weeks, or months—long enough to have gotten their energy levels "rebooted" from what they were out in the rest of the world. And because the contrast in work experiences is still fresh in their minds, they're usually especially enthusiastic about what we're doing here at Zingerman's. It's not hard to understand why—when you've been told to turn off your brain for years, it's got to feel good to turn that naturally present energy on again!

This diversity makes for a much more interesting, and effective, class. But this particular session was a bit out of the norm—while there was still a high diversity of backgrounds, this was a group of twenty-five people whom we'd hired to work only for the holidays. There'd been hundreds of applicants, and these were the ones we'd chosen to bring on board. But unlike so many of our new hires who have come here to begin a positive new piece of their lives, most of them knew this job would be ending in about eight weeks. And, other than being interviewed, this was the very first thing they were doing at Zingerman's.

Teaching the new-staff orientation is typically one of my favorite parts of my job. But in this case it was tough: twenty-five people who showed up from the far left-field corner of life all in one fell swoop. Most very clearly had never engaged with work, let alone the owner of the business, in anything resembling this sort of interactive, appeal-to-your-intelligence way. I think mostly they were stunned, or at least surprised and caught off guard. The two-hour session was like watching the "working dead" slowly wake up. You could almost see the cobwebs coming off, the gears beginning to turn again, the creativity—long stifled—starting to spark. Good, for sure, but strange. I kept thinking about it as if it were the part of a late-night horror flick where the walking dead start to come back to life.

Gradually, I could see the new staff members come out of their corporate-imposed comas. It was as if they'd been trained in other jobs to stay safely in their shells, not to show too much emotion, share insights or ideas, make serious suggestions, or even act as if they cared. Which would then, understandably, be the sort of low-energy approach they'd bring to work their first day. For them, that was what a job was anyway. They might well have been thinking that as holiday help it might actually be even worse here than it had been elsewhere. I don't blame them—when you've been beaten down a lot, you naturally flinch when anyone bigger comes close. To quote artist Jon Onye Lockard, "Treat a man like a dog long enough and he'll bark." He goes on:

"You don't know what being human means until you are treated humanely."

I saw this kind of extreme energy gap again about six weeks later when I went to speak on the campus of a very well-known, large university. Now don't get me wrong—I'm a graduate of a Big Ten school and a big believer in higher education. I'll leave out the name—I get around a lot so it could have been one of any number of institutions. It was on a Monday, about 6:30, still early in the evening. As it happened, I ended up walking in something of a circle while searching for the room. Frustrating, but also eye-opening: I certainly saw more of the building than I might have otherwise.

While the talk itself ended up going very well, the experience outside of it was *not* uplifting. There was paper littering the floors. The walls were mostly empty. People were staring down, typing on their computers or texting on their phones. I'm sure most of the people I saw were smart or they'd never have been admitted to this school in the first place. But no exaggeration, the energy was—if I'm being generous—at best about a 6 out of 10. Most people were walking the halls looking glaringly glum, their eyes looking mostly down or straight ahead into space, and their energy low. Their body language was not screaming, "Hey! We're having lots of fun here!" Clearly, the energy crisis has hit the educational system as well.

A couple of days later I was back at work, headed into the Deli. Coincidentally, I got there at 6:30, as well. But this time, I mean 6:30 in the morning. It's half an hour before we even open, but I go in anyway because I know I can get coffee, sit down, and start working. In complete contrast to what I'd experienced during my evening on campus, everyone at the Deli was awake in every sense of the word—setting up, smiling, laughing, looking at and talking to each other, engaged, interested, and interesting. It was still dark outside but the lights in their eyes were very clearly on. Remember here—I'm talking about people who were at *work,* a condition which much of the nation seems to feel is grounds for going into depression (or a depression?). People clearly cared, felt cared for, and believed in what they were doing. Coming so close on the heels of my early-in-the-evening walk across campus—in a place where people are supposed to be having the most enjoyable experience of their lives, and paying a lot of money for the privilege—the energy gap was beyond glaring.

When organizations live the Natural Laws of Business, almost everyone in them will operate at high energy.

My hope is that here at Zingerman's—along with all the other sustainable businesses out there—we are modelling a better way to work. Tapping into people's natural energy is a better way to go. As I write, although economic indicators are nowhere near excellent, the energy level here at Zingerman's is high. As are our sales. I'm getting similar reports from friends and colleagues across the country. The headlines can still be horrific, and, I know, many people are still suffering, but the companies that are living the Natural Laws are doing pretty darned well.

Our job, the way I see it, is to help keep it that way. Or more accurately and more appropriately, to raise energy levels even higher regardless of which direction others' economic winds are blowing. In truth, the way we're working with the Natural Laws here gives us a very natural advantage over most of our competitors—it's not like we're paying people two or three times as much money. And, although I think we do a lot of good hiring and training, I honestly don't think the people who work here (me, Paul, or anyone else) are ten times better than everywhere else. They're just operating at close to full capacity, high in creativity, with positive energy in play, pretty much every day, while others elsewhere are stuck in low gear.

Positive energy brings a big competitive advantage.

It does seem a bit odd to give away our natural advantage in the marketplace. If everyone else in our industry caught on and started to live according to the Natural Laws, I suppose that would make it harder for us here at Zingerman's to stay successful. But, you know, that would—as per Natural Law 9 ("Success means you get better problems")—be a really, really good problem to have. As a big believer in sustainable business, I'm adamant that the better everyone around us does, the better our town's going to do, the better we're going to do as well. So, please, go for it—eat away at our current natural advantage. Living them is pretty much free and, frankly, also a lot more fun.

I know that for many organizations, starting to live the Natural Laws might be easier said than done. It's not just some switch you throw or a new supplier to simply start buying from. But, emotionally challenging as it may be, I fully believe that living the Natural Laws *is* the solution to the energy crisis in the workplace. Anyone who's interested, who's ready to do some reflection and is willing to change the way they lead and run their organizations, can get the work going in the right direction. And, quite honestly, you don't have to be a boss to do what needs to be done—leadership work isn't limited to people whose names are listed at the top of corporate org charts.

While there is work involved, building positive energy is mostly about an intellectual and emotional commitment to introspection, better communication, effective collaboration, and living in harmony with nature. The more effectively we do those, the more mindful we are of them, the more the energy in our organizations is sure to go up. When all this works in harmony, people start to make the transition that Wendell Berry described—they go from "bad work" to "good work." Good work leads to good energy. If we improve energy quality, we increase effectiveness. Raise the quality of the work people do and we raise their energy again. You get the idea. If you think that won't impact GNP, product quality, service scores, fun factors, and fifteen hundred other things—think again.

Living the Natural Laws of Business creates radically more rewarding ways of relating to work, to the world, to our organizations, and to ourselves.

On the odd chance that you've read this far but are still skeptical, let me steer you towards Sharon Compton. Sharon's worked at Zingerman's Mail Order for nearly seven years. She's not a manager nor is she on the fast track to being a Zingerman's partner or trying to take over the corporate world. She's a very kind and thoughtful person who contributes positively to what we do in meaningful ways. The other day, Sharon stopped by where I was sitting in the Mail Order service center and asked if I had a minute. Which, of course, I did. She wanted me to know how much she appreciated being able to be part of Zingerman's. She'd come to work here only at the close-out of her "real career," from which she'd retired after twenty-five years on the job. She wanted to share with me that, having worked here, in a positive and rewarding setting, one in which she was having fun at work, appreciating and being appreciated at a really high energy level every day, . . . well . . . she'd started to realize that her entire first career had been almost, in her words, "a waste."

Before you start feeling badly for her, let me add that Sharon was smiling when she said it, and she said straight off that this revelation wasn't really bothering her. She told me that it had become clear to her early on when, six months into working here, her husband said something like, "What's up with you? How come you're not complaining about work anymore?" It was confirmed more recently when an old friend they hadn't seen for a long time came to visit. As he was leaving he stopped her, smiled, and said, "Wow. You sure don't complain like you used to." So, take Sharon's story and add back in the positive energy lost during her "real career" at wherever it is she worked all that time. If you're doing the math, you can also eliminate the twenty-five years of negativity that, almost needless to say, she also unwittingly unloaded on her family and anyone else she dealt with. Multiply the differential by however many millions of Americans are in the workforce. You can subtract from those the relatively small segment of folks doing "good work" in sustainable businesses whose energy is usually positive, and the equation is downright overwhelming.

If we put the power of positive energy back into our economy, great things could get going.

When I presented my views on the energy crisis at last year's Gathering of Games (the annual open-book finance conference), they asked me what song I wanted them to cue up when I went out on stage. After giving it a good bit of thought, I opted for Bob Dylan's "The Times They Are a-Changin'." The economic struggles in which we've been enmeshed make clear the obvious ineffectiveness of the old model. But positive energy, creativity, innovation, and the effort tapped into simply by living the Natural Laws of Business can turn the country in the right direction. Living in synch with nature certainly feels better, it's a lot more fun, and the bottom line is, it just plain works better. You really can feel the difference. To quote Gustav Landauer, in a line that makes me think again about the way our employees work every day: "During revolution, people are filled by spirit and differ completely from those without spirit. During revolution, *everyone* is filled with the spirit that is otherwise reserved for exemplary individuals; everyone is courageous, wild and fanatic and caring and loving at the same time."

The Inside Scoop on Working Here at Zingerman's

Judy Hayes, Zingerman's Customer and Wife of Chad Hayes, Zingerman's Delicatessen

I hope you don't mind, but I feel compelled to share this story with you after reading your essay on "Fixing the Energy Crisis in the American Workplace." I loved reading it, and the further into the article I read the more I enjoyed it! It got me thinking about my career as a teacher and how the economy has changed so much of our structure, our education system, and our passion for teaching. I can see how the educators I so highly respect around me are losing that energy as each year progresses, our staff decreases, and our performance expectations increase, and how it affects the next generation of children we are paid to "energize"!

I became a teacher back in the day when I was single and felt so blessed to find a career that I loved. I loved to get up every morning and interact with my students, and felt that I was making a positive impact on others in the world (as they were on me too!). After getting married and my husband Chad's illness dragged from one year into the next, our energy was gone (both individually and as a couple). My teaching position changed at work, Chad wasn't able to work, and I was exhausted from being a "single" parent while he was repeatedly hospitalized. I don't say this to be all gloom and doom; here comes the good part.

Since Chad's health has improved, so have *our* lives! Without a doubt, I know in my heart that his energy has been restored by his employment at Zingerman's. His physical health had been improving for the months leading up to his work at the Deli; however, after he began working in a "positive" environment, his emotional and physical health has improved to an entirely new level. He has found not only one, but many new purposes in his life. He loves going to work and learning about the business, new products, new trainings, and more cheeses! He is thrilled to help people, work with people he likes, and sell products he loves to consume! He loves his Zingerman's family and we spend much of our time outside of work with our Deli friends and their families. I never would have guessed him to be the guy that loves getting up early and taking the bus to work! He is a different man now that he feels he can positively contribute to our family. I find myself stopping by the Deli for a sandwich just so I can say "hi" to our friends, be treated with great service, and avoid the miserable food elsewhere even when Chad's not at work! (Oh, yeah, and enjoy the great food! Sorry, I almost forgot about the food!)

Chad's renewed energy from work has spilled directly into our lives at home. Our kids are so happy to see Chad when he gets home from work, and they ask to go visit him at the Deli regularly. I now have the best relationship with my husband that I've had since the day we were married. Despite the economic crisis in our school district, that energy from Chad, his work, our family, and our home continue to inspire me to keep the passion and energy at my workplace, where I can still make an impact on the next generation regardless of the happenings of our politics in our state capital! Even if that energy isn't present in all aspects of our lives, the more we build on it, share it with others who can see and feel it, the more it will spill into other aspects of our lives and those around us.

While so many people never find passion in their workplace, I think it's healthy to remind those who have how fortunate we are! Your article inspires me to appreciate and hold tight to that energy that belongs to us free of charge! I would like to share and hopefully reiterate that positive energy with some of my colleagues in a time when there is so much "deadness" in our workplace.

Walking into the Deli or seeing Chad after he's been working is all the proof I need to understand the energy you write about. Thank you for sharing your concept of energy with our family through your essay, your company, your employees, and your willingness to continue "bouncing" ideas out into the world! I am surprised at myself for having this much to share with you! I hope many people consider how they can impact this energy crisis (for free) before spending another dime trying to fix the economy with refinancing . . . again!

Katie Garlinghouse, Retail Counter Person, Zingerman's Delicatessen

I applied to the Deli on a bit of a whim, a suggestion from my then-boyfriend, now fiancé. A few months before that, Rick had put an application in my hands while I was sitting in the Next Door working on finishing my senior thesis. I guess he knew that the best place in Ann Arbor for a college graduate with a degree in Russian history is Zingerman's Deli. I asked Ari for a job after my graduation, and up to this point in my young life, it's the best thing that's ever happened to me.

I am so lucky to have been surrounded by all of you incredibly passionate people. I've never had so many wonderful friends, the kind that you can call at 2:00 a.m. if your house is burning down. I love Zingerman's as a business because it's the kind of place that encourages personal and professional growth. And I've always felt that my opportunities at Zingerman's were only limited by my imagination. I've grown up here, and the lessons I've learned will follow me wherever I go.

sider Pangman leveling a wedding cake at the bakehouse

Raising the Energy Bar

A 12-Point Plan for Better Energy Efficiency

Having gotten that rather grim assessment of the average American workplace out of the way, let me move on to a better and more positive place. Although I know that most big companies will likely think our work on energy management a bit odd and a stupendously silly use of organizational resources, I would posit that it's actually the other way around. The work that we've done to teach, define, live, measure, and recognize positive energy has very clearly helped to meaningfully enhance a culture that was already very energized when we started that work back in 2010. If I were you, I'd give energy management a shot—the risk is low and the cost is lower still. Ultimately, the only one stopping each of us from going after ever greater personal heights of positivity is each of us! What follows is our overview on the subject—a dozen ways to do better at managing our energy every day!

Learning is a big thing for me. Among other benefits, it helps me continue to move forward when I feel confused, frustrated, or unfocused. All I usually need to do is find a great book, listen to an insightful speaker, or attend an interesting training session, and my brain is back to moving actively along creative paths in a matter of minutes. Perhaps it's because I love learning so much that I have such great respect for anyone who's willing to share their knowledge. Which is probably also why I'm adamant about giving credit to those from whom I've learned. What follows is all inspired by, and learned from, a friend of mine named Anese Cavanaugh. You can check out more of her work at her website, which is www.daretoengage.com, and get her take on this subject and a host of other interesting insights from her unique approach to organizational leadership.

It was at another *Inc.* magazine conference, this one in the fall of 2009, that I heard Anese share her strongly held views about energy and the essential role it plays in the workplace. It took only about two minutes before the clarity and compelling nature of her point hit me in a way that Stas' Kazmierski (one of the two managing partners here at ZingTrain) calls "a belated glimpse of the obvious." You know, one of those things you hear and it's so immediately, incredibly, clear that you can't believe you never noticed it before. Once I heard Anese talk about energy, I couldn't believe I hadn't paid attention to it years earlier. What I learned from her has changed the way I—and our entire organization—work every day.

So what do I mean by energy? While I'm interested in global warming and alternative fuel sources, they're definitely not my areas of expertise. What I'm talking about here—what I learned from Anese—is that I need to pay very close attention to the energy that I bring with me to any interaction I have. To become mindful as well of the energy level that every person in our organization brings with them every day to their work; the impact that that energy—high, low, upbeat, angry, flat, furious, or fantastic—has on their co-workers, customers, and everyone else they come into contact with; the energy that one can sense—for better or for worse—within a minute and a half of walking into a business. Good energy, I realized after meeting Anese, is a hallmark of good leadership. You can feel its presence almost immediately in any well-run organization.

In hindsight, this work around energy management is what Maggie Bayless, the other managing partner at ZingTrain, taught me many years ago could be called "unconscious competence." Paul and I, and other effective leaders, have long been good at managing our own energy; we just didn't *know* we were good at it. While it's better than unconscious incompetence, unconscious competence generally leads to frustration, dependence, and ultimately organizational failure. Thanks to Maggie, we long ago learned that for Zingerman's to grow and get better it's imperative for us to figure out how to turn these areas of unconscious competence into teachable, learnable, practical "recipes" that people can put to work every day in meaningful and measurable ways. What follows is my approach—a dozen aspects of energy management to be aware of.

1. Getting Clear—Good Energy versus Fast and Frenetic

I'm going to start by stating what should be obvious, but I'm sure actually isn't. When I talk about raising the energy level, I'm *not* talking about getting frantic; frenetic energy is definitely not productive. We've all been around it: it raises quite a racket, there's a lot of motion and a sense of near-hysteria that, while intended to get people fired up, mostly just send staff firing off in an uncoordinated and unproductive manner. Frenetic energy is dissonant, distracting, discouraging. Taking energy in that direction is probably worse than having flat, neutral, or next to no energy at all. Unwittingly, fear and foolishness take the place of focus.

There's more to bad energy than being frantic. Bad energy can be negative, crabby, antagonistic, oppositional, or outright rude. It's not fun, it's not friendly, and it's anything but productive. Bad energy is always bad news. Good energy, by contrast, is . . . energizing. It feels good, it's fun, it's inspiring, it's exhilarating and enjoyable. It's fairly fast paced, but calm. Good energy is healthy, it's life giving, and it contributes positively to pretty much everything from spiritual well-being to sales building. It puts nearly everyone who comes into contact with it in a good mood. People feel safe in its presence, which means that their natural abilities, normally held back for fear of failure, start to emerge.

Ultimately, the call is ours on which type of energy—good or bad—we want to bring to the table. Both are very powerful, and each casts an odd but almost inexplicable spell on our organizations. Which makes me think that the two are much like the "good" witch and the "bad" witch from *The Wizard of Oz*—while the results are quite different, each type of energy has a certain magic about it, and either can produce strong stuff that's hard to explain but happens anyway. Each of us has the power to choose the energy we bring— which "witch," I wonder, do you want to be?

2. Overall Organizational Energy

Anyone who's been to a great concert, theatrical presentation, poetry reading, or sports event knows what it's like to feel the buzz. There's no way around it—those high-energy, good-vibe, high-five events are the ones people want to be part of. The same is true of businesses. High-energy organizations are the ones most people—especially the sort of high-energy, caring, positive people we want to cater to as customers and co-workers—like to go to. There's something special about them. While it may be hard to put your finger on what it is, there's no question about the fact that there's a positive buzz, a good feel, something special, at work. Good energy is appealing, attractive, and very conducive to getting consumers to spend their money with us.

Good energy is when you come to work and people are smiling, they're nice to each other, they actually engage with customers and co-workers in meaningful ways rather than just going through the motions. The vibe is positive, and people are upbeat even when there are opposing views on the table. You know the energy is good when you go to a meeting and people are having fun and are engaged, even if they are dealing with difficult issues. Well-run businesses have really positive energy nearly all the time. You can feel it on the phone, it comes across on their website, and of course when you walk into a place in person. Quite simply, there's good energy in the air.

Then there are all the businesses that live on the low end of the energy scale. Think about your visits to most chain stores or restaurants that felt so flat that you backed quietly out the door before the hostess could spot you. Or the meeting that felt so uncomfortable you wished you'd missed it altogether. Or that time you asked someone how their day was going, and their answer was, "Two more hours and I'm out of here!" I'm pretty sure we've all had those sorts of experiences. The feeling I take from them is, at best, flat and, at worst, downright destructive. It ain't much fun, and it's not a feeling I want to be around. To the contrary, I'll actually go to great lengths to avoid it. Good people want to flee when faced with bad energy. Think about what that means for your best customers and most committed co-workers—I'll posit that consistently bad energy will lead almost inevitably to going out of business.

3. Good Energy Is Fun

Back in 2006 we began writing the third of our long-term organizational visions; the first was done in 1982 when we opened, the second in 1994. The latter was called "Zingerman's 2009" and outlined what our future was going to look like when we arrived at the then super-distant days of 2009. Eerily, but not really surprisingly, it *very* closely resembles the Zingerman's Community of Businesses that exists today. Our newest vision is called "Zingerman's 2020." Number seven of its nine key components speaks to the subject of fun; specifically, it states that we'll be having 380 percent more of it in the year 2020 than we were in '06 when we wrote it. (If you want a copy of the whole vision, see the back of the *Guide to Good Leading, Part 1,* or email us at zingtrain@zingermans.com.)

I bring this up here because including fun in our vision has stimulated a great deal of discussion within our organization about how one actually defines fun. My take is that *fun* in the professional sense of the word is really all about good energy. "Professional" is the key here—we're not talking about what each of us likes to do outside of work, but rather what it means for the organization to have fun while doing the work at hand. Differentiating between the two is similar to when we once had to get employees to understand the difference between our professional assessment of quality and their personal taste regarding food. Both are legit, but it's imperative that we learn to distinguish between the two. I realized the same was true of fun; what we like to do on our own is great, but it's almost completely unrelated to much of what goes on at work.

The reality is that when the group's energy is good, pretty much everyone involved is having a good time while still doing the work needed to make the business successful. Good energy is both an outcome and a contributor—it helps the group do better, and the better the group does, the better the energy, and the more fun the group members have en route. All of which consistently leads to better customer service, better quality control, and better everything.

4. Monitoring and Mentoring Others on Energy

While I've long been fluent in the language of good food, until I met Anese, "personal energy" wasn't even in my vocabulary. That has, of course, changed completely. I'm now watching, feeling, listening, and learning about people's energy the way I've long tuned in to the flavor and quality of our food. For the first time, I was able to be much clearer about my expectations around an issue that I'd previously thought of as too vague to be explicit about. While many leaders are probably unconsciously competent in managing their own energy, hardly any of us, in my experience, are actively teaching and talking about the subject to our co-workers and colleagues. Energy awareness, then, is a huge opportunity for organizational improvement. Coaching on this subject is one of the most meaningful gifts I can give to any up-and-coming leader at Zingerman's. If I do nothing more than get them to pay close attention to their own energy and then modify their behavior to make their work more effective . . . Wow!

Even a small improvement in energy "administration" by the manager of a twenty-person team makes for a huge improvement in the group's performance. It's not rocket science; it's just good business. When the energy is better, sales go up, stress goes down, tensions decrease, fun goes up, everything just works better. And best of all? An improvement like this in energy management costs nothing! It's really all about flipping an internal switch through more effective self-management, and then just doing it. Anyone who's ready to do a bit of self-reflection and then modify their behavior to do what's needed for the benefit of the business can make a big difference in a very short time.

5. Better Energy Management at Every Level

Of course, it isn't just leaders who bring energy to the business. Everyone on the team is in some way adding their energy to the mix. It doesn't take a degree in organizational studies to figure out that when a business is working really well, most every staff member is bringing good energy to the game every day. The best teams pull together—even in adversity—and the energy stays fairly positive throughout. Conversely, when an organization is sinking, the energy will almost always be bad. After operating that way for a while the organizational "soil" is depleted; there's no reserve of goodwill or cache of creativity to call up in hard times, so when trouble comes, things will go downhill quickly.

All of which means that, while it's essential to improve energy management at the leadership level, it's also of great help to teach these ideas to everyone. Towards that end I've started to comment regularly about energy to individuals, in groups, and even when we go offsite to visit other organizations. I've made a particular point of complimenting entry-level folks when I feel like they're putting good energy into play each day. I have a feeling that until I point it out, most of them don't even realize that they're doing anything out of the ordinary—at that stage of their careers, it's most likely that they're just as unconsciously competent in the field of energy management as most effective longtime leaders. If they bring high energy to a new job, it's probably because it comes naturally to them, not because it's some learned behavior that they're expected to develop. It's worth encouraging them—the more frontline people we have who are bringing great energy every day, the better we'll do as an organization. Everyone likes to hear a good, heartfelt word of appreciation. What's the risk? The compliment alone will, very clearly, improve energy in and of itself.

Exercise: Business-to-Business Energy Assessment

Here's some practical, hands-on homework. Go out and visit a dozen businesses—including your own. Assess the energy as soon as you enter the door. Make note of the vibe, how it makes you feel. I'll posit that after two or three stops you'll be darned good at noticing the nuance. Check the feel that the staff gives off. Do they acknowledge your presence? When they do, are you glad they said something? Or did you find yourself wishing they'd wandered right by you and ignored you? Is the place exciting? Does it feel grounded? Calm? Phony? Over-the-top? Calmly confident? Or as boring as a bad restaurant in a tourist town during the depths of the off-season?

As you leave, give the spot a score on a scale of 0 (makes you want to flee five seconds after you get in) to 10 (you want to go work there or at least shop there all the time!). A score of 6, let's say, would be indifferent—no strong feelings one way or another. You didn't hate it, but you're definitely not going to make any effort to go back, either. To elevate this exercise to real heights of effectiveness for your organization, I'd suggest taking two or three co-workers along with you. We've had quite a few ZingTrain seminar attendees go home and do this exercise with their staff, who have found it to be very eye-opening. The experience you get from assessing the energy together will create a common awareness, shared language, and a higher level of energy around good energy!

6. Paying Attention to Your Own Energy

When you've got your finger on the energy pulse of a place, stop for a second and think. Based on what you experienced in the business overall, what would you estimate the energy levels of the leaders of that business are likely to be? I'd forecast that it's very much the same as the energy of the business overall. There's just not really any way around the reality that the energy—good or not so good—starts at the top. You already knew this, but let me say it again for the heck of it—as with pretty much everything else in leadership life, we need to behave as we want others in our organization to do. If I want good energy in a meeting room, one of our restaurants, a staff retreat, or anywhere else, I need to start by making sure that my own energy is pretty darned positive.

I can't guarantee that I'm right all the time, but I think I have a pretty good handle on this. There is a little list I run through: Am I being mindful of the moment? Am I being appreciative of all the little things going on around me? Am I having fun? Am I smiling? Is my body language good? Am I breathing regularly and evenly? Am I making positive eye contact with others around me? Are all my interactions meaningful? Am I listening well? Am I giving out heartfelt compliments? Have I successfully managed to avoid obsessing over stuff that's either already happened or that's still in the future but over which I have no real influence? Energy spent fretting over things that are out of our control is almost always negative, and it generally detracts from the personal energy pool we've got to draw on.

Think quickly of almost anyone you really like, or liked, working with. It might be a manager whose shifts were always more fun and more effective than the rest. Or it might be a leader who helps the people around them rise to ever-greater heights. If they're like the great leaders I've been around it's safe to say that they almost always radiate positive energy. Something shifts up a notch when they walk into the room. Others feed on their energy, and the feeling in the entire group gets better almost instantly. Somehow, they bring that aura of good energy most everywhere they go. They always seem to stay upbeat, but never superficially so. They move quickly and with purpose. They come across as confident but never really cocky. When you look in their eyes, the "lights are on."

I like this quote by mid-20th-century psychologist Emma Gilbert (named actually for Emma Goldman): "There are some people you meet whose eye catches you and you feel they are interested in you." They're paying attention to what's going on around them. They're appreciative of both small contributions and big wins. They connect with people as they pass, and when they can, they greet them by name. They give credit liberally to others and to the organization around them, and take it for themselves only rarely. They ask good questions and actually listen to the answers. They may challenge others, but it's done in a good spirit, one in which the best around them feel caringly pushed to rise to ever-greater heights. They laugh a lot. They talk about all the great things they've learned. They work hard but they have fun doing it. And the group somehow seems to always do better when they're a part of it.

These are people whom customers want to buy from and staff members want to work hard with! Becoming consciously competent on this subject has made me realize that most all of this stuff around personal energy management can be taught, learned, and taken forward with ever greater ability by any self-reflective leader. Sure, it might come naturally to some and not so much to others. But anyone who's ready and willing can do it—they just need to have seen some of it in action when it's working, and then commit to themselves and maybe those around them that they're going to make it a reality over time.

The Gift That Keeps on Giving

To make this emphasis on energy a bit more tangible, think for a minute about succession planning. It's certainly a big subject in any organization, like ours, that's been around for a while. So, I know it's a little strange, but I'd suggest you start to look at the energy you bring to work as a critical element of good succession planning. I really believe the energy we bring may well be the single most important thing we're going to leave behind, the legacy that, like some strange organizational DNA, will be replicated over and over again long after you and I have moved on.

With that in mind, I want you to imagine a small box. You can decide what it looks like—utilitarian, wood, metal, simple, or artful, decorated in a style of your choosing. Imagine filling your box with whatever energy you've brought to work today. Good, bad, fun, frenetic, indifferent, insane, or otherwise—you get to decide what kind it is. Then imagine passing that box around to everyone you work with. Imagine further that, right after you've given it to them, Martians make off with you mid-day (hey, it could happen!). That little energy box, it turns out, is the last thing you've left for your co-workers. You, of course, will be gone (don't worry, I hear Mars is a nice place to hang out), but the energy you left with them will live for years to come. It becomes the core element of your organizational culture.

This analogy may seem odd, but it really isn't far from the truth. As leaders, we are the primary source of energy for our organizations. Like it or not, we will always get back from others what we first give to them. I'm going to put this image in my mind every day as I head in to work. The concept definitely gets me thinking, makes me pause before I start to pout or complain or slide into acting like an unhappy eight-year-old. And while I'm all about also getting the proper succession plans set up on a formal level, the reality is that the energy we give and the culture it creates is going to last at least as long, if not longer, than some notarized, ninety-eight-page legal document. For better or for worse, our energy is very much the gift that keeps on giving. Which is why, whether I wake up in a good mood or not, I'm going to do my best to make it a really good gift. In fact, I'm going to start looking for a nice box to leave on my desk.

7. Building One's Own Energy

Ultimately, you're the only one who knows what contributes to raising and/or lowering your own energy levels. The key is knowing what it is that helps you to build, restore, maintain, and sustain positive energy, then to manage your life accordingly. There are no absolutes. Introverts like me like to be alone; extroverts prefer to engage with other people to recharge. The things that increase my energy are learning, reading, running, journaling, sitting in the sun, listening to good music, cooking, and connecting one-on-one with people I like to be around. While everyone has their own version of my list, there are a few themes that I've noticed consistently come to the fore from folks I respect and have asked about this issue. Generally, though definitely not always, people who can keep themselves at high rates of positive energy engage in very regular routines that somehow include positive and planned physical and emotional workouts, do regular learning, and create a lot of positive connecting time (in whatever way works for them). Most are also pretty generous, and nearly all are actively and highly appreciative.

Part of keeping my energy up is also managing when and how I will engage with the things that lower my energy. This is, of course, also a personal thing. I try to tackle tasks I don't want to do early in the day so I can get them over with. If I have a meeting that I think is going to be stressful I'll try to schedule time to go running right afterwards. And I've long since stopped reading financial statements and customer complaints late in the day—once they get into my head I just can't get them out, and my energy when I head home is awful.

One less pleasant point to raise in terms of staying on the "ups" of the energy spectrum is the simple, yet super-important, challenge of keeping time spent with the people that drain our energy to a real minimum. Louis de Bonald once wrote that, "There are people who do not know how to waste their time all by themselves. They are the scourge of active people." I'll transpose that onto the world of energy. There are some well-meaning folks who aren't satisfied just having bad energy; they want to drag everyone else's down, too. They're the people who complain endlessly, the ones who find the problematic aspect of every situation, the people who persist in seeing what's wrong, no matter how much the rest of us try to focus things on what's going well first. Granted, we all have bad days, but the people who are like this all the time are not fun to be around. While we certainly need to be kind and to interact respectfully where needed, I try to keep my time with these folks as brief as I can—the better to keep my own energy level high. And when I'm feeling a bit down, tired, stressed, or distracted, and I know that I'm all the more vulnerable to absorbing their bad juju, I just politely but pretty firmly avoid them with ever greater diligence.

When we have people like this in our organizations, there's just no way around the reality that they're having a negative impact on our culture. One way or another, respectfully and caringly, we need to help them to either alter their energy or help them find another place to work. Basically, these people are like the gas-guzzlers of the organizational energy world. They take about ten times as much energy to go the same distance as our best, high-energy, high-performance players. If you want to subsidize them in your organization, by all means, go for it. Unwittingly, I've certainly done it in the past. But seriously, these people are draining good energy out of everyone around them faster than even the most positive leader can put it back in.

8. Check Your Energy at the Door

I don't mean leave it behind; I'm talking about pausing ten seconds *before* you enter a room, make a phone call, teach a class, start a dialogue, a meeting, or an email. And then using those few seconds to make sure that the energy you're bringing to it is really what you want to bring. It's the emotional equivalent of putting on your seat belt and making sure the mirrors are okay before you start your car. I guarantee it many times over—the energy I put in the room will have a major impact on the way the interaction goes. As the leader, the energy I bring will have an even bigger impact than that of others in the group—the better mine is, the better theirs is likely to be. The better theirs is, the more fun I have. The more fun I'm having, the better my energy. The better my energy, the better theirs is. It's a virtuous, totally sustainable, high-energy cycle. So take pause before you turn that door handle to enter; getting your internal energy properly calibrated is a small, no-cost contribution to the success of your entire organization.

9. Four Energy Faux Pas to Avoid

Sometimes, despite my efforts, I still start to slide. My energy slips down towards the middle range of the scale or, if I'm not careful, straight into the negative end of the spectrum. When I start to slip, I start to bring down the energy of our entire team. Here are four things I've tried to teach myself to avoid. All four are downers. Each drains energy faster than we can infuse it, much like trying to heat your house in the middle of a Michigan winter with your windows wide open. You can keep throwing resources at the problem by putting more energy into play, but it's way more effective to just close the windows.

   a. Looking unhappy. It may sound silly to say this, but start watching how many people out in the world just look miserable most of the time. They're frowning, even grimacing, looking glum; it's amazing how many people walk around muttering, complaining under their breath about customers and co-workers. Even if they mean well (and many do), I guarantee that their look and the commensurate energy that comes off it contribute negatively to any group they're a part of. Unwittingly, they drag down most everyone around them, and pretty soon, the whole team looks terrible.

b. Negative body language. This overlaps, I suppose, with item *a* above, but I separate it because bad body language isn't always about being unhappy. When the leader is curling up in the corner, slouching, has bad posture, or won't make eye contact, the rest of the room will, consciously or not, pick up on these silent signals. It's obviously *not* a good thing. Imagine the quarterback coming into the huddle looking all hunched over and timid, and then think about what that would likely do to the confidence levels of those around him. Looks alone can drop the energy level of a group by half in about thirty seconds. A couple of sighs and eye rolls can deflate even the most dedicated staff member. Pretty soon people spread the word—"stay away from the boss"; "don't bother making suggestions"; "keep your opinions to yourself." Even though no words to the effect might actually have been spoken, people aren't stupid. They simply shut up, take their good energy elsewhere, and the organization suffers.

c. Bad acting. Sure, all service jobs and all leadership roles are partly about acting. But it's supposed to be a good performance! The best thespians deeply connect with the core of the part they're playing, so that from the minute they hit the stage the audience feels like the actor actually *is* the character that he or she is playing. By contrast, people who are trying too hard, who aren't coming at this from the heart, come across as slick, superficial, phony, and awkward. Their energy is just *not* good, and their efforts are almost always ineffective. Most everyone around them, knowingly or not, starts to shift away, to pay less attention to what they have to say, to take them less and less seriously. Respect goes down, and when respect for the leader falls, the energy in the organization won't be far behind.

d. Sarcasm and gossip. Hey, we've all done it. But we also know in our gut that neither gossip nor sarcasm is a great thing. And we know that neither contributes to raising the energy levels in our business. That gossip is destructive and distracting is pretty much a given. Sarcasm, in the right setting, can actually work well, but take it from one who can easily overdo it: too much can bring the energy of the group down in about eighteen seconds.

All that said, this is real life, and we all slip sometimes. It's silly to say we won't. Heck, I've probably screwed up on all four of these behaviors simultaneously a few times (it's not easy being an overachiever!). But even a small bit of increased consciousness helps us cut our incidences in half, which in turn has a huge positive impact on our organization. If you don't believe that, just multiply each time we *don't* do one of these by the impact each of us has as leaders on everyone around us, times the number of people on our team, and you'll start to realize that each small slip we make might seriously mean days of productivity gained or lost in a week. It's wild, but do the math. Now that I think about it that way, every eye roll and sarcastic remark I've made over the years has probably cost us big time in terms of wasted energy and the commensurate decrease in productivity.

10. Keeping It on an Even Keel

Another element of effective energy management is the ability to read a group and the environment in which it's working, and then alter one's own energy level accordingly. You can see this at play regularly in sports, or equally so in the classroom or in board meetings. If people are starting to get discouraged or fall flat, the leader needs to step up, raise the energy bar, rally the team, and bring more enthusiasm into the room. Quickly the team starts to feel more optimistic, the energy of the group shifts up, and success, while not guaranteed, becomes a lot more likely.

Conversely, a group can actually get too high—they get a bit full of themselves and lose focus. On the surface, their energy might seem okay, but a closer look tells you it's not grounded, not anchored in the realities of what's really going on. Often there's *a lot* of motion, but most of it isn't very meaningful. In sports, this is the young team that's high-fiving and whooping it up all over the place, acting like they've pulled off a big win just by getting off to a nice lead in the first quarter. Every good veteran and coach knows that this is actually the time to slow the rookies down, to mellow out their instinctive response to celebrate way too soon. To do that she brings her own energy down a notch, gets the group to take a deep collective breath and be more cognizant of the realities of their situation. The team will be a bit quieter, but significantly more solid; the leader has led them to the sort of energy that's needed to keep their heads in the game and get to the desired outcome effectively.

Easy Energy Assessment Exercises

Small bits of attention can go a long way in building learning, and from that learning, improved performance. Here are a few really simple, exceedingly low-cost ways to get to work on better understanding energy in action in your world.

1. Self Assessments

a. I'll bet if you simply keep track of what you're doing, you'll learn a lot—awareness is an excellent way to get going. Try scoring your energy level at the start of every interaction, again halfway through, and then again at the end. Score it from 0 (a ton of unproductive energy) to 10 (super-excellent positive energy). Look at how the three scores compare. What was happening that led to the changes? More importantly, what can you do next time in similar situations to take charge of your own energy, to keep it high even when the inevitable downers come your way? Conversely, what can you do to make the most out of the positives so that you can store up the good energy?

b. Pay close attention to the energy each of your team members brings to work each day. Again score it from 0 (totally sucks) to 10 (so great you can barely contain yourself). I guarantee that in even a day or two you'll learn a ton, all of which will help you to manage and mentor your team members more effectively than ever. Again, try scoring their energy at the beginning of a shift, halfway through, and again when it's over. How did each individual's energy influence that of the group? Who formally, or informally, set the pace? Did the folks with bad energy rise to the levels of an otherwise positive group? Or were one or two bad-energy apples able to take the rest of the group down?

2. Group Assessments

a. Have each person on your team do a self assessment and then talk about their learnings. Getting energy management into peoples' minds, combined with a modicum of meaningful leadership work, is almost guaranteed to get the energy level headed in a positive direction. The dialogue around what they're learning is sure to make a big difference in the way they work.

b. Have everyone score the energy of the group on the same scale. In order to avoid group-think, it's important that they actually write down the score they gave, why they gave it, and what they'd do both personally and organizationally to make it better on the next shift or meeting or whatever it is you're measuring. Then go around the room and find out how each person assessed the group's energy. Guaranteed to make for very interesting conversation, especially the first few times through. I'll also guarantee that, given good leadership, over time the group will work together to raise the energy level higher than it was when you started.

11. Energy Alchemy—Turning Trouble into Organizational Gold

Alchemy is an ancient art focused on transforming mundane things into something marvelous. The name actually originates with the Arabic, *al-kimia*, meaning "the art of transformation." The most profit-driven among medieval alchemists focused on turning common metals into gold, but other, more spiritually minded masters worked to transform any number of commonplace materials into elixirs and solvents (from the same linguistic root as "solve") that would serve as solutions to all the universe's problems.

I can't say that effective energy management will turn old auto parts into profits, but it really does work wonders of alchemical proportions on the people part of our organizations. At no cost other than a bit of time and attention, better energy management can take anyone's leadership effectiveness up at least a couple of notches. The benefits to them as individuals, and to us as an organization, are literally enormous.

Here's how it works. Think about a few of those settings where we know the energy is likely to be negative, either because the group is having a hard time collectively, or because we've let a couple of determined doubters bring it down. I've learned that, more often than not, if I go into the engagement with the belief and hope and effort to actually raise the energy to a more positive—if still imperfect—level, I can often overcome the negativity. When that happens, it's like found money in management. The alchemy gets the whole group thinking and acting more positively. The better the energy, the better people feel, the more effectively they're able to focus on the work at hand. Mind you, this doesn't always work—it's an art, not a science. In some settings, despite my efforts, I just can't get the combination to click back to positive. Like any skill, managing group energy takes practice. But when I do, it's all upside!

12. The Endlessly Renewable Nature of Good Energy

Perhaps the greatest thing about having my awareness raised so suddenly by Anese was the realization that, with a bit of increased effectiveness on my end as a leader, I could tap into a totally natural and completely renewable energy source. Unlike conventional energy sources such as fossil fuels, which, quite clearly, are limited in supply, this is one we never have to run short on. In fact, it's really the inverse of more conventional energy sources—positive energy actually builds on itself. The more good energy you and I put out, the more we manage it well in ourselves and others, the more good energy will be built around it. Which in turn attracts customers, partners, and staff who already put out good energy on their own, which in turn adds to the effectiveness of the positive energy producers on our team. The better the energy, the better everything works, the better our results, the easier it is to work, the better the results and . . . on we go.

The Inside Scoop on Working Here at Zingerman's

Melina Hinton, Server, Zingerman's Roadhouse

The list below came to me courtesy of Melina Hinton, who at the time she wrote this was a server at the Roadhouse. She's since moved out West, but her six years with us were good ones. While I was writing the essay on energy, I also happened to be gradually getting back into work after three different surgeries in a period of sixty days. Melina mentioned to me one evening that she was happy I was back because the energy was noticeably higher. Since I was in the middle of writing about that very subject, I asked her for a bit more info—far better to go to the source to suss out what works and what doesn't work than to sit at home trying to figure it out on my own. So, here, in her own words, is what I've quietly come to call, "Melina's List." I refer to it now and again to help make sure I'm on course and staying true to what I teach. Use it or ignore it as you like.

Ari, I'm glad that you are doing well, and that you are out of the hospital. In response to why things are not quite the same here without you . . . there are a lot of reasons but here are a few offhand.

- You always acknowledge each and every one of us when you arrive, so we feel important.
- You follow up with us personally, which makes us feel that you really care.
- When you are here I find that I strive more for your approval. You have a "good conscience" quality about you (like the good angel on your shoulder).
- You have a great way of empowering us all, which comes back to us in a very positive way—we are allowed to feel good about the decisions we make here at work.
- What you do with our guests is always so positive that they, in return, treat us better.
- The energy builds here just by you walking in the door, which we all pick up and then our energy is better.
- It's great that you always offer your help, and encourage us to take that extra step that we might not have.
- It provides a very comfortable atmosphere here—that the CEO of this company wears jeans and a t-shirt every day.
- You joke and kid with us; yes, you're the boss, but you are humble, kind, and friendly.
- And I will never forget that you changed the Wednesday night meatloaf special from spicy ketchup to gravy after listening to Dorothy's and my suggestion.

Hope that helps; once again you're missed, feel better.

In honesty, I'd completely forgotten about the gravy and meatloaf until she wrote the note. It was, to be frank, a fairly unimportant incident in my existence and had happened four or five years before she sent me her list. Melina and Dorothy, another server, mentioned casually in the middle of a shift that the meatloaf would be better served with gravy than with the spicy ketchup it was coming with at the time. I must have mentioned it to our partner and chef, Alex Young, and the next week, the meatloaf magically appeared at the pre-shift tasting for staff served with gravy. The fact that this small act of listening to, and then acting on, a simple suggestion from a staff member could have such a powerful impact on everything is almost unbelievable to me.

kristen hogue bringing sandwiches to a table at the deli

Defining Positive Energy

On the Way to 380 Percent More Fun!

In the interest of taking our newly established emphasis on energy out of the ethereal and into the everyday work world, we've turned what we learned from Anese Cavanaugh into another of our very teachable, learnable, repeatable, and effective organizational recipes. Like our 3 Steps to Great Service or 3 Steps to Great Finance, the 4 Steps to Effective Energy Management that follow make up a recipe that literally everyone in our organization learns and, I hope, uses almost every day. We now teach it in every new staff orientation and have woven it into any number of our other classes and ZingTrain seminars as well. It's become a pretty common thing to hear staff members mention "energy" in post-interview debriefs to describe what they liked, or didn't like, about applicants. Each business reports on and forecasts its energy level every two weeks at our Partners' Group meetings.

Like all our organizational recipes, having the clarity that the 4 Steps bring really does make a big difference. New staff members feel more comfortable more quickly when they learn it, managers have a tool to take with them on shift every day, and we develop common language around an area of our work to which we're giving ever greater importance. The recipe has, I'm confident, helped everyone here be more mindful of, and effective at, managing our own and the group's energy. Which in turn translates directly into better customer experiences, a more enjoyable workplace, and better . . . everything! Feel free to adapt these ideas at will—my energy goes up (and so, I know, does Anese's) every time someone benefits from her teachings.

Having fun at work has long been a high priority for us at Zingerman's. It's explicitly written into our guiding principles, and is referenced regularly in our staff handbook and our training classes. Fun, I hope, is on most people's minds here every day. While most of the world seems to believe that you have to leave work before you can start to have fun, we've believed from the beginning that the two are anything but mutually exclusive. To the contrary, in our experience, the more effectively we work, the more we've found that the fun will follow. And also, conversely, the more fun we're having—in a professional way—the better the work usually goes. It is, after all, the basis of the twelfth of our Natural Laws of Business: "Great organizations are appreciative, and the people in them have more fun."

Although we'd all agreed we wanted to have it, we'd never really gotten clear over the years on what "having fun" meant to us as an organization. And

I'm sure you won't be shocked to learn that most everyone here had a different definition. Most of us take "fun" to mean doing the stuff that we each personally enjoy, but of course one person's fun is, inevitably, another's frustration.

The problem got much more serious when we put fun into our 2020 vision. It states that we will have successfully quantified fun, measured fun, and increased our fun factor by 380 percent. Unfortunately, we actually ended up in a lot of arguments over what was "fun" and what wasn't. In all honesty, the whole thing had started to make me a little crazy. Extroverts wanted more parties; introverts asked for more time alone. Athletes advocated for more physical activities; others wanted fishing trips, winter camping, shots of tequila, sewing circles, or poetry slams. To prove their points, people started bringing in data about fun to back up their arguments. No offense, but knowing what percentage of the world prefers to go bowling or how many people it takes to make an extracurricular activity productive is not high on my life list. All I knew at the time was that all the in-depth research was actually anything *but* fun!

At the time, I worked hard to remind myself that all their data gathering and point making was a good problem—we'd agreed on the vision and people were taking their commitment seriously and trying to get going so that we could make our 2020 vision a reality. As the months went by, I realized that we weren't going to go anywhere until we could get clear on what we really meant by "fun" on an organizational level—it's almost impossible to operate effectively if everyone involved isn't speaking the same language. I realized that with other core ideas in our organization, we'd done a lot of (not very glamorous) work over the years to clarify our terminology; to define what we meant by oft-used terms like "vision," "on time," and "great service." They're phrases that almost everyone uses but few companies get clear about what they mean.

In particular, one day it dawned on me that we'd done a very good job of defining what we meant by "quality." We make clear when we teach it that there's a difference for us between what foods each of us may like personally, and what we believe tastes best on a professional level. While most of the world throws the phrase "high quality" around rather freely, we figured out what it means to us: on a professional level "high quality" at Zingerman's means "full-flavored and traditionally made." It dawned on me further that we'd failed to do any of this work for the definition of "fun." What people were arguing about was actually what each of them *believed* was fun—for them. Without a clear and agreed-upon organizational understanding, it was clear to me that we were going to have a hard time getting anything accomplished. Anese gave me the answer: in the professional world at Zingerman's, the word "fun" would mean "positive energy."

Of course, we knew enough to know that the seemingly uncertain nature of "positive energy" in the modern work world would surely raise eyebrows and elicit at least a little bit of skepticism. Without question, the concept can come across to those unfamiliar with it as being annoyingly unscientific and impossibly unquantifiable. Not surprisingly, we take issue with all of that. Although they don't teach it in business school (yet), positive energy is actually fairly easily made, self-monitored, *and* measured. What follows is our effort to give some clarity to the concept and offer up a brief recipe that can take energy management out of the esoteric realm and put it into play in real life, every-day-in-the-organizational-neighborhood practice.

The question that arises is, of course, "What is positive energy?" I figured I'd start my search for an answer by calling Anese Cavanaugh. Given that she's actively taught the stuff for so long now, it didn't surprise me that Anese had an answer at the ready: "It's the ability to create positive results through the vibe you put out there," she said. "It's the feeling, the attitude you bring to life, relationships, and all your interactions. Positive energy feels good and creates even more positive feelings in yourself and in those around you."

Fully agreed. When there's positive energy on a shift, things are flowing. People feel good. We're alert, we're smiling, we're finding joy, we're appreciative, and we're looking forward to more good things to come. Time feels like it's flying by. We may well be busy but we like it—that's why we're here. Obviously, we all will have our own personal examples or catchphrases to describe that feeling. But, application aside, almost everyone you ask will know nearly immediately what you're talking about when you start describing it. When the energy is really positive, optimism abounds, people are smiling, their eyes are alive, they're helpful and appreciative. They like what they're doing and they're glad to be doing it. They're laughing and joking with each other, teasing but in a loving way, paying attention throughout. Pretty much everyone will tell you straight off that, when the positive energy is present and flowing, it's just way more fun to be at work!

Anese breaks the overall idea of positive energy into three categories:

1. Physical energy is marked by pace; people are focused, having fun, and moving fast, but not at all out of control. They're quick, yet oddly calm at the same time. Moving too fast, moving frenetically and anxiously around a room, may mean there's a lot of motion, but it's *not* great energy. When the energy is positive, people's posture will generally be good, their eyes look alive, they're alert, listening, smelling, sensing all of what's going on around them with a high level of attention to detail. Not only are they having fun, they look like it! Good physical energy also manifests in high stamina—the ability to keep going forward effectively long after others have opted out.

2. Mental or Emotional energy is when we're feeling grounded, centered, and appreciative. We're anticipating the positive, even while preparing for possible problems. We feel open, welcoming, appreciating the little things, calm, aware, enjoyable to be around. When things go wrong, as they're bound to do on occasion, people with positive emotional energy will pull together, acknowledge the stress, and then calmly address the problem. We experience positive emotional energy when we're learning and teaching, when we're excited about new opportunities, new information, and new experiences. It also comes, conversely, when we're comforted by familiar foods, family, friendly faces, or a gentle touch on the shoulder from an old friend. While physical and emotional energy certainly feed into and build off of each other, one may feel fully rested physically, but still be an emotional mess. Conversely, we can be physically exhausted but emotionally engaged. Sometimes, of course, the two can conflict—everyone will have their own issues; my Achilles energy heel is that I can get so emotionally jazzed by good learning that I stay up way too late reading and writing.

3 Elements of Energy

1. Physical
2. Mental/Emotional
3. Vibrational

3. Vibrational energy might be the most interesting of the three. It's not something they talk about in boardrooms, but the truth is, vibrational energy—the good, the bad, and the in between—is all around us. And although they don't teach it in business school, it's hardly a new concept. Vibes are akin to waves that flow out and impact everything around them; in this case, that would be our organizational culture. Food writer Vertamae Grosvenor authored an entire book called *Vibration Cooking*. The Beach Boys sang about "Good Vibrations." Mihaly Csikszentmihalyi, whose name hardly anyone can pronounce (it's roughly "Cheek-sent-me-high"), is a fairly famous, Hungarian-born psychologist who's written about it extensively; he refers to the feeling as "flow." In *Small Giants*, Bo Burlingham calls it "mojo." Athletes and musicians regularly talk about being "in the zone" or "on fire." Anese says it's "Your vibe; your impact; how you show up; what others feel around you, what you invite in others; what you create." For better and for worse, vibrational energy carries into all the interactions we have.

Vibrational energy, to be clear, can only be effectively judged by others—it's not the energy we "think" we're bringing, it's the energy *others* are experiencing. It's the energy we give off into the room, or through our phone calls, emails, texts, or rapid eye movements. Like service, vibrational energy is always and only really judged by the recipients of it. When you get a good handle on yours, you can, more often than not, probably be close in your assessment. But at the end of the day, the only real way to know is to ask others.

From a leadership standpoint, the vibrational energy we bring to work every day will have an enormous impact on everyone else. Remember that we're talking unseen, unspoken, unacknowledged, and often unintended energy here. Words and intentions are all well and good, but it's the vibrational energy that, more often than not, will get people going. Or not going, as the case may be. When we as leaders bring negative vibrational energy into any situation, it's going to detract from the work quality of everyone around us.

Vibrational energy is also a great coaching tool—it gives leaders a constructive and meaningful way to help ourselves and others to be more effective and, I suppose, reflective as well. If someone's vibrational energy is exhausting to others, or driving them away, we have an obligation (in the interest of helping them succeed—see page 137) to share that with them. If you do address it, what you'll often get back is an argument—"That's not how I feel!" or "I'm totally fine." While anyone may choose to argue, there's really no argument to be had. While they may be accurate in assessing their *intent*, they're likely way off when it comes to judging how they're coming off to others. Just as we're always going to honor a customer's view about the quality of the service they received from us, so, too, do we always need to respect the feedback others might give us about vibrational energy. If everyone involved is up front about how vibrational energy is coming across, it's far easier to recalibrate if things start to slide away from the ideal.

If you blend all three of these elements—physical, emotional, and vibrational—you have a read on your energy.

Building Positive Energy at Zingerman's

We generally measure our energy on a scale of 0 to 10. A score of 0 is really low: probably annoying, very unpleasant to be around. A 10 is great: calm but moving quickly, confident, nice to be around. When someone's at a 10, others will usually and often unconsciously gather up a bit of the positive energy that's being exuded. Jenny Tubbs, who's worked here for nearly fifteen years and is one of our best service trainers, suggested, quite beautifully I think, that we change the scale to "Zero to Zen." Raised my energy half a point as soon as I heard it. We do tend to be biased towards "Z" words, so maybe down the road we'll make the formal change. In the meantime, it's a great teaching tool because it quickly makes clear that high energy is *not* frantic or frenetic—on the contrary, when we're at "Zen" we're calm, cool, collected, focused, positive, productive, and enjoyable to be around!

I teach the 4 Steps that follow every few weeks now in our new-staff orientation class. My hope is to make clear from the get-go that each of us is responsible for the quality of the energy we bring to work, and then to give everyone a simple tool and technique for effectively managing it. With even a modicum of mindfulness, the recipe can make a serious difference in anyone's— and, ultimately, everyone's—day.

4 Steps to Effective Energy Management

1. Read it
2. Vision it
3. Manage it
4. Repeat it

1. Read it: Reading your energy is akin to taking your emotional pulse. On the Zero to Zen (or call it ten if you're feeling more traditional) scale, where's your energy right now? There's no "right" answer. You may feel up, down, or otherwise. The question, here, is only one of awareness. In the beginning, this calls for a very conscious level of activity. It probably requires really pausing and breathing mindfully and getting some sense of where you're at on all three levels. Over time, as you get better and better at it, you'll likely become what we call "unconsciously competent"—you just check your energy at the door, and then over and over again throughout the day without even knowing you're doing it.

2. Vision it: As with all of our visions, this is about getting clear on our preferred future. By the end of the day (or shift, or class, or, I suppose, this essay) where do you want your energy level to be? In essence, what's your vision? As Anese asks her clients all the time, "What impact do you want to have on those around you?" Remember, forecasting is a leadership act—it's your call: Where are you going to lead your energy level today?

3. Manage it: Once we're mindful of our energy, and we have a clear sense of where we want to take it, it's well within our ability to effectively (though of course never perfectly) manage it. How we do that is different for each of us. Some need to take a break, others need to break out a good joke. Some need a quick breather, others just need to do deep breathing. Some should speed up, others have to slow down. Some need to vent, others will want to voice appreciation. The key is realizing how much influence we have on our energy: to paraphrase Gandhi, it's all about how much we need to "be the change we want to see."

4. Repeat it: Effective energy management means running repeatedly through steps 1, 2, and 3. The more we're monitoring and mindfully modifying our energy at regular intervals, the more likely we are to attain the positive future, the vision, of positive energy we're after. It's easy to get thrown off—anything less than an optimal interaction is likely to cause an energy dip amongst any of us. Anything from a difficult customer to a dropped loaf of bread; from a bad tip to unseasonably high humidity; a dropped phone call from a mail-order customer part-way through a big order . . . almost anything can bring energy down. It's normal for that to happen. The key is to keep running through these 4 Steps repeatedly during the shift so that we can catch it when it's starting to slide and, on the upside, so we can ride it and appreciate good energy when we're "in the zone."

As good as our energy already was at Zingerman's before I met Anese back in '09, it's most definitely even better now. Without question it has helped to improve our service, the quality of our workplace, and the quality of the daily experience we deliver to everyone we interact with. I have no doubt that the improvement in those areas has helped us to grow sales, reduce staff turnover, etc. Energy management is taught in our orientation, our service training, and our classes on leadership. We also use it extensively in our work at ZingTrain. Anese has come to speak to our leadership team, and we've had a few of our up-and-coming leaders go through her "energy circle" training program. Bo Burlingham and Jack Stack, co-authors of *The Great Game of Business* and the granddaddies of open-book finance, taught me years ago that if you track anything—that's right, pretty much anything—you're going to get about a 10 to 15 percent improvement just by tracking it. I'd say we've easily gotten that and then some. I'm happy and honored to pass it on to others!

The Inside Scoop on Working Here at Zingerman's

Dana Laidlaw, Retail Counter Person, Zingerman's Bakehouse

Seeing how other people struggle with their energy really forces me to see the impact I can and *do* have on others when I'm at work. That is *really* educational. Most of the time I'm concentrating on my energy—what do I have to do to stay between an 8 and a 10 (for myself and the customer's sake) and still support the closers and make them as ready for a great close as I can? Some days it's pretty easy to stay in the "Zen" zone, while other days I feel I spend all my time trying to stay focused getting X number of things done. It's hard to focus on tasks and energy at the same time, but I'm sure it'll eventually come more naturally.

I have spent this year trying to not mutter to myself under my breath when I make mistakes, and I think it has helped. In hindsight, I think that the comments I have gotten this year from people about my being a "calm" or "comforting" presence can be traced directly to my efforts to not lower the energy in the room by anything I'm doing or feeling in the moment. This is definitely good service in action—both to others and to myself.

mike white sampling cheese at the deli

SECRET #22

We're All Leaders

Getting Frontline Folks to Step to the Fore

Of all the ideas in this book, the one that follows may, ten years from now, turn out to be one of the most powerful. It's a sleeper, something that's sort of still in the background even here at Zingerman's, and one that's only a faint whisper of a thought out in the world at large. While I'm sure others have had the same insight many times in history, it came to me—a belated glimpse of the obvious—only a few years ago. It is, as Emile DeFelice said about his approach to alternative agriculture (see page 13), pretty much the opposite of the way the rest of the world does it. But I'm confident that, for us at least, it's a way better way to work.

The idea of everyone here being responsible for leadership follows fully in the footsteps of our long-ago decisions here to redistribute responsibility and authority for customer service, finance, organizational change, and almost everything else. Just because the accountants are the ones counting the cash, and the owners of the business are the ones putting in the capital, it doesn't mean that everyone else here isn't also accountable for our financial success. Same, of course, now goes for leadership— like every other good-sized business, we have an org chart and a whole lineup of supervisors, managers, partners, and the like. But the bottom line is that leadership isn't limited to just those who happen to have a title; here, at least, it rests—really, radically, and regularly—on everyone.

Although I wrote the original essay well before I reconnected with my anarchist mentors, it's quite remarkable how closely the concept correlates with what they were all about. The truth is that, while the concept may sound simple and soft enough to the unsuspecting, I think that starting to get everyone to think and act like a leader has the potential to radically redistribute the power within an organization, in a very good way.

There are, I know, "secrets" in this book that are easier to buy into than this one. But if you want to pick up on an approach that will make a meaningful, lasting, and life-affirming change in your organizational culture and the lives of everyone in it, give some thought to spending your intellectual capital on the concepts that follow. Convincing everyone to think and act like a leader, as if their decisions have a significant impact on the rest of the organization, may not be the easiest work you'll ever undertake. But it might be some of the most impactful; if we sell the approach well, it will, I guarantee, alter your organization for the better, and probably, forever.

I'm sure that there are still many old-school business thinkers who will be skeptical about this sort of stuff. Frontline people, that approach would argue, are here to work, not to lead; they're hired to follow orders and implement decisions that have been delivered decisively by brilliantly charismatic bosses. At least that's the way they seem to see it. It's not, however, my sense of the way the world really works. The truth is, I think, we at the "top" need all the help we can get. There are others all around us, even in "lowly" frontline positions, who know things we don't know but would unquestionably benefit from. Old-school bosses may have all the authority, but they hardly have all the answers.

The other big issue on the table is that although most upper-level executives would probably never acknowledge it, the seemingly small decisions that front-line people make all day long have a huge impact on organizational success. Strategic plans are great, but a scowl, smirk, and some bad vibrational energy from an uncaring counter person could send a potentially big corporate gift customer spinning away in a matter of seconds. While the old-school norm is to act as if the work frontliners are busy with every day is basically brainless, the truth is that every small service interaction, every tiny judgment about quality, every bit of energy they put—or don't put—into their work with their colleagues can, and does, make a big difference in the organization's health and welfare. Which leads me, through one of those odd paths my mind tends to meander down, to an anarchist folk singer few Americans will ever have heard of.

Let me introduce you, then, posthumously I'm afraid, to Utah Phillips. I'm not sure how best to describe him—like so many of the men and women I admire and learn from, he was a whole lot of things; "hard to categorize" would probably be the easiest label to lay on him. He was a folk singer, Korean War vet, peace activist, poet, humorist, hobo train rider, and also, as I said, an anarchist. If nothing else, Utah unquestionably walked his own path. It wasn't, from what I know, always an easy one, but it was his. The man worked hard at finding his own way in the world. He lived his values, and brought joy and insight to people everywhere he went. If Hugh MacLeod's marvelous book *Ignore Everybody* had come out in his day, Utah would surely have been in it or, at least, written a blurb for the back. Born Bruce Phillips in 1935, he came to be called "Utah" in honor of his later life in Salt Lake City. Although he slipped through life unnoticed by most of the world, during his long career Utah caught the attention of those in the know. His songs have been covered by Emmylou Harris, Joan Baez, and Arlo Guthrie, amongst others. In the mid-90s alternative folk singer Ani DiFranco took him under her artistic wing and put him on her

Righteous Babe record label (featured in Bo Burlingham's book *Small Giants*), and in Utah's later years the pair performed together regularly. The Folk Alliance gave him a lifetime achievement award in 1997. Sadly, he passed away in 2008.

The funny thing is that I actually met Utah Phillips, unexpectedly, one evening out at the Roadhouse. He was performing in town that night and his booking agent, Jim Fleming, a regular Zingerman's customer, had brought him in for dinner. I spent only about ten minutes with him, but he made a very lasting impression. It was at table 206 in the bar room, and he was sitting at what any server there would formally know as "position one"—the first seat on the left of the table when your back is to the front door. Why I remember that it was that table, and that he was in that seat, I don't really know. I have a feeling, though, that Utah was like that—I'm guessing his influence on those he was close to remains rather large. Once his spirit entered your life, I don't think it ever left. Big white beard, broad smile, gentle laugh, soft voice: he was definitely a presence in the room. Having gone on at length earlier in this book about energy, I will say with total certainty that his was exceptional—calm, positive, affirming. And peaceful. Jenny Tubbs would have probably said his energy was at a "Zen" on the energy scale.

As it happens (unrelated to any of this at all), Utah told me that he loved Jewish food. Now, as my mother would have said, "Utah Phillips" was definitely "not a Jewish name" so that was hardly what I expected to be talking to him about that evening. But it turns out that he'd grown up in a Jewish neighborhood in Cleveland, with a Jewish stepfather, and a high affinity for chopped liver, rye bread, mandelbread (see page 354 for the recipe), and the like. Later the family moved out to Salt Lake City and he was Bar Mitzvahed there, in the capital of Mormon culture. While I was at the table, he rattled off a raft of Yiddish words to show me that he knew what he was talking about. Even my mother would have been impressed. For whatever reason, living in the moment, I sent Utah a gift box of Jewish culinary treats from the Deli, along with a thank-you card, set to arrive on May 12th of that year. My mother, impressed or not, was in Israel at the time. She actually entered the hospital there with pneumonia that very same day. She died, rather suddenly, four days later. Utah turned out to be on equally unsteady ground—he, too, passed away that same month, May 23rd to be exact. Not surprisingly, I guess, while dealing with the grieving around my mother's loss, Utah's death slipped by me with only a small bit of attention.

It feels a bit strange to meet someone so special so close to the end of such an exceptional life. There's a lot of Utah Phillips lore if you look into it, but one of the best-known bits is a song he did about an incident that took place nearly a century ago. Actually, it happened back in the era in which Emma Goldman et al. would have been active. In fact, I'd venture to guess that had he lived in that era himself, he'd have spent much of his time sharing jail cells with Emma and her anarchist associates. Anyway, the incident in question occurred in 1916. In a rather interesting, though nearly forgotten, footnote in American history, a ferry full of free speech activists tried to dock in Everett, Washington. The local sheriff boarded the boat and demanded to know who the group's leaders were. "We're all leaders here!" was the men's unified response. The statement was, seemingly, so provocative that the sheriff and his deputies immediately attacked. A dozen and a half people died in the ensuing violence.

To be clear, I'm a completely non-violent person with no affinity for conflict of any sort, but the story and the statement have stuck with me, along with the personal recollection of meeting Utah here at the Roadhouse. I realize now, too late, that I should have sat longer with him. But, at least I met the man, and have a chance here to add a small asterisk to his already exceptional resume—Utah Phillips has now officially appeared in a book on business leadership. Fortunately, the voices of Emma Goldman and Alexander Berkman are here, too, to keep his spirit company.

In my fantasy version of our organization, should some similar event ever take place here and someone were demanding to see our leaders, I'd like to imagine that the response most everyone (other than, understandably, the newest staff members) would give would be something along the lines of, "Hi! How can we help you?"

Which, in a Utahian nutshell, is what this whole essay is all about. Back at the time of the Everett massacre, the idea of everyone being a leader was clearly a radical, almost riot-causing concept; at Zingerman's, I want to make it an everyday reality. I mean, I'm all about clearly defined job responsibilities and leaders stepping up to serve the organization. But the more I work my way through and around the idea of this whole thing, the more strongly I feel that the time has come. Maybe the 21st century will be the era in which we free the idea of leadership from the old prejudices and preconditions that have surrounded it for most of the 20th. Maybe instead of just turning the old pyramidal org chart upside down (you know, the old inverted triangle), it's time to, at least conceptually, flatline the whole thing once and for all. If we're getting out of the old-school hierarchical structure and into a more inclusive, creative, free-flowing, fun, and egalitarian approach to work, why limit leadership thinking and activity to a tiny slice of organizational life? Instead, I'd say, let's share the learning, the stress, the success, and all its other elements throughout the organization. To paraphrase the boys on the boat in Everett, "Let's all be leaders here!"

Managing versus Leading

Many business books will argue that there's a big difference between leadership and management. They rarely paint a pretty picture of the latter; management is mostly associated with maintaining the status quo; at best, a bit of petty bureaucracy. For the most part, management is made to seem myopic; the bad guys in the story of business. Leadership, by contrast, is the one that we're meant to look for, aspire to, and appreciate—it's generally far more favorably framed as the thinking person's way to the future.

I, on the other hand, have always used the two terms—management and leadership—interchangeably, and have been very insistent that there was really no difference between them. I couldn't ever figure out how one could *manage* an organization of any size without *leading* others towards something. It just seemed clear that if you were managing a group well, you must also, by definition, be leading or else nothing would be getting done. Conversely, I'd never understood how you could lead effectively without also managing to make something happen; charismatic speeches without action plans to implement them make for great theater but are hardly effective leadership. The point is, I saw leadership and management as one and the same.

Of late, I've changed my view. I've realized, after my most recent round of reflection, that, in a way, neither of those two angles is accurate. I still don't like the way most business books present the subject, but I'm abandoning my old approach (of using the two terms interchangeably) as well. As I was working on this essay, a third option came to me. It goes like this:

A "manager" is a job title, a position with specific responsibilities, clear expectations, and some range of control to be used in ways that benefit the organization. If you have an org chart, the manager will, for sure, show up on it somewhere. Becoming a "manager" means that someone else took action to hire you, and gave you a set of responsibilities and an area over which you have some authority. Management, I believe, is neither good nor bad—like business itself, it's really just a tool you can use to get your work done. And a manager can do good work, or bad. More often than not, intentions aside, we all do some of each, often simultaneously.

A leader, I now believe, is *not* the same as a manager. Being a great leader requires no title and no particular experience. No one necessarily appoints a leader; leaders don't necessarily have any particular set of responsibilities and they're often invisible on an org chart. There's no age requirement. Education can help but it hardly counts for anything if what you learned in the classroom isn't applied in a constructive way. Although leadership is most often associated with power and hierarchy, the truth is that it's not all that connected to either. In fact, I've come to believe, *the only thing that truly gets you into the ranks of leaders is the decision to lead combined with the ability to actually start leading.*

Mohammed Bamyeh, modern-day anarchist, author, and professor at the University of Pittsburgh, posited that "freedom is the exercise of freedom." I'll adapt his approach: Leadership is the act of developing leaders. The more everyone in our organization buys into, and then in turn teaches, leadership— as opposed to just following direction—the more effective I'll be as a leader. Basically, what that means is that if you get others to lead well, to go for greatness in all they do, you in turn become an effective leader. In this context, rank and resume mean nothing; it's all, ultimately, about results. Please note, I don't mean "results" in that hard-assed, take-no-prisoners, "the bottom line is the only thing that counts" kind of way. Rather, I mean results that correspond with your values, your vision, and whatever else you're working on. Which for us means being profitable while having fun, honoring freedom, and supporting the community around us, living our values and delivering on our mission in meaningful ways.

In this context, I'm resetting my mindset on the subject—all managers, even minimally effective (assuming they get anything done at all) ones, are, by definition, also leaders. They may not be great ones, but they're still leading. But what's different is that, quite clearly, when I thought this all through, *not all leaders are managers.* The latter is a set of specific job responsibilities. The former is a mindset. While we clearly have managers who are responsible for managing—and leading—their areas of responsibility, every single person who starts to work here is now responsible for the effectiveness of our leadership activity at Zingerman's.

Let me repeat that just to make sure my point isn't lost in the slew of sentences I just shot at you. *Everyone who works here is fully responsible for the quality of the leadership work we do.* If we have a leadership shortfall, we're *all* on the line for it. Please note, though, that this is *not* about abdication, and I'm not trying to slough anything off on new staffers. I'm still one of two co-founding partners and the CEO or whatever other titles you want to lay on me. So regardless of whether you go with our approach to Servant Leadership (see page 113) or whether you take a more old-school, "I'm the boss" angle, the buck still starts and stops with me, Paul, and the other partners. But the point is, we expect everyone here to think and act like leaders and to go for greatness in all they do. If I screw up, it can't and won't wash for everyone else here to just look the other way and act helpless.

There are, of course, a thousand definitions of what "leadership" actually means. I like what Peter Koestenbaum writes in *Leadership: The Inner Side of Greatness:* "Leadership means greatness in all you do." If we want people to buy into our emphasis on "going for greatness," and leadership is greatness, then I am back, effectively, at Koestenbaum's construct—if we got everyone who worked here to buy into being effective leaders, that would mean they were going for greatness in all they did and . . . really, what more could one hope for? "Leadership," Koestenbaum adds, "is a mindset and a pattern of behaviors. It is to have made a habit of a new way of thinking and a new way of acting." Our work, I realized then, is to sell everyone here on that new way of thinking. If everyone here thinks like a leader and that means that they're going for greatness in all they do, then it will also lead them towards a more fulfilling life, in which case their energy is better when they get to work, which means we all can and will win together.

The more the culture of the business coalesces around this leadership mindset, the more everyone thinks, feels, and acts like an owner, the more every single staffer here will go after greatness all day long. It shows up in both big and small ways. In literally the last eight hours I've read a draft of a vision of greatness written by a waitress, overheard a pantry cook caringly, unexpectedly, and effectively express his gratitude to a customer for coming in to eat, and had a busboy thank me for picking up some scrap paper off the floor. My appreciative, anarchist, live-in-the-moment soul celebrated each of those for the great acts of leadership success they were.

Busser Bowls Over MBAs

Not long ago we had a group of executive MBA students at the Roadhouse for a one-hour ZingTrain presentation, to be followed immediately by dinner. After I spoke, while they waited for their pulled pork sandwiches to come out of the kitchen, we put together an impromptu panel of staff to answer questions on what it was actually like to work here. Turned out to be a couple of servers and a manager who happened to be on shift at the time. I'd referenced many times during the talk how many great teenagers we had on staff, and how they consistently did wonderful work, were intellectually and emotionally engaged, and consistently crushed the social stereotype about today's young people having a bad work ethic. I should have seen it coming, since the people we'd put on the panel were all probably in their twenties. As the three panelists took turns effectively answering the group's queries, one of the audience members raised his hand and said, "This is great, but where are these mythical eighteen-year-olds?" Fair question. I thought quickly about who was on shift and then asked one of the servers to go get Leo Bayless-Hall.

Leo began his bussing stint at the Roadhouse when he was, I believe, all of sixteen. After two years at the Roadhouse, he graduated high school and went on to attend Clark University in Massachusetts. He had recently come back to work with us again for the summer. At that moment, he was the only eighteen-year-old I knew who was actually in the building. Two minutes later, Leo appeared from behind the curtain we use to cordon off the room for group gatherings. "So who exactly are you?" one of the audience members asked. "I'm Leo Bayless-Hall," he answered. "And what do you do?" someone in the group shot out. "I'm a busser," he replied. Stopped, smiled, and started up again. "And I'm also in charge of managing morale." Made my day. A busboy back from college to work for the summer comes out as a consummate team player. A creative kid who will, I'm sure, go on to do other great things in his life had turned out, much to my delight, to be a self-made manager and leader.

If Only I'd Known

Had I only known Utah Phillips's story when I was fifteen instead of fifty, or maybe if I'd studied American history, rather than Russian, it might not have taken me so long to get this glimpse of the obvious about leadership. It came to me one blue-skied August afternoon, while I was getting ready to speak to our entire organization, presenting at the kickoff of our plans for the year.

We'd committed this particular time around to really pushing ourselves that year to ever greater heights, to "going for greatness," particularly—as per our newly (at that time) agreed-upon 2020 vision—in regards to bringing our customers radically better food and radically better service. It's not like we hadn't been working this way before—we just wanted to take it all up a notch that year. Not exactly sure how I was going to frame things, I went back through Koestenbaum's book.

Like Utah Phillips, Koestenbaum's got a big gray beard and, in the book jacket photo, at least, a broad smile. I've never met the man, but I have a feeling his energy would be equally excellent. His writing touches on many of the same subjects we focus on here—the importance of bringing meaning into everyday work, an emphasis on self reflection, the value of teaching at every level of the organization. One thing I like about Koestenbaum's book is that it applies different language to ideas that we'd already been working with: he has a way of explaining what was already clear in my head but that I wasn't quite able to clarify to others. One passage in particular really piqued my interest. The challenge in business, he explains, "is to teach your customers leadership, whatever else your product or services may be." I had to really stop and think about what he was saying—at first intellectual glance his statement kind of confused me. But the more I reread it, the clearer the concept became, and the more it made sense. "Selling anything," he goes on, "means helping customers buy leadership in support of their own values."

Our obligation, Koestenbaum says, is to constructively teach our clientele how to be leaders in whatever ways our products and services help them to do that. "If you teach leadership to your customers," he continues, "then you will prosper, for you will have created a satisfied customer." In other words, in our case, since we're selling traditionally made, full-flavored, handmade, high-quality foods—products that are, by definition, at the upper end of the market—we need to sell our customers on the idea of being leaders in the food world. Those who want to shop and eat in the middle of the market aren't going to feel terribly inspired to spend time and money in one of our places. Same goes for other areas in which we hope to be leaders—service, sustainability in business, open-book finance, etc. Customers who don't share those values, who don't want to lead in those areas, Koestenbaum concludes, aren't likely to feel fulfilled when they spend time and money in our businesses. By contrast, he argues, the people we want to sell to are likely leaders in other areas of their lives; if they weren't, they probably wouldn't be buying the sort of food we're selling in the first place.

The more I pondered Koestenbaum's point, the more it made sense. Followers tend to buy in the middle of the mass market; the leaders we want are, by definition, out front, finding better food, better service, and better ways to work. The more their values are aligned with ours, the more comfortable they are with being in a leadership role, the more likely they are to be effectively leading in all aspects of their lives, the more they feel that their values are in synch with ours—all of which means multiple wins for all involved! Like it or not (and I like it, actually), leaders are the people we want to be around; whether it's in business, music, school, sports, art, or anything else, leaders are likely to be circulating positively in our organizational ecosystem. Koestenbaum's concept has interesting implications for our approach to service and to selling. But at that particular, pre-presentation August moment, my mind took his views one step beyond where he'd been in the book.

Given that our belief in Servant Leadership says that we'll treat our staff as if they were our (organizational) customers, it struck me that if you like Koestenbaum's "teach leadership to your customers" approach, then *we need to get our staff to buy leadership, too.* We've long believed that everyone here is capable of leading, and we've always opened our leadership classes to anyone in the organization. But, seeing things from Koestenbaum's perspective, I realized that while we'd offered everyone the opportunity, we'd never actually *closed the sale* as we should have. Frontline people here had the chance to learn leadership if they liked, but *we'd never actually come out and made clear that—even if they weren't managers—leadership was part of their work.*

To many people here that shift might seem subtle, but I think that getting everyone who works here to buy into the belief that leadership belongs to them (and not to some amorphous, often antagonistic "other") is huge. It's the difference that I keep coming back to in all our work between "empowerment" and "responsibility." The former is far better than enslavement, and it certainly makes tools available to those who want them. But there's not a particularly solid connection between being empowered and actually taking action. Given the chance, some frontliners, for sure, might "buy" leadership. But we know that, realistically, most won't—it's like an optional, after-school study session: everyone *could* attend, many will consider it, but only a handful will actually show up and study. Successfully getting our staff to "buy" the idea of leadership means getting them to believe that each of us owns responsibility for the effectiveness with which we *all* lead.

This shift beyond making a passive offer to one of "closing" an actual, sign-on-the-emotional-dotted-line "sale" is a big one. If leaders at Zingerman's need to be ready to step onto the dish line to help when the dishwasher's feeling a bit overwhelmed, then my anarchist orientation clearly dictates that, conversely, dishwashers also ought to be prepared to step up and help lead if and when a manager starts to slide off course. We are, after all, all in this together: knowing what position we've each agreed to play is important, but at the end of the day, it's all one team. Regardless of title, we all need to lead. So, let me say it again. *The commitment to being effective leaders has to be part of what we expect from every single person in the organization, regardless of seniority, job title, or anything else.*

This entire construct came together even better a few years later, after I'd had the chance to assimilate all of my anarchist studies. If you start with our commitment to treating everyone as an equal, if you believe that most everyone is creative and intelligent and able, when you stop sucking up to people in positions of authority, when you lead by serving others instead of by stepping on them, then getting everyone to take leadership responsibility for the effectiveness of our work is the only reasonable way to go. In a way, I think that at times too much of the anarchists' work was focused on bringing down leaders. I've got a different twist on the subject: *Instead of beating down the leaders, I'd rather bring everyone else up.*

"Every normal human being is competent . . . "

Murray Bookchin, writing in *Remaking Society*, said that "every normal human being is *competent* to manage the affairs of society and, more specifically, the community in which he or she is a member." Just to reinforce his—and my—belief in the abilities of all those often-overlooked, but I think insightful, individuals who do the majority of the world's work, here are a few comments from Fionna Gault, a twenty-four-year-old hostess at the Roadhouse. "A leadership role," she told me, "is something given by the 'followers' and the faith that they have in you as a leader. Being a manager or a supervisor does not necessarily mean that you are seen as a leader by the staff. Leaders are those who are sought out to solve problems. I would go so far as to say that the majority of the leaders in an organization aren't recognized by a title, and that often the most effective leaders are those who have not been promoted. I have worked for and heard stories about countless workplaces in which the managerial types are generally considered useless, so employees lean on each other to make things work. Obviously this is not ideal, but it is certainly no worse than an organization in which employees forsake each other and rely blindly on supervisors and managers simply because they carry the official title of leadership."

Balancing the Equation—Effectively Making Everyone Responsible

One of the things that's made us so different as an organization over the years is that we ask everyone here to take responsibility for the broad functioning of the entire business, not just their own day-to-day duties. Don't get me wrong—we certainly have job descriptions that detail who needs to do what, and by when. We have supervisors and managers and partners and each of us has pretty clear lines of authority and responsibility as well, and we most definitely assign tasks and areas of work to specific individuals. But whatever the specific sets of duties are, we don't contract and cut off by allowing only a few head honchos to have decision-making authority—instead, we *expand* the responsibility for service, quality, and finance in what I learned a long time ago are "multiples of 100 percent."

For example, as owners of the business we are fully responsible for the quality of every single service interaction in the organization. If a customer comes into our retail Bakeshop, I'm responsible for the quality of their experience even if I happen to be out doing a ZingTrain talk in Boston or on a beach in Bermuda. That's a given, right? I'm the boss. Same goes for the manager of the shop—she's *also* fully accountable for the quality of each customer interaction (even if it happens on one of her days off). Neither of us is more or less responsible because of the involvement of the other—rather, we each have full, 100 percent responsibility. As does every employee as they wait on guests during their day. And, in fact, as does anyone and everyone in our organization who might find themselves working in, or even just passing through, the retail shop at the Bakehouse. Our mission is to bring a great Zingerman's Experience to everyone we interact with, and it matters not how old we are, what our job title is, where in the organization we formally report to work, or whether we've just begun to work here, gone on break, or are heading into retirement. Everyone here knows that—service is very clearly understood here to be *everyone's* responsibility.

What we do *not* do is take the more typical, sort of isolating approach of assigning responsibility for service quality solely to, say, "customer service representatives." To the contrary, we're very clear from day one that whether you're hired into a formal customer service position or not, each of us is fully responsible for the quality of the service we give. Towards that end, we teach everyone in the organization how to give great service according to our organizational standards. Kitchen crew, candy makers, dishwashers, bakers, box packers—everyone learns it. Accountants at Zingerman's may spend most of their time on cash flow and financial statement reconciliations, but they, too, get trained on the service stuff.

Please note, though, that *we don't just empower people to give service;* it's not just an option they can take if they're in the mood. Rather, it's a very real part of each of our responsibilities to *actually do it.* It's a simple and understood expectation that we each will deliver great customer service all day, every day. It's not about empowering; it's about expecting. I mean that in a constructive and caring way, not in a callous or militaristic one. Another example of all this in action is our approach to open-book finance. One of our Rules of Great Finance says, "Success starts with each of us." This means that anyone who comes to work here in any role accepts responsibility for the financial success of our organization as a whole. Again, we haven't just *empowered* people by offering to show them copies of the financial statements and maybe opening our management meetings to anyone who wants to come. Seriously, how many waiters or bakers or bussers want to sit in on a financial meeting and make their way through a six-inch-high stack of statements? You can tell them they're welcome to come, but most will find more interesting ways to spend their afternoon. What we've done moves past an invitation: we educate each person in the organization about finances and then constructively require them to pay attention to and take responsibility for our performance.

Going on about all these leadership approaches at such length may be more background than you wanted. But the conclusion that it leads to is pretty radical, at least to me. With all that rearrangement of power and responsibility, my belated glimpse of the obvious was that the same approach that was working so well for us with service and finance was exactly the same one we ought to take when it came to leadership. We'd always essentially empowered everyone here to lead, and we've long been teaching leadership. But we'd never come out and stated an expectation as we had in those other areas. I didn't have to be a brain surgeon to realize that, just as it does in the other areas, *leadership works better in multiples of 100 percent as well.*

What's the Payoff?

The bottom line on all this stuff goes far beyond a small bit of a spiritually sound side project—the results that come from getting everyone to think and act like a leader are big. When it works, we create a totally different organizational construct. People feel better about themselves; their confidence goes up and with it their creativity, insight, and intelligence. To be more specific, here are a few things that have come out of this work.

1. An Understanding That Change Starts with Each of Us

Effective leaders understand that if we want a change to happen, that change has to start with us. That's not always easy to process, but it's true; we have to live and work in ways that are congruent with what we want to create. Yelling at people for failing to act respectfully is, of course, absurd. It's also all too common. We know, though, that it doesn't work. As early 20th-century German anarchist Gustav Landauer wrote, "a goal can only be reached if it is already reflected in its means." If we want our organization to be a great one (and I do), then we need everyone going for greatness in most all that they do.

Even the best leaders, I'm sure, have aberrations in their drive to do good. But greatness isn't just an isolated outcome—it's the collective creation of the entire crew. Remember, for what it's worth, that "going for greatness" applies in all aspects of our work—it's not just about big speeches and strategic plans. It's greatness in giving each customer an amazing service experience and in the way we pull every shot of espresso. While the expectation that everyone enter into a leadership mindset comes from the organization, the decision to actually go for greatness is an internal one. We might have hired Leo Bayless-Hall as a busser, but while his formal duties haven't really changed, it sure sounded from his response on that above-mentioned panel like he's leaving us to go back to school a leader. Best of all, the choice to take on that role was truly all his.

2. People Learn to Create the Future They Desire

In the old model, working on the future is an activity that only upper-level managers would be considered qualified to coordinate. But in our odd little

Anarcho-Capitalist world, we want everyone who's got an idea to initiate the change they're dreaming about. We teach everyone who works here how to go after the future of their dreams pretty much from their first day on the job. They all learn how we do visioning—how to write one, read one, give constructive input on someone else's draft, how to collaboratively go after what they believe is best. They're learning to do whatever they need to do to make a customer happy (see our 5 Steps to Handling a Complaint on page 127), they're getting involved in annual planning, etc. All of it is about thinking like a leader: taking responsibility, engaging, putting their hearts and minds into making a difference, initiating action to go after a better tomorrow.

To me, all that is far preferable to the old world where most of the organization is waiting for the people at the top to get their act together before others will initiate any improvement of their own. The tension that comes out of that old setting, I think, is pretty much untenable. I'd far prefer people at every level going—actively, imperfectly—after greatness than to have all but one or two of them sit around and wait for some messianic manager to come down from on high and tell everyone what to do. Looking again to anarchist Gustav Landauer for insight, I find this quote from a century ago: "To me, someone without a master, someone who is free, an individual, an anarchist, is one who is his own master, who has unearthed the desire that tells him who he truly wants to be. This desire is his life."

The people here who take responsibility for effective leadership, regardless of what job title they formally hold, are happily making things happen. And whether those improvements are in their work, their home life, their community, their art, or anything else they care about, that's a good thing.

3. AN APPRECIATION OF FREEDOM

Effective leaders also realize that everything we do is about free will and free choice. When we give, we give because we choose to. When we work hard, we do it because that's what we decided to do. When we leave early or stay late—and there are always good reasons to do both—we choose that freely, too. Getting everyone to agree to be a leader means, then, that they're also learning to accept, manage, and appreciate the freedom that we all have to make decisions in our lives. (I go over the idea of free choice in far greater detail in the essay on Anarcho-Capitalism on page 259.) In the old model, managers are the only ones who are theoretically authorized to take meaningful action. This is, of course, neither very smart nor at all realistic. Everyone in every business is taking action—or deciding not to—all day long. My point here is merely to get everyone in the organization to own the role of leadership, actively going after greatness, rather than waiting passively for a leader to figure out what to do.

Murray Bookchin, writing in *Self Management and the New Technology*, says, "The same task performed aesthetically may be a work of art; performed under the lash of domination, it is an ignominious burden. The identical task under conditions of freedom is an esthetic experience; under conditions of domination, it becomes onerous toil." The words are a bit weighty, but I think he's right on—going along passively (even if aggressively?) and feeling helpless en route is horrible; freely choosing greatness is actually great fun!

4. Better Followership

Without effective followers no leader will get anything of consequence completed. The key is that followership shouldn't be tied to hierarchy any more than leadership is. Regardless of who's leading on any given day, others of us will need to follow. Just as frontline staff will be better off for learning to lead, so, too, will I and others at "the top" be better off when we're learning to be good followers, getting on board and supporting constructive initiatives being led by others in the organization. What's different in this model is that each of us can lead and each can follow, and we all need to be good at both roles; it's not always easy, but I think it's ultimately and infinitely more effective.

As Roadhouse hostess Fionna Gault reminded me, good following is fed by, follows from, and leads to, good leadership. "Being a good leader and a good follower are pretty darn close to the same thing," she said. I hadn't thought of it that way, but I think she's right. I'm going to follow her lead and include her comments here. "I might even say that being a good follower *is* being a good leader in a way. When you decide to follow someone, to support someone's idea or initiative, you are helping them reach their full potential. Great leaders create leaders, right? Well, the main thing a new leader needs is followers, so by becoming a follower, you can lead someone to success. Deciding to follow means making a decision about the direction you want to see things go in and taking action to make it happen, even if it is under someone else's direction."

5. A World with Fewer Victims

If you ask a hundred people to tell you what the opposite of leading is, 99 percent of them will probably tell you it's "following." But it dawned on me as I was developing this piece that, as per Fionna's comments above, in this model, leading and following are mutually supportive roles. The true opposite of leadership is the victim mentality that's so pervasive in modern society. I'm sure you're familiar with it: the idea that change should probably start any place *but* with us; that we "deserve" better but, unfairly, aren't getting it; that when leadership gets its act together, then everything else will fall into place; that there's nothing managers can really do because they just don't have the "right" people to work with. That victim mindset is so common as to seem unremarkable, but I think it's a spirit-, and really an organization-, killer.

Leaders, by contrast, take responsibility for creating positive change, regardless of the challenges they face in the moment. Which means that if most everyone is acting like a leader, then, by definition, there are fewer victims out there. And that's a great thing. Where victims will lie back and wait, leaders will consistently act. If everyone here is going for greatness, starting down the road to success every day, then good things are pretty much bound to happen. Landauer said it nicely a century ago, arguing against those who complained incessantly but never seemed to move forward. "I only object to the passiveness of those who cannot find a task to pursue *right now* at any given moment."

6. Learning to Live with Uncertainty

One reason the victim mindset is so appealing is because it creates a false sense of certainty: no matter what went wrong, it's someone else's fault. There's always a ready-made excuse that almost never fails to deliver; the doom and gloom, in that case, is pretty much predetermined. Believing that things will likely be bad is almost certain to make it so.

Followers put their faith, I believe, in leaders, in part to avoid having to deal with the reality that the world is in flux and that nothing is actually guaranteed. The reality of the world is we don't know what's going to happen; it's a lot easier to just put your faith in—and then later, the fault on—the bosses. Going for greatness, living a leadership life, is the opposite—the reality is that none of us at the top fully know what we're doing either! We hope for, work for, believe in a better tomorrow, but still know full well that bad things may happen en route, that not everything works out as you had wished, and that (as per page 279), it's all actually out of control.

The truth is that when we learn to live with that uncertainty, the inherent paradox that exists in pretty much everything, the more effectively we're able to handle what's going on around us every day. There's less lashing out, a whole lot more peace of mind, and a lot more effective and enjoyable work. Effective leaders learn quickly that, while we might prefer it otherwise, the world is anything but a black and white place. And if we're all taking responsibility for leadership, then we all understand that gray is where it's at.

7. BUILDING FOR THE BUSINESS'S FUTURE

When people are learning leadership at every level of the organization, they're far more able to step up when the organization, or the world at large, needs them to. The reality is that none of us really start acting—effectively, at least—like leaders only because we got a promotion or a pay increase. Responsibilities might have changed, but it's pretty rare that our mindsets will really be altered for more than the first few days in the new role. By contrast, when we're asking—and getting—everyone to act like a leader from the time they start working here, then when the opportunity to formally take a management or partner position presents itself, they're far more likely to be ready to step up and succeed. Better preparation means that they're more likely to do well. When they do well, they feel better, they do better, we all do better. Everyone wins.

Ultimately, this shared leadership stuff is at the spiritual core of effective succession planning. Don't get me wrong. We're well along the route of getting clear, legally and ethically sound processes in place so that the organization can continue to do good things after Paul and I have both, eventually, moved on to that great big Deli in the sky (where you can eat corned beef every day and your cholesterol never goes up!). But the formal processes are only a framework. They don't really help people think any more clearly than they could when Paul and I were still sitting across the table from them.

The cool thing here is that, honestly, I think that most anyone who's worked here for a while would be able to come up with answers that are pretty comparable to what Paul and I would do most of the time. Not always, I'm sure, but even Paul and I don't come up with the same answers every time either. I see evidence of this successful, spiritual succession work every few weeks when we do our open-forum panels at ZingTrain seminars. At most every session we ask three or four folks from around the organization to come in and answer random, absolutely unplanned, questions from the audience. The crew members on the panels are so on board with the program that they almost always put the audience on its intellectual heels. It can be, even for me, almost unbelievable that frontline people could process and reflect as clearly and effectively as they very clearly do when we run these sessions.

To hear some rather randomly selected manager, frontline staff member, or partner reference vision, mission, values, Bottom-Line Change, open-book finance, or 5 Steps to Handling a Complaint, without time for preparation or practice, is kind of a cool thing. Having them do it all with poise, positive energy, and a clear sense of confidence that they actually understand what they're talking about, know why we do what we do and how it works, and can share stories of how they've personally put it into practice, is pretty powerful. They really do, now that I think about it, look, feel, and sound like leaders. I don't want to jinx anything, but I have yet to leave a session feeling anything less than amazed at how ready people are to lead. They know their stuff and they really are ready to roll!

8. THE WORLD WILL BE A BETTER PLACE FOR IT

When the people who work here are "buying" leadership like this, they're taking responsibility for the world around them, whether that's a single customer, a particular product they're preparing, the environment, their family, or anything else. I don't want to make this seem too over the top, but the more people take responsibility for what's going on around them, and work to improve it, the better off the world is going to be. It plays, particularly, I think, to the point of building a sustainable business: when we're sending people home with more good stuff than they arrived with, that's pretty clearly a really great thing. In essence, it's the inverse of the energy crisis in the American workplace (see page 35)—in this case, the business begins to serve as a sort of spiritual charging station. People often come in feeling low from things happening in their lives outside of work, but I really think that, more often than not, they leave work in a better frame of mind than they were when they arrived that morning! This work does, I believe, truly change the way people feel about themselves, and hence the way the world around them works. To quote Gustav Landauer again, "We shall not abdicate responsibility, rather, we will quietly take it on, safe in the knowledge that future generations will thank us for helping them respect themselves once again."

Can This Concept Really Work?

If you're already a believer, I can answer that with a very simple, straightforward, and unequivocal "Yes!" and you can skip ahead to page 108 (Closing the Sale). If you're not yet convinced, let me try working my way through the most frequently stated reasons opponents have argued that the approach will fail. Let me get into a more cynical, old-school character. Okay, . . . here goes:

What are you, nuts? That'll be terrible. Five hundred bosses and no one to do the real work is not a recipe for success!

Given a minute to process the point, I think that the statement is kind of silly. First of all there's not the slightest bit of evidence that everyone taking responsibility for service or finance at Zingerman's has done anything other than help to improve the results we get. We're actually doing pretty darned well (knock on wood) in all those areas. On top of which, what could really be bad? Too many people being too proactive, trying too hard to create too much positive change? Or too many people who are going for greatness at the same time? Are you serious? If that's a problem, then as per Natural Law 9 ("Success means you get better problems"), it's an exceptionally good one.

I guess it really only seems like a problem if you're stuck in the old model of command-and-control leadership—sure enough, five hundred people ordering each other around at the same time is not the way to get much of anything accomplished. But we partners and managers don't just get to do what we want either; we all need to follow our agreed-upon processes, make collaborative decisions, and work slowly but steadily to get others on board to do the right thing, even when we happen to hold the final decision-making authority. So while I am talking about five hundred people here stepping up and regularly working and thinking like leaders, I'm not talking about that same set of five hundred acting arbitrarily and inconsiderately or having their indiscriminate way with the organization, without really taking time to talk it through with others.

What if not everyone wants to be a leader?

In truth, many potential employees probably don't. But what about all the people out there who don't really want to give great service? We just don't hire them; there are plenty of other places they can get a job. And if they do get through our interviewing process but prove disinterested? We just find a way to constructively disengage as quickly and courteously as we can. Similarly, what about the people who aren't really up for carefully crafting high-quality products? Same scenario—try not to hire them, and if they slip through anyway, then simply try to move them on and out as smoothly as possible. So, seriously, why would it need to be any different when it comes to leadership?

We simply start to interview everyone with leadership in mind—over time, the culture supports the vision; the systems and training contribute as well. Over the long haul you have a culture in which leadership is the accepted way to act every day. Not much to lose, and, I think, a whole lot to gain.

The best people are already generally inclined to lead. By taking this approach, we'll give them the support and clearly stated expectations that can only help them to achieve their goals. One staff member I asked about this whole thing said, "You're definitely on to something here with this idea of everyone being responsible for leadership. If we have the expectation that we're all going to act as leaders, and there is the structural support to empower this feeling, then the sky is the limit for us. We will all push each other to new standards of greatness. Talk about radical—we're all leaders at Zingerman's!"

What if all those frontline people are trying to lead and they aren't in agreement on where we should be going?

Well, in the broad sense, we've addressed this issue already by coming to agreement on a long-term vision and values for our organization, having that in writing, and then very actively sharing it with everyone who works here. People who aren't into that vision (or our values) probably don't come to work here, and if they do, they very definitely won't last. More specifically, because we start out our work by agreeing on a vision of what success looks like to us on every project, everyone is taking responsibility and making decisions within the context of that vision. We address this challenge, too, by having a "recipe" for Bottom-Line Change (see page 337) that requires us to come to agreement on a vision of the change before we move forward. On top of which, lest anyone still have any illusions, it's not like all the partners are perfectly in alignment on every issue either. Certainly, freeing people to participate in leadership means that in the short term we're sure to have some conflict. But the clarity around vision, values, and processes means we have a pretty high likelihood of getting to success.

Aren't you inviting anarchy?

Playing that old anarchy card, eh? The simple answer is "No!" Remember, "anarchism" is not "anarchy." The latter is chaos. The former is about good people freely choosing to collaborate in a caring way in the interest of creating a better tomorrow. If everyone is leading, and leading is going for greatness, and every leader is mindful of what's best for the group, the math will clearly add up to a better organization. Even if you go to the chaotic end of the spectrum, life's still not going to be any more out of control than it was when employees were always just awaiting orders from HQ. Asking everyone to provide leadership doesn't mean that people at the "top" of the organization don't still hold authority. We have the power, if we really want to use it. In our world, of course, we also have the responsibility to use that authority effectively and ethically. Ultimately, we just want to get everyone to really use their head, and head into the future forcefully and positively, instead of standing pat and waiting passive aggressively (and often impatiently) for the owners to get their act together.

What if all these new leaders make "bad" decisions?

Hey, they're most definitely going to make mistakes. I do all the time. But I'll bet you that more often than not, when they've really decided to think like leaders, to go for greatness in all they do, more often than not they're going to make pretty darned good decisions. Look, if you know where we're going (the long-term vision), you understand the ethical framework and guidelines we go by (our guiding principles), you know the "plays" (3 Steps to Great Service, 5 Steps to Handling a Complaint, 3 Steps to Great Finance, etc.), and you know how to keep score (our three bottom lines—food, service, and finance—as measured in our huddles every week), it's not really that hard for anyone who's smart, sensitive, and even moderately savvy to step up should the boss go down. To quote Murray Bookchin again, "Every normal human being is *competent* to manage the affairs of society and, more specifically, the community in which he or she is a member."

Just for one in-the-moment, seemingly minor, but great example, the other day I asked a relatively new busser at the Roadhouse if there was anything I could do to help him. In the old business model, not wanting to look bad in front of "the boss," i.e., me, I'm pretty sure that he'd have just said "No." But he'd just been through the new staff orientation where we'd talked about some of this stuff. When I asked him if he wanted any assistance, he stopped for a few seconds to think about it. Then he said he was going downstairs to stock some paper goods and asked if I could keep an eye on his section in case a guest needed water or bread. I think that was brilliant. It's leadership on his part. He asked me politely. It was a question, not a big bad command. He couldn't have done it better if he'd have been the manager. It was great. He acted like the leader we're looking for. And everyone—the customers, me, his peers, and him—benefited from his efforts.

What if the boss starts screwing up and sets a subpar course?

That, unfortunately, is an all-too-common scenario. Leaders, I'll say again, aren't perfect. In fact, one of the points of this process is to help protect the organization from our inevitable leadership letdowns—if everyone's a leader, someone will step up and lead. It's really not "if" the boss screws up; we all are going to. The point is *when* the boss screws up, everyone around her or him is also responsible for the effectiveness of our leadership work. So if the managers or partners start to steer our organizational bus towards the cliff, it's everyone else's role to grab the wheel and help constructively and caringly straighten things out!

Closing the Sale: Leaders Helping to Develop Leaders

In closing the sale on everyone being a leader, there are two last points to make. The first is to sell those who are in positions of authority on the idea of really wanting to let frontline folks act like leaders. That, I suppose, might be easier said than done. So many old-school bosses view the world of leadership as a zero-sum game; people of "lower rank" going for greatness somehow implies that their own prestige and power would be diminished. Having only recently come to work here, Fionna Gault reminded me how hard the move might be in most organizations. "A manager on a power trip," she reminded me, "is not conducive to a horizontal org chart." She's right, but unlike the other bosses she's worked with and for, I look at it the other way. *Strong and effective leadership is actually all about helping to develop leaders.* My success as a leader, then, is measured, to a great extent, by how much leadership energy, presence, and insight are happening across the entire organization—the more frontline people are stepping up, the better!

My second closing cause is to sell frontline folks on the idea of stepping up, to convince those who have no formal authority to think like an effective leader and go for greatness in all they do! For most folks on the front line, that's far easier said than done. While they may not love being led, it's often easier to stay with the status quo—frustrating though it may be—than to break out of the old mold and politely, courteously, and respectfully start to contribute positive leadership to the organization.

The beauty of this approach is that there's so much to gain. If we can make this model a reality—"buying" leadership is actually a pretty sweet deal for all involved. The truth is, once you get over the psychological oddity of it all and break out of the social and corporate mode that most of us have been raised in (the one that tells you that frontline folks are mostly supposed to shut up and do their work), there's a lot of opportunity for all of us to grow and learn. Leading, going after what you believe in, going for greatness in all you do, learning to rally others to your cause, making a positive difference for everyone around you, seeing your efforts pay off in the form of better day-to-day experiences for your customers, co-workers, family, and community is a far more rewarding way to live.

No matter what you go on to do in life, learning to lead early on in life is going to help with everything you do, at home, at work, or anywhere else you go. To quote world-class chef Thomas Keller, in Michael Ruhlman's *The Soul of a Chef,* "You can't spend half a career as someone else's employee and then suddenly, one day, start thinking like an owner. Think like an owner and act like an owner from your very first job as a prep cook."

I can say that the same thing is true for me. I remember, probably fifteen years ago now, I was teaching service for ZingTrain at one of the local hospitals. We were going over our 5 Steps to Handling a Complaint, when one of the hundred or so frontline hospital staff in the room raised his hand to challenge our approach. "It's different for you," he shot out with more than a bit of cynicism. "You handle it differently because you're the owner." I was a bit stumped by his comment, maybe even slightly stunned; I'd presented the service stuff hundreds of times, but I'd never heard that line before. It was, I suppose, an honest taste of what it's like in the old-school sort of organizations that most people, unfortunately, go to work in every day.

I thought about it for a minute, and then realized that although what he was saying clearly made solid sense in his world, he had it completely backward. "Actually," I said, staying as calm as I could, "it's the opposite. I'm the owner because I handle things differently. This is basically what I was doing when I was an hourly employee and then a manager working for others, long before Paul and I opened the Deli." To Thomas Keller's well-considered point, those who think and act accordingly before they actually acquire any formal title are far more likely to develop into leaders, and more often than not, effective ones at that. Most everyone will have heard the old saying, "Men are what circumstances make of them." But I'm with 19th-century, Michigan-born anarchist Voltairine de Cleyre, who wrote, "I set the opposing declaration; 'Circumstances are what men make them.'"

The idea of leadership being something that anyone—regardless of title, age, resume, education level, experience, or anything else—can take on is a fairly radical one. Effective leadership, freely chosen, and respectfully delivered with a service mindset, is always helpful. And when it can and does come from every element of the organization, look out—that's some serious organizational power being put into play. With that in mind, I wish that I could turn back time a bit, maybe bring Utah Phillips back to share his thoughts on the subject. He might be able to go up to some of the folks who work here and ask, in a more gentle manner, I'm sure, than that Everett sheriff did back in 1916, "Who are your leaders here at Zingerman's?" And, in my hopes and dreams at least, they would smile, and respond, with an infinitely softer and far friendlier tone than the sailors did on that ship in Everett Bay, "Hey, we're all leaders here!"

The Inside Scoop on Working Here at Zingerman's

Mike White, Retail Counter Person, Zingerman's Delicatessen

"Are you an owner, or family, or something?" a pair of guests asked me after we met wandering the Deli floor. My interaction with these two was forty-five seconds or a minute long, and it's stayed with me for a while now.

"Are you . . . family?" touches on something that I've heard from guests around the ZCoB, that Zingerman's is a family business. I love that with however many employees and businesses we develop, Zingerman's still has that special feel. The honest hospitality and drool-worthy food are what I associate with an earnest, nostalgia-inducing family business. And though Ari and Paul came up with the name Zingerman's for the Deli, it isn't a fake name; I've met people with that last name, so I can understand why people may think there are a few generations of Mr. and Mrs. Zingerman hanging around Ann Arbor at their various namesake establishments, keeping them earnest. The way I see it, that sort of assumption is one of the highest accolades we receive.

"Are you an owner?" is a severe form of flattery, and nearly always makes me smile. I'm inclined first to slapstick; they assume this twenty-four-year-old guy is the owner of this bustling, nationally known deli! But I realize now that nearly thirty years ago, as of typing this, one of the owners of this corner store sandwich shop was a twenty-five-year-old guy.

"Are you an owner?" also touches on an important aspect of my workplace philosophy: that I am the owner of each guest experience I engage in. If I had walked past those guests, they may have walked a lap around the "bread-box" and decided to leave, having felt overwhelmed by the high density of noise, food, and people. Or if I had told them quickly that the line for food forms outside, they may have felt mistreated, misunderstood, or worse (is there worse?). Being conscious amidst each guest experience and feeling responsibility for its outcome are ownership. While training people for football Saturdays and *other* holidays, I typically tell them, first and foremost, to be patient. Maybe it would be better to follow that up with, "Be Mr. or Mrs. Zingerman—own the experience."

"Are you . . . something?" is what makes Zingerman's special. It's hard to put your thumb on that "something," but I'm pretty sure it's the same "something" that has customers thinking an hourly employee is an owner. I've been working with food since I was fifteen, and I truly enjoy it. No other employer has encouraged me to develop personally as Zingerman's has. And it's easy to take that for granted after being immersed in the ZCoB for a while. Still, though, I feel most effective at work when I am faced with challenges and learning opportunities, knowing that the ZCoB has bet the bank on my ability to be me.

So, to paraphrase, if you were wondering the outcome of the conversation with those two guests, I smiled and replied, "Yeah, I own some of it."

pitmaster ed mitchell from raleigh, north carolina, and roadhouse managing partner alex young making barbeque at the roadhouse

A Recipe for *Servant* Leadership

Thinking about, and in, Servant Leadership

As I'm sure you well know by now, I'm all about the conceptual, intellectual, and emotional end of leadership work. But at the same time, there's also the other end of the leadership spectrum—the daily struggles that we all need to work through if we're going to get to the greatness to which we aspire. As anyone who's been a manager for more than a month knows full well, leadership is not all love and positive learning experiences. As much as we all try to stay on the high side of things, there are still those days where, all of the visions and values and mission statements and missions to Mars aside, everything feels like it's falling apart. While the vision and values can give some solace and a sense of direction, the truth is that we also need something that we can, almost reflexively, fall back on when the inevitable in-the-moment crises come.

Speaking of falling, as I'm writing about Servant Leadership, my mind keeps coming back to fumbles. You know, in football, when a player suddenly, inadvertently drops the ball and everyone then scrambles desperately to be the first to fall on it. Even though every player knows that they're supposed to do this, football teams still regularly run loose ball drills—knowing you should fall on the ball is one thing, but being able to dive for it, instinctively and effectively, is another thing altogether. Recovering fumbles, clearly, is not rocket science. But doing it in a game is far harder than you would think. Which is also what I think about leadership. It's not rocket science either, but being able to do it, instinctively and effectively, is another thing altogether.

Now, football, as I'm sure virtually every North American knows, is not about fumbling. The point is to score points, and then keep the other team from scoring more than you do. In leadership work, most everyone knows that we're going for greatness, working to attain bottom-line results, create a special place to work, and deliver great customer experiences. The challenge is that things don't always go the way we want. Like them or not, fumbles and flub-ups happen almost every day. And it's safe to say that—in football and business both—the better teams do a lot better job of handling those unexpected events than do bad ones.

The business equivalent, I think, of the loose ball drill would be training managers on what do when, despite the best-laid plans, all hell breaks loose. In the madness of the moment you need an inner default, a drill you've done over and over again, something that puts you into the right frame of mind to maneuver through the madness. One of the many things I love about Servant Leadership is that it allows us to do that training. If we practice it regularly, it builds the ability—the management muscle memory, so to speak—that over time becomes instinctive, the way a well-trained linebacker knows how to dive for a loose ball.

Servant Leadership says, when in doubt, do what's right for the organization and the people in it. When you're in doubt in any situation, simply give more service. When there's a problem, look inward first. When you're confused, be kind. When there's not really enough to go around, give more to others before you take for yourself. In every case, the "decision arrow" points clearly in the same direction. When in doubt, serve. Which is why I can't stress enough the import of drilling ourselves on Servant Leadership. When in doubt, give service to the staff, the customers, the organization, and the community. Try it for a week or two—it's amazing how much difference a service focus can make!

The phrase "Servant Leadership" may sound like one of those nice throwaways they always write into the opening section of employee manuals. But please don't let any perception of passivity fool you—Servant Leadership is very strong stuff. If you really live it, Servant Leadership changes everything.

Our approach to the concept is based on a book written back in 1977 by Robert Greenleaf entitled, simply, *Servant Leadership*. It's very much worth reading the whole thing—I've gone through it in detail at least ten or twelve times. Over the years we've worked with, adapted, and adjusted various elements of his teachings, translating them from the theoretical into the practical world of day-to-day leadership here at Zingerman's. What follows is our interpretation of Greenleaf's approach—the Zingerman's recipe for effectively implementing Servant Leadership.

To get you going, here's a small taste of Greenleaf in action: "[W]e should move," he writes, "towards a new institution that embraces both work and learning—learning in a deep and formal sense and all of the learning influence most people need. This requires a new type of leader, one who can conceptualize such an institution, generate enthusiasm so that many good able people want to be part of it, and provide the strong focus of purpose that builds dynamic strength in many. Great things happen when able leaders create these conditions." Servant Leadership is, quite simply, one of the easiest ways I know to help make our organization more effective and the world a better place in the process. Best of all, it's free. You can make an enormous impact without investing anything other than your own intellectual and emotional energy.

The basic belief of Servant Leadership is that our job as leaders is—first and foremost—to serve our organization. To paraphrase John Kennedy's magnificent 1961 inaugural speech, "Ask not what your organization can do for you. Ask what you can do for your organization." To those who already think that way, this statement might sound obvious, or even inevitable, but in my experience, it's actually neither. In fact, in most traditional organizations the service flows in the other direction—the rest of the organization exists primarily to serve the needs of its leaders. In a servant-led world, by contrast, we do the opposite—here, *we* serve the organization. Instead of just being about the boss, Servant Leadership is about success for all involved.

Servant Leadership is all about giving, and it's all about service. It requires that each of us come to work every day committed to doing what the organization needs done, to serve the entity as a whole even when that means that what we would like as individuals may get short shrift. It means treating those who "report" to us as we would our customers, not like hired help who are there only to serve our every need. It means that the more we succeed, the more we grow, the more people I get to give service to. And if I serve well, we'll likely keep growing, and then serving and growing still farther into the future.

It's safe to say that, although he's hardly a household name, Robert Greenleaf's ideas are much better known in the business world than anything ever put forward by Emma Goldman. But hearing them and living them are two totally different things. Paying lip service to Servant Leadership is easy, but doing it well is another story altogether. For those of us (which would be most) who were raised in a hierarchical world where success is all about earning privilege and power, Servant Leadership is actually completely counterintuitive.

Seriously, to live Servant Leadership effectively is no small thing. It's not a hobby, and it's not about sending an annual donation to the Greenleaf Center for Servant Leadership in central Indiana. It is an entire reorientation of the way most all of us are "raised" in the work world. When we live it well, Servant Leadership means that

- I, as the leader, come last, not first.
- We get promoted in order to serve more, not to be served more by others.
- We respond to staff complaints with the same sort of positive, appreciative response we would give to customers.
- It's more important for me as the boss to bring coffee to the new cashier than the other way around.
- When there's a conflict between what's right for us as individuals, and what's right for the organization, we have an obligation to do what's good for the group.

A RECIPE FOR SERVANT LEADERSHIP

- We hire people in order to help *them* succeed.
- We lead the way in making an appreciative workplace.

Here's how it works in practice. My major "customers" here at Zingerman's are the managing partners of the ZCoB businesses, people like Frank Carollo and Amy Emberling, the managing partners at the Bakehouse. In turn, Frank and Amy's primary customers would be the Bakehouse managers. The managers' major customers would then be the frontline staff. The idea throughout is to keep the (positive) energy flowing *out*, towards the frontline staff. They, after all, are the ones who are dealing with paying customers and/or making the products we sell. Servant Leadership means we have an obligation to make sure their energy is upbeat, available at all times to give the best possible service to customers. The better their energy is, the better our service, the better the outcome will be for the entire organization.

Paradox and Servant Leadership

Having lived it for so many years now, I think that one of the underlying requirements for successfully living Servant Leadership is the ability to work through paradox—people who have a hard time with it (and many do) won't, and don't, do well in this system. If you haven't looked it up lately, according to a quick, online search's in-the-moment definition, paradox is "a statement or group of statements that leads to a contradiction or a situation which defies intuition." And that's exactly what Servant Leadership sets out to be. Quite simply, while the theory sounds straightforward, when you start to put it into practice, you'll find it's way more difficult to deal with the paradoxical realities it presents than it might seem after just a couple of pleasant-to-read paragraphs.

I don't know what it is about this subject and sports that use balls, but getting new managers to understand Servant Leadership is like teaching someone who spent a lifetime playing soccer to learn basketball for the first time—it's completely counterintuitive, and much of what you did to succeed in one setting will cause you big problems in the other. A guy who spent his whole life learning to keep his hands *off* the ball, now has to learn to grab hold of it and handle it with grace for a good two hours. In soccer, when you kick the ball you're doing the right thing. In basketball, if you kick it they stop the game. If you kick the ball on purpose you get a technical foul. Kick it again and you'll probably get kicked out. Same with Servant Leadership. What brings success in the old-school business world would probably get you kicked off the team at the Greenleaf Center for Servant Leadership.

Perhaps the toughest Servant Leadership paradox to tackle is that the higher up you move in the organization, the greater your obligation is to serve. It's simple, but counterintuitive for anyone who's been trained in the corporate world. *In our servant-led world, the higher you get promoted, the harder you'll probably have to work and the more you have to give of yourself.* The whole system runs completely counter to the traditional American image that "we're going to get promoted so we can kick back and reap the rewards of the efforts we made earlier in our careers, taking advantage of a large staff who's there to serve us." Servant Leadership turns that idea upside down; success in the "servant" sense often makes our work *more* challenging, not less so.

Another of the Servant Leadership paradoxes is that we commit to treating staff like customers (not like low-level servants brought in solely to do our bidding). In the straight sense of service, as we define it here at Zingerman's, that really would mean doing whatever a staff member asks of us. Of course, that's neither possible nor advisable. Which just makes for more paradox. As Servant Leaders we're regularly faced with this dilemma: When should we give service to an individual staff member and when is it time to give service to the *group* by *not* doing what that staff member asked? The problem can come up in any number of ways. I can easily imagine an employee asking us to transfer one of his colleagues to a different department because he doesn't like working with them. Or demanding to have his pay doubled because his house payment went up. While I certainly don't begrudge either employee asking for what they want, clearly those are requests that we can't, in good conscience, fulfill. An even tougher situation to handle would be when we find ourselves having to fire a staff member because it's become the right thing for the organization for them to move on.

One final, related, paradox: Servant Leadership creates a setting where what we want for ourselves may conflict with what is best for the organization as a whole. Sometimes we, as leaders, have to choose to give up what we want for ourselves in the short term in order to provide more for others around us. It's hard to know where to draw the line—which is a big part of why learning Servant Leadership is hard to do: the old model calls for lots of straight lines, command and control, and good and bad sides to every decision. But *Servant Leadership lives in the gray and the uncertainty that is everyday life in the real world, dictating all the while that we err every day in favor of the organization rather than ourselves.*

Even with all the best intentions and a lot of attention to learning, Servant

Leadership is not a skill most people can master in a month. I think it's a whole different way of thinking. My friend Meg Noori, a poet, writer, editor, and one of the leaders in the work to transcribe and keep alive the Ojibwe language, has demonstrated for me regularly that two languages are not just interchangeable words for exactly the same things. To the contrary, the way living languages are constructed, they actually create different thought patterns, and, from those, different ways of relating to the world and of speaking, writing, and working. Similarly, Servant Leadership is its own business language. It's not just a nicer way of talking about "being in charge" or a more polite tactic for taking power. Servant Leadership is a wholly different way of relating to the organization and the people in it. And, like Robert Greenleaf, I think it's a better way.

Why Bother?

After all that you could well be wondering, "Wouldn't it be easier to just do this the old way?" Or "Isn't it kind of crazy to give employees service when we're actually paying them to perform?" Or "Why would we want to work hard to get promoted so that then we could have the chance to work harder?" Ultimately, we all have to answer that for ourselves. But at Zingerman's we believe that Servant Leadership does the following:

It's the right thing to do for the world: In any element of life, service is the highest form of contribution we can make to those around us. While there's certainly a lot to be said for self-improvement, ultimately, it's really much more what we *give*—not what we *get*—that defines us as leaders and establishes the legacy that we leave behind. Service, and the spirit of generosity behind it, puts positive energy out into the world, makes everyone and everything around us better—it's a natural and organic nutrient to enrich the "soil" of any organization.

It makes for better service to customers: This is just Natural Law of Business 5: "If you want the staff to give great service to customers, the leaders have to give great service to the staff." *The service our staff gives to our customers will never be better than the service we give to the staff.* If we want to give our guests exceptional, extra-mile service, then we absolutely, one hundred percent, have to do the same for the people who work for us. We are the ones who will either set the standard for or, alternatively, hold back the organization's service quality. The better we get at giving service—to both staff and guests—the better our business is going to be.

It helps our staff to grow and succeed: When they choose to work in our organization, staff members entrust us to deliver effective leadership. In return, we as leaders are responsible for *providing an environment in which staff members can fulfill their dreams and live up to their potential.* As Robert Greenleaf wrote, "The first order of business is to build a group of people who, under the influence of the institution, grow taller and become healthier, stronger, more autonomous."

Providing great service to our staff can only help to make the ZCoB a better and more desirable place to work. And since we are competing with hundreds of other companies to attract the most creative, hardest-working, food-lovingest staff we can find, this offers us a huge strategic advantage. The better we serve the staff, and the more likely they are to spread the word about what we do in a positive way, the more likely we are to get more good customers and more good co-workers. Again, everyone wins!

It helps each of us grow as leaders: I really believe that the more you give, the more you get. And because Servant Leadership is all about giving, it only makes sense that if I get really good at it, it's going to reward me with a more satisfying and meaningful life. For starters, I get to make a positive difference in the lives of our staff. And because Servant Leadership pushes us to look inward first before we start assuming others are to blame, the most successful people in our organization are almost always the most self-reflective. And since self-reflection very often leads directly to self-improvement, that means I'm moving forward in my work, while simultaneously serving those around me.

It sets the right tone for everyone else: In *Sacred Hoops,* basketball coach Phil Jackson wrote that, "creating a successful team . . . is essentially a spiritual act. It requires the individuals involved to surrender their self-interest for the greater good so that the whole adds up to more than the sum of its parts." Like it or not, as leaders, we set the example for everyone in our organization. If *we* don't put the organization's interests above our own, who will? If the leader sends a message that "I come first," then it's kind of inevitable, don't you think, that the staff will adopt that same "me first" attitude?

Putting an Inspirational Idea into Practice

This is where the intellectual rubber really hits the organizational road, where we leave theory behind and figure out how to actually put our beliefs to work on the line in a very practical sense. As with so much of our other work, we've taken the broad conceptual approach that Robert Greenleaf writes about and come up with very specific ways to put it into practice every day. In this case there are six elements—*providing vision, giving service to staff, working in an ethical way, learning and teaching, helping staff succeed, and saying thanks.*

1. Provide an Inspiring and Strategically Sound Vision

At Zingerman's the Servant Leader's number-one responsibility is to provide vision for his or her part of the organization. There's much more on the subject of visioning (as you probably already know) in *Zingerman's Guide to Good Leading, Part 1*. As we use the term, a vision is a descriptive and fairly detailed picture of what success will look like for us at a particular point in the future. It's the big picture, the lofty and inspirational edifice that we're all working to construct collaboratively. The vision, as we view it, is an answer to the simple yet radical question, If we're really successful in our work, what will our organization look like (fill in the blank) years/months from now? In our model, a vision should be

- **Inspiring.** To all who will be involved in implementing it.
- **Strategically sound.** We actually have a decent shot at making it happen.
- **Documented.** You really need to write your vision down to make it work.
- **Communicated.** Yes, if you want your vision to be effective you have to not only document it, but actually tell people about it.

Writing and sharing a vision is, straightforwardly, great service to the group—it gets all of us on the same organizational page; it lets the staff know where we're headed, what tomorrow will look like, and how that future will be better than the present-day reality in which we're currently working. The vision is, in essence, the "cathedral" that all our work is contributing to building and that we believe in, every day. Here at Zingerman's we want to provide a vision for pretty much everything we do. The most critical would be a vision for the business as a whole. For us, that is Zingerman's 2020. We also need a vision of greatness for each business unit—we have one for the Bakehouse, Roadhouse, Creamery, Mail Order, and all the other ZCoB entities. We also write inspiring, strategically sound, and documented visions for each department or operating unit. Literally, we write visions for every new project, every new product, and every process we're trying to put in place.

Don't underestimate how much people who work with you want to know where you're going. They may not ask the questions aloud, but in the privacy of their minds, or in conversation with colleagues, they're all wondering "What will things look like a year or two down the road? How will things be the same? How will they be different? What big successes will we have had? How will people be working together? What products will we be offering? How much of them will we be selling? How will our financials look? Our workspace? What will our customers say about us?" Don't hold back when you write the vision. Detail makes a difference. People want to know where they're going, why they're going there, what's in it for them and those around them.

If the staff is clear on where we're headed, we can all avoid wasting energy on unnecessary conversation—staff members feel calmer and more confident when they know what's going on. We know here at Zingerman's that we're not opening anywhere other than the Ann Arbor area (as one example), so when offers come in for us to open in other cities, we can quickly and politely say "no," without wasting any time assessing the opportunity. And if we start to lose focus or forget where we're going, that written vision is easy to access and provides us with a quick answer.

One subtlety to stress: while Servant Leadership dictates that we make sure *there is an effective vision in place, it doesn't mean that we need to dictate that vision from the top down.* We may be the primary author or just another person on the team who decided to contribute. Our job is mostly to make sure there is one. Good Servant Leadership might well mean giving someone else in the organization the opportunity to lead by writing the first draft. Or if we write the first draft ourselves, to then go out and gather input from others and adjust accordingly. The key in all of this is effective collaboration; the best visions almost always blend the insight and intuition of whoever's in the leadership role (who may not be the one with the title) with the wisdom of the rest of the group.

2. GIVE GREAT DAY-TO-DAY SERVICE TO STAFF

For anyone who's taken our service training classes or ZingTrain seminars, this next element is all about applying our 3 Steps to Great Service and 5 Steps to Handling a Complaint to our interactions with staff, just as we would with customers. Seriously, pretty much all the same stuff applies. For more in-depth info on our "service recipe," see *Zingerman's Guide to Giving Great Service,* but for the moment let me quickly walk you through.

3 Steps to Great Service, Servant Leadership-Style

1. Find out what the customer wants.

In a Servant Leadership context this comes down to simply greeting and engaging with staff members as we would customers. If I see staffers coming towards me, I live our "10/4 Rule"—when I get within ten feet of them I make eye contact and smile, and within four feet I greet them. If they've worked here for many years, I'd probably greet them with the same sort of familiarity I would use with a regular customer of long standing. If they're new and I don't know them, I need to reach out and introduce myself and welcome them aboard. (Just so you know, this last act isn't easy for me. I'm actually very shy, and a total introvert, but Servant Leadership dictates that I need to do it anyway. So I do!)

As with customers, I engage staff members, spending as much time with them as I can in order to get a solid sense of what they're feeling and thinking, how their energy is, what's going on in their lives, etc. The more I know, the better I'll be able to serve them, and the better, in turn, they'll be able to serve the customers. Just as I would do with a customer coming in the front door, it's good to get things going by asking the staff member what I can do for them and then actually (whoa!) listening to the answer. Just as it does in giving great service to guests, paying attention to staff adds immensely to the quality of the service work we do. Throughout the interaction, as a leader, I'm reading the energy, body language, and nuance in the tone of voice of the staff member.

The Power of Listening

Listening is a hugely important element of literally everything we do, but it's particularly important in Servant Leadership. Greenleaf is adamant about this and has a lot to say on the subject: "I believe," he begins, "that the first step in good communication, anywhere, is listening. In planning, deciding and communicating, on matters concerning how people think and feel and act and grow, one has only two general ways of getting at the data needed to manage: observing and listening. And a great deal must be gotten by listening. I have a hunch," he adds, "that most managers are poorer listeners than they are observers."

I'd agree. In fact, I put myself in that category. While Paul is probably naturally good at it, I think that by nature, I'm a lousy listener. But I've worked hard to get better and, while I still slip more often than I'd like, I'm probably now pretty good much of the time. Without question, improved listening skills have helped me get better at almost everything I do, in every part of my life.

"Listeners," Robert Greenleaf points out, "learn about people in ways that modify—first the listener's attitude, then in behavior towards others, and finally the attitudes and behavior of others." How well we listen says a lot about how much we value (or don't value) other people's views, and also the results we get in the organization. The whole element of active listening—not just being able to repeat the words you heard, but rather putting your whole emotional, reflective, caring, sensitive, empathetic, vulnerable self into it—puts me in a different place in the world than when I focus on defending or proving others wrong.

I'm convinced that Greenleaf is totally right to add, "Listening is an attitude, an attitude towards other people and what they are trying to express." Adding to that I'll share what I heard from Stas' Kazmierski, one of the managing partners in ZingTrain, who long ago taught me to try listening "with my heart, not just with my head." This, I will say with certainty, is a huge element of good service to staff. To really listen closely, not just to hear the words but to hear the spirit of what people are communicating, the cry for help, the sense of success . . . to suss out the small inner smile forming slowly but still so deeply inside they barely hear it themselves, is a great service.

This listening work is well worth the effort—I've found few more effective ways to expend my own energy. It does take work, though. Practice probably won't make perfect (nothing does, really), but it does make a difference. As Greenleaf elucidates, "Everyone who aspires to strength should consciously practice listening, regularly. Every week, set aside an hour to listen to somebody who might have something to say that will be of interest. It should be a conscious practice in which all of the impulses to argue, inform, judge, and 'straighten out' the other person are denied. Every response should be calculated to reflect interest, understanding, seeking for more knowledge. Practice listening for brief periods, too. Just thirty seconds of concentrated listening may make the difference between understanding and not understanding something important." And who knows what good things could come out of that?

2. Get it for them.

We have three facets to this second service step, which, when done well, are delivered to staff members just as they would be with customers.

Accurately. This is fairly simple, although all too rarely done in the daily work world. Someone told me years ago that, on average, American executives deliver on only about 50 percent of what they say they're going to do. While that may be disheartening, it actually seems pretty accurate. But that stat won't fly in a servant-led world. Imagine if we only did one of two things we promised our customers? We'd be out of business in no time.

Quite simply, then, if we say that we're going to do something for a staff member, Servant Leadership dictates that (duh!), drum roll, we should *do* it! If they leave us a voice mail . . . yes, we should call back in a timely way. If they text, email, or write a letter, we should write back promptly. Not three weeks later because we were busy or in a bad mood. I know you knew all that but not responding in a timely way is quite common and, as good service states clearly, is really not okay. Imagine not calling a customer back for a couple weeks because you were busy! You'd never do it (I hope!). Accurate and timely responses, deliverables delivered, paychecks paid, etc., usually go unnoticed, but their absence undercuts almost everything.

Politely. This means that we greet staff members or colleagues as the smart, caring professional human beings that they are. Courtesy counts inside the company as much as it does outside of it. All those nice words we teach staff to say to customers we need to use inside the organization as well. "Please," "Thank you!" "Sir," "Ma'am," . . . you know the drill. The key is that we have to actually do it, not just talk about it. And do it, with meaning, at every level. Whether it's a new staff member in our call center or a new CEO, everyone should get the same polite greeting. Being exceedingly courteous with the new counter person will likely count for a lot more than you might think. And it will be one of the most inexpensive strategic initiatives you ever implement.

Enthusiastically. Enthusiasm is a tough one for many managers with old-school mindsets. It's understandably difficult to get over, but it's what Servant Leadership is all about; yes, *we're* paying people to work, but we still need to act enthusiastically every time we see them. Even, I should add, when you don't really like them all that much. The organization's overall energy, of course, starts with the leaders—if we want staff to be really enthusiastic, we'd better be acting pretty darned upbeat when we greet them. The energy we put out there is going to set the tone—the more positive we are, the more motivated, the more grounded, the more fun we're having, the happier we look when we see the staff, the more likely it is that they're going to do a great job with guests.

3. Go the extra mile.

This third step is really just as we would do it with paying customers. Extra miles for us are generally small things—the stuff that, more often than not, costs next to nothing but leaves staff members smiling. Open the door for them, give them a small gift or thank you card, let them leave early on occasion, provide them with additional time off or additional resources to do their work. Extra miles aren't magic, and they generally don't cost much, but they definitely make a difference. If we were in a ZingTrain seminar I'd probably have the whole group brainstorm a bunch of extra miles on white sheets on the wall in order to get them thinking, but I'm sure you get the concept already. (Of course, if you want some practice, flip to the "Notes" page at the end of the book and jot a few extra miles down while the concept is fresh in your mind.) It's usually pretty simple—schedule an extra session of a class you offer for a staff member who couldn't make it to your last one, offer them a cup of coffee, a ride home, empty their trash so they don't have to, buy them a good book or a bouquet of flowers.

I know this probably seems like small stuff, but I will say from experience that, just as is the case with customers, these little things go a long, long way towards helping staff members feel cared for, believing that they, and their work, make a difference, that the small things matter. Which means that they in turn are more likely to go the extra mile, to care and take care, to do the little things that add up to making a big difference in the way the business is being run. Extra miles may seem like minor asterisks on a very complex and fast-paced production, but they add up and make a very big difference.

5 Steps to Handling a Complaint, Servant Leadership-Style

When it comes to complaint handling, Servant Leadership leads us to almost, though not quite, the same process we would follow with paying customers. There's much more on these in *Zingerman's Guide to Giving Great Service*, but in a Servant Leadership nutshell, here's what I try to do when someone who works here complains to me.

1. Acknowledge the complaint.

With staff, as with customers, the whole complaint-handling process works so much better when we just start by letting the person know that we've actually heard what they've said. So instead of refuting, denying, explaining, excusing, or any of those other things that I often instinctively want to do, it's important to just get grounded, swallow hard, take a deep (mental, if not physical) breath, and say "Oh," or "Wow!" like I really mean it. Really big complaints call for a combo package—a big "Oh, wow!!!" can work pretty well. Mo at our Mail Order likes to say "Sheesh!" Someone else here (I can't remember who) told me they use "Yow!" You can, of course, have your own catchphrase. The point is to let the staff member know you heard them, which is a fairly rare occurrence—bosses in the old school usually give the staff commands, not confirm that they've heard concerns.

Acknowledgment sounds easy. But it's far easier to know that I should do it than it is to actually come through under pressure. By nature, I take things pretty personally and I'm often a bit tired and operating at a high level of intensity, so when someone on staff is unhappy with something that I've worked hard to make go, it's easy to slide into being defensive or to start explaining why things are the way they are. This is not, I can say with the voice of way too painfully much experience, at all effective. Which is why practicing, role playing, and a lot of mental discipline can add up to make such a difference with stuff like this!

2. Sincerely apologize.

This one's pretty counterintuitive for most people in positions of power. It was for me at least. Service has never come naturally to me; I've just worked hard at it for many years now. But just as it does with customers, cutting to the chase and sincerely saying, "I'm sorry" to a concerned or frustrated staff member will go a long way towards reducing stress and helping get everyone on the same side of the problem. Please take note that an apology does not mean that the

127

staff member (or the customer for that matter) is necessarily correct about the content of their complaint or criticism; we're just appropriately apologizing for the fact that they're upset or concerned. And we follow that acknowledgment with a simple, but sincere, apology. Something along the lines of, "I'm really sorry you were so upset," or "I'm sorry you were caught off guard," or "I'm sorry it didn't work out as you wanted it to," or whatever way you can come up with to convey an apology. (Caveat: Sorry to say it, but "I'm really sorry you're acting like a jerk" won't cut it in this context. Although, I'll say that *thinking* it for a brief second might at least get you smiling to yourself and help you get over yourself and get focused on giving good service instead of being frustrated.)

3. Take action to make things right.

It's a given that we're going to field a wide range of staff concerns. Some new one is sure to come up and catch me off guard almost every day. A lot of them—and a lot more than most old-line managers might want to believe— are totally legitimate. Paychecks might not have been prepared as they should have been. The schedule wasn't up on time. We promised them something but forgot to take care of it. We failed to return a call in a timely way or forgot to come to a meeting we'd scheduled. In these situations, we need to find a way to make things right, just as we would with a paying customer. I try hard not to get caught up in proving points or playing politics; my job is just to effectively find a way to make things right.

That said, there are certainly occurences where, although the staff member is truly upset, things aren't quite so simple. Realistically, there will always be situations where people who work here are asking for, or complaining about, something that they may well not fully understand. It could be that (we believe) they've inaccurately assessed the situation; perhaps they just don't agree with the way we do business, or their scheduled request said "Saturday" but they meant to say "Sunday." There are, unfortunately, no shortage of these sorts of disconnects.

In these sorts of situations there is actually room for a significant departure from the way we treat *staff like customers,* and how we treat *customers like customers.* With paying customers we're almost always going to act like they're right, even when they're wrong. But with staff, that doesn't really work for us organizationally. For example:

- The staff member's reality is way off base.
- Their behavior is unethical or inappropriate.

- We believe the organization at large is going to suffer for something the staff member is demanding.

In those sorts of situations, it's incumbent on us as leaders who are serving the organization to find a way to constructively and kindly address this reality gap, and, as gracefully as we can, guide all involved toward a positive, mutually agreed-upon resolution. The key is that we handle it in a respectful, dignified way and go for win-win solutions whenever possible—just because someone's done something that's out of step with reality or the rest of the organization doesn't mean we need to step on them in return.

4. Thank them for letting us know.

Again, this is no different than it would be with a paying customer. A simple, "Thanks for letting me know you were frustrated," or "Thanks for sharing your concerns. I really appreciate it," goes a long way. The key is making sure they feel good about having voiced their concerns. Although it may not feel that way in the moment, the reality is that they're doing us a favor. If they don't complain to us, guess who they're going to be complaining to? You got it—everyone else.

5. Document the complaint.

While we haven't yet fully integrated this fifth step into our management work, there's really no reason not to be moving in this direction. Documenting and sharing staff concerns about operational issues, leadership shortfalls, or opportunities for improvement could bring many of the same benefits to our leadership work that it is bringing to our work with frontline customers. At an extreme level this is the stuff HR departments appropriately advocate for. But the truth is (and I could and should take note of my own advice as well), making a note or two in your computer about what happened could only help later. It certainly won't hurt!

A Few Service Subtexts for Servant Leaders to Be Mindful Of

a. **Treat the staff with dignity at all times.** We don't have to agree with them, we don't have to like them, we don't have to be happy to see them, but we really do need to always treat them in a dignified manner if we want this Servant Leadership stuff to work.

b. **Show that you care about them as individuals.** This doesn't mean you're responsible for their lives, nor does it mean you have to fix their problems for them. It does mean that you take a minute to ask how their vacation was, to find out how they're feeling, how school's going, how their family is, or where they're from. Show them that you know they have—and have had—a life outside of work. Small questions and a bit of recall to ask again a week later make a big difference; caring people like to know someone cares.

c. **Don't hold grudges.** Although most of the world continues to carry them, our experience here is that grudges get you absolutely nowhere. At least nowhere good—they just suspend you in an angry, unproductive past that poisons the organization and, actually, our own spiritual state as well. Hey, I know that employees err; sometimes they completely screw up. But the past is the past, and it's over. Because we're committed to giving great service to the staff, and because we're not living on Planet Fair, as Servant Leaders we commit to taking a forgiving approach. This doesn't mean that you don't hold firm on appropriately agreed-upon consequences or that you completely forget what happened. It just means that you're going to look forward to—and work towards—a positive, mutually rewarding future rather than let yourself get locked into an old grudge for past behaviors.

d. **Cut the gossip.** Yeah, I know, gossiping is good fun. For about five minutes. Until you find out someone overheard you say something, or until you realize you've talked yourself into a poisonous corner that's hard to work your way back out of. So, hey, do yourself a Servant Leadership favor of great proportion and stay away from gossip. It really never, ever helps to talk ill of the organization or its members in front of frontline staff members. Telling tales out of school is not in synch with Servant Leadership.

---

3. Manage in an Ethical Manner

It's not new news that we as leaders have a huge responsibility to actually live, not just pay lip service to, our values. You definitely *didn't* hear it here first—it's in everything from the Bible to Jim Collins's *Built to Last* and the writings of anarchists. It's also safe to say that there aren't a whole lot of leaders who actively announce that they *aren't* going to lead in an ethical manner; everyone says they will, and most, I think, actually believe they are most of the time. So what goes wrong? Probably much of the same stuff that goes wrong with everything else—unclear expectations, bad communication, decisions being made in isolation, failure to follow through, misconceptions, misperceptions, and missed opportunities all make for some pretty big ethical shortfalls.

To get a bit more specific about it: one simple and all-too-common problem is that so few organizations have actually put their guiding principles down in writing—it's hard to really live up to a set of standards when the standards aren't clearly documented. Reading minds is rarely a healthy way to run a company. And it's more than a little frustrating when the only way to find out you screwed up is for someone to set you straight after the fact. Without a sound ethical orientation, people start to lose hope, integrity falls, their belief in what they're doing starts to drop, they stop doing the little things, they lose respect for themselves, their leaders, and the organization. If you don't have your guiding principles (or, if you prefer, ethics or values) written down, . . . write them! Details on how to do it are in *Zingerman's Guide to Good Leading, Part 1*.

Another simple but all-too-common problem is that even when organizations put their principles in writing, they tend to leave them languishing somewhere out of sight, which quickly puts them, also, out of mind. If you've had them, unwittingly, under cover, now's a good time to bring 'em back out and start actively sharing them with everyone in the organization. There's little to lose and there's a whole lot to gain! Even just making time to reread them regularly will make a difference. You'll quickly see where you're already doing well and where you might find opportunities to improve. The more you work with a written set of values, and the more you teach them, the more meaningful they're going to be. Here at Zingerman's, Paul and I cover them in all the new-staff orientation classes, we reference them regularly in doing our daily work, and we do actively bring them into difficult discussions and use them to help us frame decisions of all sorts.

Please note that I'm not talking about preaching, which I've never found to be productive. This is all about effective implementation, not lecturing or handbook thumping. It's more in the mode of storytelling—sharing insights and experiences about where the values were lived or, conversely, where we fell short and how we then recovered from our shortfall. Storytelling of that sort is the easiest way I know to make our guiding principles come alive, to keep ourselves as leaders more in line with what we're trying to do, and to demonstrate to everyone in the organization that our values actually have value! To quote Robert Greenleaf, "Ethics, in the abstract, does not interest me. But ethical people trying to do their creative, responsible best, do interest me."

I'm sure none of that will shock anyone who's given even an iota of thought to the issue of ethics in business (which I'm guessing you have, or you'd not likely be reading this in the first place). What I want to suggest next, though, might seem a bit more out of the box, uncomfortable, odd, or unwise, depending on whom you're talking to. *I propose that we actually come out of the leadership closet and actively share the struggle—with staff and colleagues —that's at the core of all ethically sound business.* That we actively let people in the business know that, more often than not, we're not all that sure what to do in difficult situations. And that figuring out a good answer is often about making peace with various shades of gray, not going straight to some simplistic black or white extreme.

---

6 Elements of Effective Servant Leadership

1. Provide an inspiring and strategically sound vision
2. Give great day-to-day service to staff
   - 3 Steps to Great Service
   - 5 Steps to Handling a Complaint
3. Manage in an ethical manner
4. Be an active learner (2 hours/week) and teacher (1 hour/month)
5. Help staff succeed by living the training compact
6. Say thanks

I know this is not how most of us have been trained to do it. In the old model, when the going gets tough, the bosses get going—usually that means retreating to the back room to talk strategy, then showing up not long thereafter, with big decisions already made and everything well in hand. Everyone else, in turn, is essentially asked to just follow orders. Rarely, though, do people "lower down" in the organization know that those "at the top" actually had a hard time determining the best course of action. The frontline crew is told what to do, but they hardly ever hear the discussion that was behind the actual decision. Again, I advocate the opposite approach. I think it's far more effective to actually bring people into that struggle and let them share in the decision making.

Sure, there are some things that really require privacy—difficult HR problems, salary issues, and that sort of thing. But those aside, most any difficult decision has an ethical element to it; by bringing a lot more people into the dialogue *we start to teach everyone in the organization how to effectively manage in an ethically grounded manner.* While managing in an ethical way sounds simple (just "do the right thing," right?), it's actually pretty darned difficult to pull off. Even the best of the best don't get it right all the time. In one way or another, there are dozens, and probably more like hundreds, of places we knowingly accept ethical shortfalls on any given day—products that could be better; staffers who aren't yet superb but we still allow to serve guests; a customer we know we probably should have gone back to one more time to check if they were okay. In school this stuff is an academic exercise, a chance to discuss the theory behind ethics in business. For us, it's about real food, real people, and real money, and the decisions often need to be made in the moment and under a great deal of pressure.

By involving "everyone" in sorting out those ethical uncertainties, we serve the organization in (at least) three ways:

a. **By effectively teaching ethics to everyone.** Few folks frame it this way, but deciding how to handle a difficult customer; whether to serve a sandwich that's almost, but not quite, good enough when the customer has had to wait a bit too long already; how to respond to a colleague who's not working in a very service-oriented way—all of these are ethical decisions that get made, mostly on the q.t., all day long, without anyone from the upper levels of most organizations even acknowledging that they're happening.

We teach everyone up front the importance of collaborative, ethical decision making—when they're making all those small decisions all day long, I feel better knowing that their thinking is grounded in much the same ethical soil as that of the partners with the broadest strategic responsibility. Personally, I think it's great— it's real, it's realistic, and it really makes a difference. The more we train everyone to work mindfully at this level, the sounder their decisions are going to be, the more successful the organization is likely to be. The power, the wisdom, the safety on this stuff, is all in the group.

b. **By guarding against a narrow view from the top.** Second, *we protect the organization from the inherently unstable reality of the* *one upper-level executive (or small group of executives).* The problem occurs all over the country every day: people at the top making decisions that, in the privacy of their corner office, seem totally sensible, but in truth are completely unsound for the company. To quote Robert Greenleaf, "To be a lone chief atop a pyramid is *abnormal and corrupting.* None of us are perfect by ourselves, and all of us need the help and correcting influence of close colleagues." And, he points out, "The pyramidal structure weakens informal links, dries up channels of honest reaction and feedback, and creates limiting chief versus subordinate relationships which, at the top, can seriously penalize the whole organization."

Dean Tucker, writing in *Using the Power of Purpose,* points out that over 80 percent of the knowledge in American organizations is actually still held only in the heads of its employees. Which means that a small, isolated set of leaders can't possibly make consistently sound decisions—they're missing too much information. Worse still, most of the executives aren't even aware of how much info they're missing. Speaking as a CEO who's probably more in touch than most, it's still, I think, inevitable that, left to our own devices, we're going to go off course or often do something stupid. What usually saves me is that I'm around good people who help keep my shortfalls from seriously damaging the organization over the long haul.

c. By backing up the belief that we're all responsible. When a business makes a major ethical error, even in a command-and-control setting, most everyone in the company is still sort of complicit. Sure, the lone chief could go solo and screw up completely in secret. But, more often than not, everyone involved suspected something was wrong but chose to look the other way out of awkwardness, apathy, uncertainty, past frustrations, or fear of getting fired. More often than not, a big ethical shortfall starts with small, seemingly uncritical decisions at every level. Sure, we as leaders have a lion's share of the responsibility. But, then again, if everyone's a leader, everyone also shares in the responsibility for what the organization is doing.

My hope here is to build an organization in which, through great service from the top, an overt commitment to active communication and collaboration, and systems that require us to self-monitor (like open-book finance, for instance), we can create an environment in which people will actually speak up when they sense that something is wrong, rather than let me or Paul or anyone else drive our bus(iness) over a dangerous, unethical, cliff.

Have the Courage to Engage in Caring Confrontations

Sometimes Servant Leadership calls for us to do what seems, at first glance, to be the opposite of the usual congenial approach to customer service. When someone we work with isn't living up to clearly communicated expectations, when allowing them to continue as is, is undercutting both their and the organization's success, then we need to sit down with them and have what we call a "caring confrontation." It could be with anyone we work with—partner, manager, boss, employee, or anyone anywhere in the organization whom we're struggling to work well with. It's caring because we do it with dignity, respect, and a positive (even if uncertain) outcome in mind. It's a confrontation because, by definition, it's not about all the good things the other person might be doing. For me at least, these conversations are never anything I look forward to; they're usually at least somewhat, if not very, difficult. But to *not* have them when things aren't going well is a disservice to whomever it is that we're trying to work with more effectively, and to the organization overall. To quote again from Robert Greenleaf, the challenge for each of us is, "Am I willing to say the words and take the actions that build constructive tension? The act may seem hard and unreasonable to the recipient at the time, but it may be the most constructive kindness."

To read our recipe for Productive Resolution of Your Differences, see page 338.

4. BE AN ACTIVE LEARNER AND TEACHER

As Paul often says, "There's a lot of information out there that we need to know. And no one of us is going to get all of it—if I'm not learning it and you're not learning it, we're probably missing out!" I agree. In fact, the reason this application of Servant Leadership appears as it does on our list is, actually, the result of the two of us going out and doing more formal learning in the first place. The story dates to a sunny autumn day; I think it was the fall of 1992, if I remember right. The two of us had taken time out of our regular work routines to fly out to San Francisco to attend an *Inc.* magazine conference. The highlight of the conference was the chance to hear Skip LeFauve, then head of the Saturn Corporation, present on what he and his crew were doing to make a new kind of car company at their plant in Tennessee. One of the many good things he shared was their expectation about leaders learning and teaching. We loved it and we've been using it ever since.

To be clear, it's not like the idea of learning was new to us. Both Paul and I have always been big readers, conference-goers, and generally avid students on almost any relevant subject. We've always made time to go to seminars and classes, we've happily paid for others here to do the same, and we started teaching—both formally and informally—very early on in the life of the business. I don't think either of us could imagine doing it any other way; it just seemed incredibly obvious that without that learning and teaching we were never going to have even the slightest shot at getting to where we wanted to go. But as the business grew and brought in more managers, we found ourselves increasingly frustrated that many of them didn't seem to have the same passion for training that we did. Which was why we were so excited to hear what Skip had to say. At Saturn they were way more out front about it than we'd ever been—*every manager was expected to do two hours per week, on average, of formal learning.*

To be a bit more specific, here's what we look for from anyone in a leadership role:

> **Two hours a week of formal learning.** Following Skip's lead, we ask that all Zingerman's managers and partners do an average of two hours of formal learning a week. The immediate question that almost always comes up is, "What is *formal* learning?" I can tell you more quickly what it isn't—osmosis is out, and hanging around with interesting people (even at work!) isn't included either. That said, almost everything else is in. Books, audio, websites, attending seminars or classes within our organization or without, educational websites, newspapers, consumer magazines, trade magazines, etc.
>
> The other question that comes up is, Why ask people who are already so busy to take two hours out of their week to learn?

There's a whole host of reasons that I'll list below, but before I even get to those, it's important to make clear that this learning (and teaching) is not "extra" work—it's part of the work that we expect. So someone saying that they don't have time to do it (which, of course, I've heard too many times) is akin to saying that they don't have time to wait on a customer, clean their coolers, or any of the other eight hundred tasks that we all have to do every day.

One hour a month of teaching inside the organization. We also ask that all Zingerman's managers and partners make time for an average of at least an hour of formal teaching per month. The more we teach, the more we learn, the more we clarify our message, and the more clearly we understand what it is we want and what we want to say. That is a very virtuous and positive learning cycle that I love being a part of.

(Although I didn't know it when we heard him speak in San Francisco, it turned out that Skip and his family actually lived in Ann Arbor, and had been good Zingerman's customers for a long time. Over the years I had the opportunity to wait on him many times and to casually share thoughts and learn from his experience and insight. Sadly, he passed away suddenly in January 2003, at the young age of 68. While we never worked together directly, I have the feeling that he lived much of what's in this book in creative and inspirational ways. Members of his family continue to be good customers. But I'm sad that, although we were friendly and I saw him in the Deli regularly, he and I never quite managed to make the time to talk at the length that I'd have liked.)

The learning mindset is very much at the core of Servant Leadership. "Perhaps," Greenleaf says, "we should move towards a new institution that embraces both work and learning—learning in a deep and formal sense and all of the learning influence most people need. This requires a new type of leader, one who can conceptualize such an institution, generate enthusiasm so that many good, able people want to be a part of it, and provide the strong focus of purpose that builds dynamic strength in many. Great things happen when leaders create these conditions."

5. HELP STAFF SUCCEED BY LIVING THE TRAINING COMPACT

Servant Leadership does turn standard 20th-century business thinking on its head. The old model says that when we're successful we'll want to hire more people in order to help us succeed. Here, we actually hire people in order to help *them* succeed. That's right. If we're successful, if we grow, that means we get to bring on more good people so, quite simply, we can help them do a great job, too. While all that might sound strange, it's actually incredibly logical. Think it through—if all the people we hire are attaining great success in their work, how then, is the organization overall likely to be doing? You got it. If they're all rocking the house, it's pretty safe to say the house is gonna be rockin'—in a good way—as well.

This approach, really, is fully in synch with the whole idea of giving great service to the staff. The better we serve them, the more success they garner, the better they do, the better we do; the better we do, the more we give them—and through all this the community and the customers are coming out better and better for it every day. The key here is that it starts with us as leaders committing to helping everyone we hire become great at their work. What that work is, and what "great" might mean, will of course vary from person to person and project to project. But the point is we're out to overtly assist and support everyone in getting there.

When we first started teaching these elements of Servant Leadership at Zingerman's, this fifth section used to simply say, "Help the staff succeed." But in early 2000 we added the line "by living the training compact." What drove us to add it was the release of one of the better books of the new century, *First Break All the Rules* by Marcus Buckingham and Curt Coffman. The book detailed a project put together by the Gallup Organization that surveyed 1,000,000 frontline employees and 75,000 managers to find out what it was that kept the best people in their jobs for the longest period of time. The authors distilled their results down to twelve questions, ranked in order of importance, to which, if you could answer in the affirmative you had the best shot at successfully keeping the best people in your organization.

The funny thing was, when I read through the list, I realized almost immediately that there was an uncanny correlation between what the Gallup folks had found to be most important, and what Maggie Bayless had put onto our training compact ten years or so earlier. If you look at the Gallup findings you'll see that the number one question on their list is exactly the same as what was already in our training compact—"Do I know what's expected of me in my work?" The second most important query, "Do I have the tools I need to do my work?" was, uncannily, the second point on the left side of our training compact. The third Gallup question, "Do I have the opportunity to do what I do best?" is, I think, the right side of the training compact. Only if we each take ownership of our own career can anyone truly have a good shot at doing what they believe they do best. The fourth question, "In the last seven days have I received recognition or praise for good work?" follows along with the left side of the training compact again. Anyway, you're getting the point. It was wild—what Maggie had put together in the mid-90s was being verified by a Gallup study of over a million people. It was pretty obvious that what we needed to do was just get better at doing what we were already supposed to be doing—living that training compact with ever-greater effectiveness. (For more on the training compact, see page 53 in *Zingerman's Guide to Good Leading, Part 1*.)

Quite simply, it's way easier to do a good job when you know what "good" is, when you have the tools you need to learn what you need to know, and are clear in the measurements and the rewards for work well done. Good service dictates that we give staff members all of those things from the get-go!

Zingerman's®
training compact

trainer agrees to:

(1.) document clear performance expectations

(2.) provide training resources

(3.) recognize performance

(4.) reward performance

trainees agree to:

take responsibility for the effectiveness of their training at Zingerman's

6. SAY THANKS

The sixth element of Servant Leadership here is probably the simplest, the most elemental, and easiest to do on a day-to-day basis. It's not fancy and it's really not all that hard: just be actively appreciative of everyone and everything you work with. No, I'm not saying you need to send sappy ecards to colleagues every day. I'm talking about meaningful ways to let people know that you noticed the quality of their work—actively sharing that you saw that they did something special and that you care about them and what they're doing. It's letting people know that they make a positive difference for the organization, for their colleagues, and for their community. You don't really need me to tell you how to do this. It's hardly difficult to do. But it is important.

To be blunt, saying thanks is the kind of thing that high achievers (like me) can forget to do with far too great a frequency. Natural Law of Business 10 says that strengths lead to weaknesses. It only makes sense that self-motivated, internally driven, high-achieving leaders who are totally good with long-term gratification would slip up on saying something nice about the small, short-term stuff that might seem almost insignificant to us but is actually enormously meaningful to most of the people doing most of the work in our businesses. Saying thanks makes an enormous difference.

- Everyone—you and I included—works more effectively when their efforts have been noticed and appreciated.

- Ultimately, saying thanks by recognizing people's contributions is one of the best ways to let people know that their efforts have really made a difference.

- It's more effective and enjoyable to lead with appreciation than to lead with criticism.

- When we say thanks, we set the tone to move our organizational culture towards a more appreciative, positive future.

(For more on this subject, see "Creating a Culture of Positive Appreciation" in *Zingerman's Guide to Good Leading, Part 1.*)

Postscript: Servant Leadership and the Free Sharing of Power

To be really clear here at the conclusion, Servant Leadership is not a scam. It's not an irrelevant nicety, and it's not insignificant. Neither is it some modern, new-agey way to delude people into doing what we want, just by smiling and being nice to them. Servant Leadership is solid; it makes sense, and, for us at least, it's been very, very successful. It is, without question, a hugely important element of the organic garden that is the Zingerman's Community of Businesses. Quite simply, Servant Leadership serves as a simple seed that we can quickly plant in new managers, something that they can consistently learn to fall back on without having to worry too much, or overthink things, when they're under pressure. Servant Leadership has long been the core component of our orientation class for new managers, and we reference it regularly in almost every element of our work. It's a huge help to new managers from the minute they start because, I think, its basic direction is so easy to remember. It works in much the same way that the imaginary football team I describe in the intro to this essay learns to dive for loose balls. When in doubt, Greenleaf says, serve. And when the pressure's really on, serve more still.

Although Robert Greenleaf was clearly very critical of the old-school approach to organizational life, he didn't (to my knowledge) ever envision himself as an anarchist. That said, a lot of his writing was well in synch, I think, with anarchist intent. The way I read it, Servant Leadership is separated from the community-minded, collaborative, free-thinking, supportive elements of anarchism by far fewer than six degrees. Servant Leadership is about the belief that service to the organization is the key to pretty much everything; that when we do it well, we bring out the best in everyone; that when those at what are usually considered to be the "lowest" levels of the business are getting better, then the entire organization is getting better too. Although we at the top may know a lot, there's actually a lot more that we don't know. And to really build a great business requires real respect, collaboration, and communication across all lines, initiative from every area, and accountability by everyone, not just each of us for our own activity, but for the success of the entire organization.

The leader, in Greenleaf's construct, still leads, but primarily by serving; he asks us to use our power as little as possible, leading always with service, gentleness, and generosity, the better to build a positive future for everyone involved. The power and wisdom, he posits over and over again, is actually in the group, in the collaborative, collective, creative people in the organization, not in the hierarchical order and special privileges that take up so much space in most of the work world. Although he worked in it his whole career, he was very critical of the old model. "The prevalence of the lone chief," Greenleaf posits, "places a burden on the whole society because it gives control, priority over leadership. It sets before the young an unwholesome struggle to get to the top. It nourishes the notion among able people that one must be boss to be effective. And it sanctions, in a conspicuous way, a pernicious and petty status striving that corrupts everyone." Greenleaf (like the anarchists) envisioned a future in which people "will freely respond only to individuals who are chosen as leaders because they are proven and trusted as servants."

Servant Leadership, then, provides each of us with a framework in which to function: a mindset and set of guidelines to which we can return again and again as we grapple with the difficult, ever-challenging issues of effective leadership. While considering the idea of it may be easy, actually living Servant Leadership fully, from the inside out, is anything but. The concept is so contrary to the way most of us have learned to be the boss—or to be bossed—that it can take a long time for it to really take hold. Living Servant Leadership isn't just lip service; it's about real, meaningful, from-the-heart, authentic service to the organization and to the people who work in it. To really think *in*—not just think *about*—the language of Servant Leadership is a long, probably a lifelong, project. But it's one I'm happy to be engaged in and to work at, however imperfectly, every day. In that regard, I'll throw my own intellectual and emotional lot in with Gustav Landauer—change isn't easy to master. "I am only starting," he said, "to free myself from the spider webs [of traditional society]. I have to learn to speak very differently."

I've reread Robert Greenleaf's book many times now, and I uncover new insights each time through. The last lines here go to him: "This is my thesis: caring for persons, the more able and the less able serving each other, is the rock upon which a good society is built. Whereas, until recently, caring was largely person to person, now most of it is mediated through institutions—often large, complex, powerful, impersonal; not always competent; sometimes corrupt. If a better society is to be built, one that is more just and more loving, one that provides greater creative opportunity for its people, then the most open course is to raise both the capacity to serve and the very performance as servant of existing major institutions by new regenerative forces operating within them."

notes from the
back
dock

The Inside Scoop on Working Here at Zingerman's

Amos Arinda, Line Cook, Zingerman's Roadhouse

People often ask me, "Why do you think Zingerman's is such a great place to work?" I used to answer that question with a shrug and a shake of the head, usually followed by, "I don't know. It just is." That response would usually frustrate most people—if not outwardly, then probably on the inside. They were looking for something more profound, something magical, or at least more concrete. But I had nothing I could put into words. After a while my underwhelming answer for why I, and others like me, enjoy working here so much began to bother me as well. After much deliberation I realized that the answer was, plain and simple, that we practiced Servant Leadership. Because, no matter what concept or philosophy we practiced as an organization, I have found that at the root of each one lay the notion that the leader was in a place of servitude to the collective staff. It all centered around the fact that at Zingerman's, the leader was there to serve the staff and not the other way around. Take, for example, the concept of open-book management: at the very core of this style is trust that the direct reports you manage are capable, and in some cases even more capable, of making key decisions that affect the business. And as a leader your responsibility is not so much to dictate to others but, rather, to create an environment where they can make the decisions that in turn run the organization! Quite honestly, a business does not run without the staff. Until people in positions of leadership realize that fact, they cannot effectively lead.

What makes this concept paradoxical here at Zingerman's is that we encourage everyone here to be a leader—so, in a way we are to be servants to each other, right? So, when you really think about it the people who are the best servants to each other make the best leaders! Funny how that works, huh?

j atlee and mail order managing partner mo frechette
discussing the vision for the shift

The Secret of Stewardship

Building Power without Using Authority

I first read Peter Block's Stewardship *not long after it was published in 1993. While Block writes about an array of subjects, the one that made the biggest impression on me was his argument that authority is usually best left unused, and that peer-to-peer relationships make for a far healthier organization than the old parental model of command and control. In preparing the piece that follows for publication, I went back and reread Block's book. I was impressed anew by how much wisdom Block worked into the 241 pages of the book, but also by how much of his fairly radical approach we've successfully woven into the way we work here at Zingerman's. Our frequent use of the consensus process is a direct reflection of what follows.*

I was also surprised, in my framework of the moment, channeling early 20th-century American anarchists, by how much of it is, again, based on encouraging and requiring conscious and individual choice, and on how much of that, again, reflects the anarchist emphasis on free individuals pursuing lives that they feel good about leading.

Stewardship is probably the least glamorous "secret" in this book. By contrast, the work on energy is . . . well, immediately energizing. The idea of everyone being a leader, if you go for that sort of thing, is equally uplifting. Servant Leadership lays a foundation of giving, an orientation of favoring others first that's really the total opposite of the old-style, uncaring, owner-oriented capitalism. But Stewardship is the heavy lifting without the excitement. It's very much about the nuts-and-bolts, below-the-surface, relationship-building focus that makes it possible to really make all of what we do work. Saying we believe in equality and democracy pretty much goes without saying in North America, but actually acting as if everyone is equal regardless of the formal authority anyone may or may not have isn't all that easy. Stewardship is where it starts.

—✏—

Peter Block, I believe, is one of the most interesting thinkers of modern business writing. I'm not sure what they think of him in the corporate world—his approaches are anything but mainstream. I know, though, that he's had a big, and very positive, influence on us. Fortunately he's never had to go to jail or into exile for his views, but they are truly about a very different, nonhierarchical way to work. Stewardship and its core concept of building an organization based on peer-to-peer, equal-to-equal relationships in place of the more parental, patriarchal, and authority-based way things work in most of the work world are probably as radical today as Emma Goldman et al. were a century ago.

In Peter Block's words, "Stewardship is the willingness to hold power without using rewards and punishment and directive authority to get things done." I'm down with that. Maybe it represents the "lapsed" part of my anarchism—Emma Goldman would have probably just said, "Get rid of the power and authority and you won't have the problem." I'm saying, keep the authority and the power . . . but other than in really extreme, emergency cases, keep 'em in your pocket. Stewardship will rewire your reset button—instead of defaulting to domination, Stewardship tells us to take a step back and see if we can't convince everyone to get on board, working with them as if they were our partners, not the hired help. In trying to work through pretty much any situation that involves staff members, Stewardship pushes us to ask, "What would partners do?" The obvious framing in our own organization would be, "What would Paul and Ari do if they were in disagreement?"

Peer to Peer at the Starting Point

The truth is that, although the formal concept for it is adapted from Block's book, Stewardship at Zingerman's is basically just the way that Paul and I worked together from the get-go. We didn't call it Stewardship; we just called it common sense. Here's the backstory. When we opened the Deli in 1982, our original thought was that it would be much like the fish market where Paul and his partner, Mike Monahan, were working at the time; a couple of cold cases, a couple extra staff, and a couple of hands-on, on-site owners. Paul, we figured, would come help me run the Deli for the first few months we were open, then head back to the fish market, which—having already been in business for three years—was likely to be the busier of the two businesses. I was the one who was going to run the Deli, while Paul and Mike would man the fish market.

With that model in mind, we divided up the ownership accordingly—as the managing partner of the Deli I would have half of the shares; working from a distance (across the street actually), Paul and Mike would own a quarter each, totaling up, of course, to 100 percent. Over the years, the fish market, while still a really fantastic spot (I'm firm in my belief that it's one of the best in the country), stayed small. The Deli, on the other hand, grew. And grew. And grew some more. Gradually, Paul started to spend more and more time with me running it and commensurately fewer and fewer hours at the fish market, so much so that by the mid-'80s, Paul was practically full time at the Deli.

Throughout, though, the percentages of ownership remained as they'd been—I had half the business, Paul only a quarter. We eventually bought Mike

Monahan out of the Deli in the mid-'90s, at which point our ownership evened out at fifty-fifty. But throughout those first fifteen years, although the share split didn't really reflect the way we were working, the reality of the relationship was that *the disparity in legal authority never came up*. If we couldn't agree on what to do, we agreed that we wouldn't take action until we did. For whatever reasons of affability, emotional makeup, or fate, the fact that I technically had the ability to pull rank on Paul was never an issue; laying formal legalities aside, *we always operated as if we both had the same percentage of ownership*.

The approach worked well for us then, and it's still working well now, three decades down the road. We gradually built that same mindset into the way we worked with other people, too. The whole habit of pulling rank on our staff—so standard in most of the work world—was a card we almost never pulled out. No matter how difficult a day might have been, we always worked hard to talk things through, not just order others around; neither of us has ever felt like we were "better" than anyone, so treating people as peers really just seemed reasonable. It's not like we never used our authority—we just didn't use it very often. Instead, we relied on our willingness to negotiate respectfully with employees, even though, technically, they worked "for" us. We hadn't read *Stewardship* yet, and the way we were working wasn't some well-thought-out and deeply researched philosophical construct.

The "problem" that reading *Stewardship* solved is one that started to arise as we grew and hired more supervisors and managers. Although Paul and I were clearly living and modeling a very egalitarian approach, our new managers still seemed to pull rank on their employees a whole lot more than we ever had. To say the least, we were a little miffed—it was not what we were modeling and it clearly (to us at least) was not how we wanted them to work. But when the pressure was on, people would start acting like the old-school authority figures that Paul and I abhorred. Our intent was always to treat everyone like an equal; not to use our authority to make single-minded, command decisions unless we absolutely had to. After regular rounds of feeling frustrated, confused, concerned, and, at times, angry, we finally realized that what we took for granted wasn't obvious to everyone else.

As has proven to be the case so many times, the problem, really, was ours, not theirs—we had an expectation that we'd failed to explain. While the oversight wasn't malicious on our part, it might as well have been; we were unwittingly starting down the all-too-well-traveled road of "hidden agendas," which are always followed by unfortunate frustration and understandable anger. Fortunately, we figured out the error of our ways fairly early on—when we read *Stewardship*, we realized that we needed to be far more up front about our expectations. That if we weren't clear with others about our issues with our managers' use of authority, their authority issues were going to undermine everything we'd worked so hard to build up over the years.

The entire approach then, while it's based on things we learned from Peter Block, really just was an attempt to more effectively clarify what I suppose our insurance provider might call a "pre-existing condition." Peter Block did a beautiful job of clarifying concepts that Paul and I had failed to communicate. Teaching Stewardship was a positive step towards setting our organizational outlook on the subject straight. What we originally just called "common sense" (wrongly!) has become a fairly consistently applied leadership approach in our organization. Making the move from the old school model of command and control to Stewardship may sound simple but, like Servant Leadership, the concept is probably easier to convey than it is to put successfully into practice. For most people, Stewardship is completely counterintuitive.

Stewardship is about getting done what needs to be done while exercising our formal authority only when we actually need to. In contrast to the more typical, top-down, command decision-making mode, effective use of *Stewardship builds on peer-to-peer, partner-to-partner relationships with everyone we work with.* Frontline staff may not hold stock shares, but, more often than not, we're going to treat them as if they're equal partners anyway.

Over the years, Stewardship has become a model we use for all our decision-making work—including both manager to staff and peer to peer—all the way up, down, and across our organization. While, in honesty, we do far less formal teaching on the subject than we do on other things, I think we've done a reasonably good job of building Stewardship effectively into our culture. New managers who come from the outside find out quickly—our culture isn't very receptive to people on power trips ordering others around. That said, what's working now could erode very quickly if we're not careful. This gentle, mindful, minimalist approach to applying authority could quickly come apart if a new generation of Zingerman's managers were to move unwittingly back into the old model of more authoritarian, top-down management.

Stewardship, I've come to believe, is a bit of a safety lock on the weapon of authority that managers in any organization are handed shortly after they're hired. Without getting into anyone's politics on issues of gun control, I think it's safe to say that everyone will agree that safe gun handling is important, and that it only makes sense to keep loaded weapons away from loaded settings. Back in the frontier era of the Old West, gunslingers were commonly requested to check their guns at the door when they entered a saloon. In case some disagreement got out of hand, it was better that they had no firearms to fight with. Similarly, Stewardship asks us to put our authority away before we enter into our day-to-day work. If we really need it, it's still there waiting safely by the door. But by voluntarily setting it aside (other than in extreme situations), we and everyone else around us are considerably safer. The sort of sudden, spur-of-the-moment decisions made in anger that wreak havoc in so many organizations can be pretty effectively avoided when Stewardship is the order of the day.

Authority versus Agreement; or It's Better Not to Blow Yourself Up Just to Prove a Point

Here's the scoop on Stewardship. It's no big secret to those we work with that, as managers or owners, we have the authority to act unilaterally, to pull rank in an emergency or crisis, whenever we need to. As Peter Drucker says, writing in *Management Challenges for the 21st Century*, "Someone in the organization must have the authority to make the final decision in a given area." Certainly, as majority partners, Paul and I hold ultimate authority over the managing partners (and I guess everyone else) in our organization. Our commitment, however, is to work with them when at all possible (and it pretty much has been all the time) using a consensus—not a command—model. Similarly, as CEO, I guess I technically have formal ultimate authority over all organizational operating issues, but our commitment, again, is to work collaboratively and by consensus. This same model holds true within each part of our organization. The managing partner has ultimate authority over the managers in his or her business, but attempts to operate first by gaining agreement rather than simply ordering things to get done. The managers have authority over the frontline staff that they hire, but again, we ask that they use it as little as possible.

What this means in practice is that the higher up we move through the organizational chart, the more we attempt to use consensus as our operating model for Stewardship. In other words, newly arrived staff members will have the narrowest range of options and probably the least amount of bargaining power in negotiations.

Over the years of working with the Stewardship model I've come to believe ever more strongly that the effectiveness of our authority is a lot like a nuclear arsenal. Having "the bomb" is a big deterrent—possession alone gives you great power, but it's more effective if you don't use it. If you do drop a bomb, even if you come out on top in the moment, great destruction almost certainly will ensue. While you retain power in a post-bomb world, you'll also have a great deal of rebuilding to do before you can get things back to normal. Far better, I'd say, to get to an agreed-upon outcome without blowing anything up. Have the weapons to ensure safety in dire circumstances, but use them only as a last resort.

It is my ever-stronger belief that *the value of our authority in an organization is inversely related to the frequency with which we use it.* In fact, I'll share with you the relevant formula that Stas' Kazmierski, one of the two managing partners at ZingTrain, came up with a while back. I was teaching the section on Stewardship that we do in our two-daylong Leading with Zing seminar. The two of us had co-taught it probably twenty or thirty times, and I'd always been the one to teach the segment on this subject. Anyway, I was sharing all this stuff I've just gone through here, talking about the inverse relationship between power and authority, etc., when, all of a sudden, out of the corner of my eye, I see Stas' stand up and walk over to the big white pad of paper that we hang on the wall to write on while we're working. As I kept talking, Stas' started writing. I continued presenting but snuck a peak at the white sheets to see what he was up to. He'd written:

$$P = 1/A \times Fu$$

I really had no idea what he was doing. The audience, not surprisingly, was starting to smile and snicker a bit trying to ascertain why this mild-mannered sixty-year-old organizational change expert was writing "Fu" on the board. I had no idea. It made no sense to ignore whatever his new insight was, so I decided to stop what I was doing and ask. Stas' smiled—that wise smile of someone who knows, and knows that he knows. "Power," he said, slowly, "is the *inverse* of Authority x Frequency of Use." I looked it over again and damn if that wasn't right: $P = 1/A \times Fu$. That was some brilliant, in-the-moment work on management theory, the equivalent of maybe Michael Jordan making one of those moves they would show on the highlight reels for the rest of the season. If you don't remember much math theory you can take my word for it, or work with your kids who probably learn this sort of stuff in eighth-grade algebra. Stas's work was, most certainly, right on—the less frequently we use our authority, the more effective it, and we, will be. In the Stewardship model, the bottom line on power is, basically, *use it and lose it*. On the other hand, if you can hold back, you'll end up holding a lot of power!

That, I can smilingly now say, is the background on Stewardship. Coming back to the basics, the Stewardship Compact that follows creates a framework within which we can make Peter Block's model a reality. On the leader's side of things, we agree to give clear expectations; to provide the tools and resources needed to do the work; and then to recognize and reward effective delivery on the expectations we've asked for. The staff member's part of the deal is *either* to deliver on the expectations we've laid out, *or*, if they don't feel right about those, we encourage them to present an alternate set of expectations. In either case, there's a negotiation that takes place until both parties have agreed on what will be delivered. Once we have that agreement in hand, then we as leaders commit to giving the staff the freedom to do the work in a way that works for them.

When it works well, the Stewardship Compact means that two intelligent, caring individuals with diverse views on the world have respectfully talked through what needs to be done and have arrived at agreement on what that looks like. And that the frontline staff member who's agreed to do the work will then be allowed to take care of business in a way that (assuming it's ethically sound) works for them (even though that may well be different from what the boss would have them do if he or she was assigning all this work in typical, detailed, top-down directives). Take note that although I've put the leader or manager on the left side of the compact, (as per Secret 22) since everyone's a leader, the reality is that any new employee might be the one initiating the dialogue, laying out expectations of their manager, providing the manager with the tools needed to do what they're asking, and then recognizing and rewarding the manager when the work is done well. In which case it would be the manager either coming through as originally asked, or presenting an alternate set of performance goals. In either case, the key is negotiation on a peer-to-peer level, not power trips or passive-aggressive interactions. This, much to the satisfaction of my anarchist soul, is all about free choice, respect, and intelligent free-thinking individuals working collaboratively to get to positive outcomes.

When I teach this Stewardship stuff, I always ask the audience, "Of the two options on the right side of the compact, which do you think I'd prefer—*a* or *b*?" Responses vary some from group to group, but in general about seventy-five percent of people say *a*. Usually the *a*'s speak up more quickly. I understand why—it certainly seems to be the obvious answer. I mean, why wouldn't I, like everyone else, want to get exactly what I want? But *a* is *not* the

Zingerman's ®

stewardship compact

Leadership agrees to:

(1.) document clear performance expectations

(2.) Provide the resources to do the work

(3.) recognize performance

(4.) reward Performance

(5.) Provide the freedom to manage the day-to-day work within the guidelines established in the expectations

staff agree to:

(a.) deliver on the expectations that the leader laid out

or

(b.) negotiate through to agreement and then deliver on an alternate set of expectations

right answer. Not mine at least, and since the question is what do *I* prefer, not what would other people want, in this case, there's only one correct response.

If I wait about half a minute, someone else in the room will, of course (reading their own intuition and my silence when someone shouted out *a*), smile and say *b*. When they do, I simply smile right back, and say, "That's right. I'd much rather have *b*." The people who said *a* almost all then look at me like I'm crazy, which, of course, I could well be. The truth of the matter is that, while I can work with either option—that's why we give people a choice—I far prefer *b*. While anyone can just nod and quickly agree to do what their boss asked, *b* takes someone who cares more about coming through and doing what's right than about pleasing me. And they have the courage to suggest that what I've asked for might not work but still propose a constructive alternative. This whole model is, after all, about peer-to-peer relationships, not following orders.

Going back to *Servant Leadership*, Robert Greenleaf writes, "The trouble with coercive power is that it only strengthens resistance. And, if successful, its controlling effect only lasts as long as the force is strong. It is not organic. Only persuasion and the consequent voluntary acceptance are organic." When we use Stewardship successfully, our power and influence, instead of going down, actually *grow*—people feel valued, we learn from them and they from us. Authority is there, but only as a last resort. Victimhood is out. We come out of the process with a better, mutually agreed-upon outcome, one that we've both mindfully committed to. To make all this into a teachable, learnable, actionable approach, we've developed six components of Stewardship; each on its own is helpful, but the six together are pretty powerful. Stewardship here starts with an effective exchange of purpose. It's followed by a focus on clear performance results and then moves into negotiation through to agreement. Throughout there's a refusal to abdicate our leadership, all the while giving people a great deal of freedom to do their day-to-day work in ways that work for them. And we finish things up with conscious commitment by both parties to take the freely agreed-upon actions.

Six Components of Effective Stewardship Work

1. An Effective Exchange of Purpose

Most typically, old-style business leaders give their staff members as little information as they have to. By contrast, Stewardship *starts with us sharing as much as we possibly can.* In the interest of getting better results for all involved, Stewardship requires that we take the time to explain to the staff member or partner *why* we have chosen the path we're on. Despite our belief that what we are asking for is reasonable, it's not unlikely that the staff member will still be unclear or uncertain about our expectations. It's important that they have time to ask questions; the more confident they are about why we're asking them to take action, the more likely they are to do a good job. That means sharing leadership thinking, giving them the backstory, how we believe they'll positively impact all involved, and how we arrived at the decision to ask for these outcomes in the first place.

Mind you, this doesn't mean we blurt out whatever comes to mind, or that we dump any and all emotional reactions on the table as soon as we have them. That would be irresponsible on the other side of the spectrum. Too much information isn't helpful either—it's likely to create an explosively charged, emotional environment—not the productive, partner-to-partner dialogue we're looking for. Staying constructive, clear, calm, considerate, and composed is critical, even if you're sharing uncertainty or emotion.

Take note that exchange of purpose is a two-way street: it's as important that we understand where the staff member is headed as it is for them to know our intentions. We need to know what they value, what they hope to attain in the coming months and years, what their vision of greatness is for themselves, what role they would like to play in our organization. Having had an effective exchange of purpose, we now have the foundation for effective dialogue, negotiation, and commitment to mutual success.

2. EMPHASIS ON PERFORMANCE RESULTS

Working through the Stewardship Compact helps us to focus more on *deliverable results* and less than we typically might on tactics, attitude, or intentions. Although effort is admirable, we can't use it to make payroll. Stewardship emphasizes the importance of getting real results that deliver great food and great service to our customers, great financial performance to the organization, and that help us to provide the high-quality workplace we desire. What we're asking for on our side of the Stewardship Compact are meaningful bottom-line results and a commitment to attain them according to agreed-upon organizational norms and values. Once we have agreement that these results will be delivered, we can, in turn, actually offer more freedom to the staff member to design the day-to-day, hour-to-hour work as they see fit. In return for this freedom the staff member agrees to really deliver the results we've both committed to.

3. NEGOTIATING TO AGREEMENT
(INCLUDING THE OPPORTUNITY TO SAY NO)

After we've shared our views and expectations, the person with whom we are negotiating may quickly agree to what we are proposing. Assuming that they're sincere in their commitment, and that they believe that they have a good likelihood of success, there's certainly nothing wrong with this outcome. No need to negotiate when everyone's already in agreement! At other times, though, partners in this Stewardship setting might decide that they don't like what we've laid out. In that case, of course, they are choosing option *b* on their side of the compact: "negotiate through to agreement and then deliver on an alternate set of expectations." They can then

- Propose an alternate vision and/or set of expectations and get us to buy into those.

- Decide that, based on this disagreement, they may choose to leave our organization. Although it's extreme, if there's a deep disagreement and we can't come to consensus on the values or vision that surround the work, then it makes sense that they choose to move on in a constructive, mutually agreed-upon way.

- Decide to actively (not passive-aggressively) commit to implementing what we've asked because, after negotiating, they discovered new information that changed their mind.

Any of these paths are actually workable. What's important to me is that all three acknowledge the power of the staff member to act freely, to opt in as a peer. None of them are about being forced to behave like an angry eight-year-old. All three options push the staff member towards commitment to a course of action, as opposed to a more typical, in-the-work-world sense of sacrifice, helplessness, or disengagement. None of these options allow for the passive-aggressive style that permeates so many manager-employee relationships. Stewardship precludes the all-too-common victim mentality: "They told me I have to do this and there's nothing I can really do about it" just doesn't work in this model.

To make this point more clearly, we're actually *asking* the staff member if they will commit to taking the actions at hand, rather than the more typical tack of telling them what to do. To quote Peter Block directly, this means demonstrating "the willingness to give more choice to the people we serve. Not total control, just something more equal." Which means that we have to be ready to accept that they could say no. After hearing what our purpose is and then getting clear about what our expectations are, they still might opt *not* to accept them. This may sound scary, but like it or not, it's the reality of modern management life. While many of us—me included—*want* total control, the reality is that everything is out of control; all we have are varying degrees of influence. (See Secret 29 for more on this subject.) We can't force someone to make a conscious commitment—we can only explain its importance, talk about alternatives, and look at what the consequences of inaction may be for the business and for the individual.

We don't have to wait forever to arrive at agreement during this sort of negotiation. While it seems reasonable for a staff member to ask you to delay a decision for a week while they consider taking on a new short-term assignment, six months of discussion seems excessive. At some point, failure to make a commitment is, in itself, a decision by the staff member. In this role we have to remember that we as leaders represent the needs of the organization and that we can very constructively use our authority to establish time frames or boundaries within which an agreement must be reached, even while leaving the actual content more open to dialogue. Having made the mistake of not doing so, I can tell you now that the earlier in our discussions we make this time frame clear the better.

In an extreme situation, staff members with whom we're negotiating may choose to leave the organization and work elsewhere. While that may seem like a "bad" outcome, I've come to realize over time that it's not. If someone's out of alignment, then it's really in everyone's best interest that they move on. If we've helped make that happen by asking them for results they didn't want to (or weren't able to) deliver on, then I'm glad we could recognize the disconnect and move forward on our separate paths constructively. More often, though, the "no" will be a partial one—the staff member might be uncomfortable with one or more elements of what we've asked for. In this case, we commit to carrying on a positive negotiation with them in the belief that, whenever possible, we'll arrive at a set of mutually agreed-upon expectations that will work for both sides.

6 Components of Effective Stewardship Work

1. An effective exchange of purpose
2. Emphasis on performance results
3. Negotiating to agreement (including the opportunity to say no)
4. No abdication
5. Freedom
6. Conscious commitment

Finally, there are situations where what we're asking someone for isn't really negotiable. Perhaps it is an essential element of the work, or it's a standard to which many others in the organization are already successfully attaining. Or it could be that not doing what we've asked creates a real conflict with our guiding principles. In situations like these, we need to restate our expectations, let our partner know we have no room to negotiate, and that if they're not ready to meet those expectations then we won't be able to work with them. If, after all that, we're still not able to arrive at a workable agreement, then we have to constructively begin working out the details of their departure. Throughout this negotiation, work can be done in a caring, courteous, and respectful way that's fully in synch with our guiding principles and our commitment as Servant Leaders to, first and foremost, serve the organization.

Six Sayings That Support Stewardship

Throughout this work, I've adopted a few sayings and techniques that help me to get past my initial desire to be right or run roughshod over the person I'm negotiating with, and that help get the two of us to a quicker and better outcome with a lot less stress en route. While none are guaranteed to work management magic, all six have been hugely helpful to me. On the chance that they might be of value to you, too, here they are.

a. **When furious, get curious.** Paul taught me this one twenty-five years ago. I use it all the time, almost always with great results. The more frustrated I get, the more I try to make myself ask questions.

b. **Curiosity is the antidote to awkwardness and antipathy.** No matter how uncomfortable things may seem when we start, the more curious I can make myself, the sooner I get past my own problems and am able to hear what the other person is saying.

c. **Active listening is essential.** It doesn't mean I have to agree, but I do need to make sure I've heard what they're saying and actually understand their message as they mean it to be understood.

d. **Get on the same side of the problem as the person you're negotiating with.** If we talk as if we're at odds, conflict almost always ensues. But when we work together to attack the problem, we can usually come up with a creative solution.

e. **When in doubt, take a time out.** They work for kids, and I think they work just as well for everyone else, too.

f. **Never act in anger.** You can (and will) certainly be angry. Just don't make decisions and act on them while you're angry!

4. No Abdication

Stewardship challenges us not to rely on our authority. But please understand that choosing not to pull out your authority is *not* the same as simply "giving in"; working as partners doesn't mean just doing what others ask us to do. This isn't always easy to do; the people who work with us, consciously or unconsciously, can make it very, very difficult for us to stand up for what's needed, for our guiding values, or for fiscally sound practice for the organization overall. Regardless of how hard others might try to make us give in and just do what they want, we're still responsible for acting as effective leaders, *still responsible for doing the right thing for the organization overall.*

Backing off isn't any better than forcing others to back down. It's often the case that what staff members (or managers or partners) are asking for isn't in the best interest of the organization. Our job then is to constructively hold firm, to learn more about why they see things so differently, and then still to arrive at an agreed-upon, organizationally sound path forward. As Peter Block says, "The difficult part is to maintain contact without control"; in other words, to challenge difficult issues without always giving answers, and without just walking off the playing field in the middle of the game because others were giving us a hard time. We remain responsible, even when we choose not to use our authority. Abdication almost never gets good results.

5. Freedom

Once we've negotiated the Stewardship agreement on the expected results, we commit to giving the staff member a chance to do the actual work in the way that they believe works best for them. That means that, while the staff member commits to delivering results, we as leaders commit to giving them a lot more freedom to move than would be done in a more typical, old-line organization. For example, if the staff member commits to completing a project by the first of June, we need to let them do what they need to do to get it done as they see fit (within the bounds of our guiding principles, of course). They might choose to work from home, work late at night or early in the morning, meet with peers to gather information in person, on the phone, via email or Skype with someone in South America. Although I might do it differently, as long as the way they want to do it is ethically sound, is respectful of the needs of others around them, and gets the agreed-upon results, I say, go for it!

With this freedom comes the responsibility of involvement and engagement. "Freedom" does not mean "no constructive criticism." Just as we welcome input from staff members about how we as leaders are doing our work, so, too, we're asking them to welcome feedback on how they might improve their work. This is, of course, exactly how any healthy partnership would work. Both parties have the courage to constructively share hopes, dreams, expectations, and concerns, and the relationship will be more robust for it.

It Ain't Always Easy

Just to be clear here, this sort of ongoing, keep-coming-back-to-the-table-until-you-get-agreement process can quite often be rather trying. Even for me and Paul—who've been at this for three decades now—it's not easy to do. The truth is that we really couldn't be more different in our daily demeanors. And we very often start coming at issues from almost opposite ends of the investigative spectrum. While I'd like to tell you that we always handle those different views with a high degree of deference, we, of course, have had at it any number of times over the years. The secret of Stewardship here is not that we get along perfectly in perpetuity—it's that we have learned to disagree without being disagreeable, and that we understand that it's often rocky on the way to resolution. While we often roll our eyes, raise our voices, and express exasperation with each other's failure to grasp the obvious, we've continually worked at reducing the tension and embracing the diversity of thinking that we're modeling for the rest of the organization. Time and time again, we've found that if we're clear on the vision of where we're going and still in synch with the values (which we are), if we just keep coming back to the table in a stewardly way, we'll pretty much always get where we're going. But please know, while we bake some great cakes here at Zingerman's, in-the-moment dialogue and collaboration are not always a cakewalk!

One of the questions I'm asked most frequently is, "What's the secret of your partnership with Paul?" Of course, there isn't one, but we have made it through thirty years and we're still going strong. The quick answers would be a) shared vision, b) shared values, and c) all this stuff about Stewardship. The willingness to keep coming back to the table—even when it's awkward, frustrating, or difficult—is a big part of it. And, I guess I could add this advice from George Harrison's second wife, Olivia.

Married for over twenty years (until he passed away in 2001), she was asked the secret of a great marriage. Her response was simple: "Don't get divorced." Ultimately, our commitment to keeping our partnership intact, to negotiating and exploring options until we come up with one that works for the business and for each of us, is what makes it work.

6. Conscious Commitment

When we use Stewardship well, people throughout our organization are learning the difficult skills of negotiation, learning to make appropriate compromises, learning all about making mindful free choices, and moving forward towards a future that's based on a foundation of commitment. And without question, committed and caring people are the type that we most definitely want to work with!

What's the alternative to commitment? One all-too-common option is action that's taken out of a sense of sacrifice, of feeling like one has no choice, all of which are usually directly tied, at best, to helplessness and, at worst, to a severe sense of victimization. It's the ol' hidden agenda thing. We think, but never actually say, "I'll do this for you now, but later you'd better take care of me." The expectations are in place, but only in the mind of one of the parties. While employees (or any of us really) are used to getting what we want in this rather behind-the-back way of doing business, it's actually very old school, and I think the exact opposite of what we're trying to do with Stewardship. The overt, adult-to-adult dialogue never happens. Nothing good *ever* comes out of people going along as if they have no choice—the sense of sacrifice, of being compelled against their will, will always come back later to bite us in the organizational butt.

People who are good at passive-aggressive interactions aren't easy to manage. Be careful when others seem to give in too quickly—while it feels like a relief in the moment, the truth of the matter is that sooner or later, this sort of passivity is likely to cause problems later. The individual who has sacrificed for the organization is almost inevitably going to strike back later when their unspoken agenda has not been addressed. This strike may come in the form of anger, resentment, victimhood, active sabotage, or, when someone really gets into it, a rather deadly combination of all four. While passive-aggressive people act as if they have no influence over what's going on, the reality is that their seemingly passive behavior is actually an inside-out way of dominating the dialogue. Stewardship undercuts that racket by asking everyone—employee, manager, and anyone else involved—to come clean with their purpose, their expectations, and their commitment. Language is key—I work hard to steer people towards making active statements. A simple question like, "Are you on board?" can be a powerful tool if you have the patience to wait for an answer.

Beware of staffers who act out of a sense of entitlement, the feeling that they have something coming to them simply because they've been here for a long time. Our view of business is that none of us are entitled to much of anything other than to be treated respectfully, to get a fair shot at going after the future of our choosing, and then to get recognition and appropriate reward for the good work we do en route. We will honor the commitments we've made, and that when we mess up—which of course we do regularly—we'll handle our shortfalls with as much integrity as possible. Certainly, we understand that everyone involved in our organization has needs and dreams and desires, and we are strongly committed to helping realize those. But in order to help fulfill those dreams, we ask people to commit to first working to create a great organization, a great business, and a great department; to sharing their vision of the future; and then constructively working in a collaborative fashion to get there. The emphasis is on conscious commitment. When people make conscious choices, in our experience, they are acting from personal strength. They own their decisions. They don't blame others. They aren't victims.

The beauty of Stewardship is that it kind of precludes most all of that negative energy. I don't mean it can't ever happen—we have cynics, slackers, and bystanders just like everyone else. But by framing things as we have, around openly shared expectations, above-board negotiations, and freely made conscious commitments, there's really no room left for helplessness or the victim mentality. As Peter Block writes, "The central point [of stewardship] is that if people want the freedom that partnership offers, the price of that freedom is to take personal accountability for the success and failure of our unit." We're all leaders, we're all responsible, and if we work well together we can achieve almost anything.

STEWARDSHIP STARTS WITH EACH OF US!

One thing to be really clear on: Stewardship works in all directions. While I've framed things here mostly around the work we as leaders do to succeed without using our authority, the truth is that the Stewardship Compact is equally applicable to everyone in every part of the organization, working in every way you can imagine. Manager to employee, peer to peer, employee to manager are all part of the process. When a new baker here wants something from his boss, he needs to take a deep breath and approach his manager as an equal partner, not as a low-level new employee, and in a courteous, respectful, open-minded way, make clear what he's looking for. Basically, he follows the same six components of Stewardship we've just been through: to be clear about his purpose, to focus on performance expectations of his boss, to negotiate constructively through to agreement, to accept his responsibility as an active member of our organization, to allow his boss the freedom to do the work as he sees fit (ethically so), and then to give, and get, a conscious, clearly stated commitment to go forward. And he needs to understand that his boss might say no or negotiate through to a different set of expectations than the ones that the baker originally brought to the table.

The same Stewardship stuff also applies from side to side, so to speak— i.e., when someone wants something from a peer who's actually on par on the org chart, someone who neither reports to them nor whom they report to. In theory, you might think that these sorts of situations would be the ones in which Stewardship was most easily applied. But in my experience they can actually be the most awkward—while most of us are used to either being in charge, or being told what to do, people have very little experience with working as peers with roughly equal power. Although it's uncomfortable and scary for a frontline person to approach their boss for something, it's at least clear what the formal roles are and then how Stewardship sort of swings those. But when there really is no agreed-upon hierarchy, when it's not clear who's in power, when it really is peer to peer, it seems to be a bigger struggle.

Stewardship applies in any case you can come up with. And, just so that everyone knows, it's pretty likely that it's awkward for all involved. I know, I know, I'm the CEO and I've been doing this for thirty years, but the truth is I still get nervous when I want to ask for something that's out of the norm from someone, or that I'm pretty sure they're not going to be very happy about undertaking. But it's my job to ask them anyway because I believe it's in the best interest of the organization. Most everyone I know has similar hesitations about challenging a colleague or raising an awkward issue. Which means that when anyone approaches us, asking for something we might not be immediately inclined to agree to, we take a minute to appreciate the other person first for even having the courage to come forward. The little things—the energy, the invitation to engage, the appreciation for the awkwardness—really do make a difference!

PARENTAL ADVISORY

One of the more interesting challenges of making Stewardship successful in the organization is the fairly pervasive element of parenting that, unknowingly, often makes its way into our mindset. It's not that hard to understand why it happens—if you think about it, the two roles all of us know well are a) the parent in charge, and b) the child who isn't, but then rebels to assert his or her independence. We read about equality all the time, but the reality is that we don't really experience it very often. True peer-to-peer, partner-to-partner relationships—where we're working with another person purely as equals—are another thing altogether and a rare one at that. Although no one will argue with you that negotiation between equals is a bad thing, few of us actually have much experience with it. What we do know is, understandably, what we grew up with—how to be the parent, or, alternatively, how to act like a kid. That same top-down relationship remains in place when we go to school. And it's still usually there when we go to work. The "parent" becomes "the boss," and the "kid" becomes the employee.

Which is why, then, most of us unwittingly (I believe) work our way into entering management with a pretty parental mindset. Granted, there's a wide range of ways one can play the parental role—there's the mean, autocratic type; there's polite but aloof; and there's the nice, caring, "looking out for the kids" model. While the latter is certainly preferable to the uncaring construct of the former, the truth is it's still way too much like parenting than the sort of peer-to-peer, adult-to-adult, Anarcho-Capitalist-to-Anarcho-Capitalist model that Peter Block, Emma Goldman, Gustav Landauer, et al. are going after.

Moving out of a parent-child mindset is not an easy shift to make. As Peter Block says, "In its commitment to service, Stewardship forces us then to yield on our desire to use good parenting as a basic form of governance. The alternative, partnership, is something that we are just learning about. Our difficulty with creating partnerships is that parenting—and its stronger cousin, patriarchy—is so deeply ingrained in our muscle memory and armature that we don't even realize we are doing it."

In this sense, I guess, without getting too weird on you, Stewardship takes things to a level deeper than Servant Leadership. While the intent of the two is really very much in synch, I think that you can actually practice Servant Leadership while still coming at things from the perspective of a "loving parent." Which, given all the horrors of the world, is hardly a horrible thing, but it is still a good long mental walk from our focus here on peer to peer. Partnership, Peter Block posits, "balances responsibility and is a clear alternative to parenting. The questions, 'How would partners handle this?' and 'What policy or structure would we create if this were a partnership?' are the two most useful questions I know in the search for the alternative to patriarchy." They really are good questions. And remembering to ask them diligently and consistently before we get going on things is no small task.

To be clear, the adjustment here is one that both parties probably have to make. People on the front line are very used to waiting for the boss to be . . . the boss. Getting everyone to own that they're as much in charge of their future and what's going on around them is actually just as hard—sometimes harder—than it is getting their managers to stop "being in charge" all the time. To quote Peter Block, "Partnership means to be connected to another in a way that the power is roughly balanced." For most of us, this way of working is almost unnatural or at least unfamiliar, and is far easier to discuss than to actually do. Doing it well takes a real willingness to continue to talk when I want to walk away, an ability to keep coming back to negotiate more when all I really want to do is hit the highway, or, if things get really frustrating, hit the other person over the head. (Don't worry, it's just a feeling—the last person I hit was David Solomon, back in second grade.)

A big part of this work is, I believe, to help everyone who works here interact as the free-thinking, creative, independent, empowered, important, and intelligent individuals that they are. Unfortunately most people will come into your workplace having been stuck by society with a whole set of standards they feel compelled to live up—or, in many cases, down—to: "I can't do that because I'm new here," "I'm too young," "I'm too old," "I'm a woman," "I'm a man," "I'm a member of a minority," or any of a hundred other hard-to-swallow (for me) stereotypes. I believe very strongly that everyone has the ability to do great things (see Twelve Tenets of Anarcho-Capitalism on page 260 for more on this subject), and Stewardship will work best when people feel good about themselves and not constrained by externally applied and inaccurate social constructs.

When we use this Stewardship stuff well, we're helping to develop the sort of leaders we need for our organization to be successful in the way that we want. People who can tackle difficult discussions respectfully can build partnerships around conscious commitment, not just command obedience. By using the Stewardship Compact, we're walking our talk, showing staff members that we mean it when we say that "you really *can* make a difference." And in the process we're helping them to learn a skill that's rarely modeled in our society, one that will help them be more successful in most everything they do.

The Start of Stewardship Success

One of the most rewarding employee experiences I've had of late was actually a complaint from a staff member. She came to me to share her frustrations, but in a way that was as much about what she needed to do to fix the problem as it was about what anyone had "done" to her to cause it. She'd been working here part-time for four or five years, had recently gotten her degree, and was now working here full-time. "I used to be totally charged about being here," she told me, "but lately, I just don't feel that energy." At first my heart sort of sank. She's someone I really value having on staff. "But," she went on, "I know I need to do something to get recharged." I loved that she took ownership of the issue. Obviously, her manager is also fully responsible, but she didn't just dump it all on him. "Do you have any suggestions for me?" she finished. Although it bummed me out that a good, long-term employee was feeling unmotivated, the more I reflected on the whole thing, the more I realized that this was exactly what we wanted. Real life includes imperfection; long-term employment entails emotional ups and downs; smart people working with imperfect managers may well get frustrated; but really great, self-actualized, empowered employees come forward to ask for help instead of just complaining to their co-workers. Stewardship asks us all to relate to each other as peers who share in the responsibility for what's going on, and also for what we're going to do about it. While there's still long-term negotiation to do, getting agreement on expectations, sharing vision, etc., this was all about adult-to-adult interaction. In truth, I can't imagine her handling it any better than she did.

Coming to Consensus

Some of the things we do here that are more overtly systemic in their nature—open-book finance, Bottom-Line Change, our 3 Steps to Great Service—are fairly easy to identify, and the recipes, while hard to do day in and day out, 360-something days a year, are still more on the overt side of the philosophical spectrum. They are, without question, keys to making Anarcho-Capitalism, as we do it here, work—everyone knows the processes, everyone can do them, everyone sees how it's going, and all are designed to be measurable and manageable.

Stewardship is a bit different. While the process is clear and overt, the actual activity around it is below the surface. It's all in the spirit. Although it's more likely to happen here than who knows where in the corporate world, the truth is that new frontline staff at Zingerman's—or anywhere—aren't likely to call their bosses out on things when the folks at the "top" get too full of themselves. To make Stewardship a reality, those with authority have to decide not to use it and to work on a peer-to-peer level. Those without it must have the courage to come forward and speak their minds and walk into work with a calm, centered belief in themselves and those around them.

One way that we have brought the Stewardship approach into a more systemic, self-regulating routine is by adopting the consensus decision-making model at the partner level. Consensus is usually a much more time-consuming way to come to a decision, but it cements Stewardship into the way we work. Since we own more voting shares, Paul and I technically have the authority to override others, but we've made a commitment not to do that except in some extreme, not-yet-ever-actually-happened situation. A few years ago, managing partners Frank Carollo and Amy Emberling made the same move at the Bakehouse; the management team there now uses consensus for making Bakehouse-wide decisions. So, too, has our Mail Order business, and others have since gotten on board as well. Regardless of who amongst us is using it, here's how we define it at Zingerman's:

- We strive to reach consensus on key decisions. By "consensus," we mean that each individual is at least 80 percent satisfied with the wording of a decision or statement and *will actively support it 100 percent and live by the decision.*

- If a predetermined deadline for decision is reached and some, but not all, of the partners' group membership are in favor of the proposal at hand, then the dissenting members have an obligation to bring additional data or a counter-proposal to the following meeting.

There are, obviously, other ways to define it, and you're of course welcome to your own. I'm sharing it as an example of a way that we've embedded Stewardship into our organizational processes—the only way one of us can effectively go around it is basically to declare the equivalent of a corporate coup, which is not very likely to happen. Even when we do inadvertently slip and slide around the consensus process—which we'll assume is done unwittingly—someone around us will raise their hand or, at times, their voice to remind us. At that point, recalibrating or rebalancing the system is mostly an effective apology (a real one, mind you) away. I have most certainly been on both sides of that caring coin—I've unintentionally forgotten to get consensus where I'd said I would, and I've been the one to remind others that we'd agreed to come to agreement before taking action. Neither of those situations is a great spot to be in, but when we have agreed to keep coming back to the table until we reach agreement—to, as Paul always says, "disagree without being disagreeable"—it all can work amazingly, if at times rather awkwardly, well.

As I've said elsewhere, I think that those who aren't fully in alignment with all this will take the consensus model as being mostly about compliance. But the intent of it is to create collaboration, to work towards positive, mutually rewarding outcomes, to encourage innovation and creativity. It also serves to protect the organization from any one of us in authority getting too out of whack with the world and making big stupid decisions. That is, of course, the point of the democratic system. For the moment, I'm sticking to the systems we use here. We, like everyone else in the world, can use all the help we can get. To quote one of Emma Goldman's funniest lines: "Those in authority have and always will abuse their power. And the instances when they do not do so are as rare as roses growing on icebergs." Rather than wait for global warming to make the latter a reality (let's hope that it doesn't happen, okay?), consensus is a self-regulating system that effectively embeds Stewardship into the work world.

Practice may not make perfect, but . . .

If you're just starting to put the Stewardship model into practice, I can give you a near 100 percent guarantee that it's going to feel uncomfortable. It's likely to be even more uncomfortable for your staff members. Making it work starts with an understanding of the concept, but ultimately we get good at it in the same way we get good at most anything else—by practice, and then more practice still. If it were easy, everyone would probably already be doing it, right? Going back to the table, "lowering" yourself to be at peer level with people who report to you, "raising" others up who are actually lower on the org chart, negotiating as equals as if you didn't hold the power you know you have in your pocket . . . hey, I'll tell you from personal experience—even having worked on it for a long time, it can be tough to do. But it's very worthwile work.

In rereading Robert Greenleaf's writings on Servant Leadership, I found this quote: "The value of coercive power is inverse to its use—more so every day." I guess Peter Block wasn't alone in his beliefs on this one. In fact, although I'm pretty sure he wouldn't call himself an anarchist, Peter Block's approach also sounds a lot like that of the anarchists I'm so interested in. His colleague, Joel Henning, writes about Block's book that Stewardship "is about revolution. Not violent revolution, but a revolution of ideas. . . . It attempts to make relevant to our economic survival the integration of the best of the human spirit with the demands for survival in the marketplace." Block adds, "Autocratic governance withers the spirit." He believes "the revolution begins in our own hearts." Which sounds a lot like Gustav Landauer, who said a century or so ago, "Revolution of spirit is, for us, the first order." I am happy to be on board with all of that. If you put Peter Block, Gustav Landauer, me, and Paul all in a room to work on a project, I'm sure we'd find many things on which we differ. But I'm equally confident that using the stuff in the Stewardship approach, we'd pretty quickly come to a freely chosen, consciously committed-to way to move forward together to create something special. Stewardship isn't always easy, but it definitely does work.

notes from the back dock

The Inside Scoop on Working Here at Zingerman's

Chrissy Abe, Retail Counter Person, Zingerman's Bakehouse

I didn't grow up in Ann Arbor. But as soon as I heard anything about the town, I learned that this magical place called Zingerman's Deli was synonymous with it. When I was about ten, my stepmom and a friend got a booth at the Saturday Artisan Market near the Deli selling tie-dyed and screen-printed clothing, and when I was feeling in need of a little adventure, I'd go with them. Most of the time, I stayed right in the market.

Eventually I made it inside the Deli, a quirky, homey, mini-maze of a space filled with shelves and racks and stacks of until-now unseen-by-me stuff. Cheeses, oils, vinegars (who knew there existed more than one kind of each? Definitely not me!), peanut butter, honeys—identifiable sometimes only because of the color, or an image of a bee on the label! And the breads. Oh, man. My mom, and my step-mom, baked bread all the time. I didn't eat non-homemade bread until I went to school. But their breads looked nothing like the breads in this place. Even as a ten-year-old kid, I was in love with those breads.

And the happy, smiling people—both the employees and the customers! Even at that age, I knew it was rare to go into any restaurant, deli, shop, etc., and see *happy* people, on either side. I knew this was a special place. I didn't care what they did in there—I wanted to do it.

Fast forward not quite twenty-five years, and I'm doing it. I've worked for Zingerman's for a grand total of six months. I've never felt as welcomed and supported by my co-workers. Everyone I pass says "hi," has a smile on their face, and asks me how I'm doing. My bosses know my name. *Ari and Paul know my name.* They're not a couple of faceless corporate suits I'll never meet, or have to quake in my boots on hearing their names. From day one, it's been impressed upon me how important I am to the continued success of this organization. Me! Little, insignificant me from nowhere, knowing nothing about anything. In the eighteen years of my life that I've held jobs, nowhere else have I felt as much ownership, as much individual responsibility—where my input is welcomed, even encouraged! Where I take care of my customers, from start-to-finish, and make sure that they are blown away, not by me, of course, but by this company. It's my responsibility to show people what the ZCoB does, what it's capable of, how incredibly special, responsible, and involved an organization it is. *And I get to be a part of that, every day.*

pouring water at the roadhouse

SECRET #25

Managing by Pouring Water

Turning Water into Wins

I know I have a lot of strange stuff in this book. Mixed metaphors, magical thinking, and people you never heard of—anarchists, folk singers, hobos, obscure business writers, pig farmers. But hey, if you got this far in the book, you're either used to it, or you're nigh on as odd as I am. As you may know, I'm a big fan of books—I have three on my table right now and not a day goes by I don't read something and learn from it. But in the last few years, I've probably learned as much carrying my water pitcher around the dining room at the Roadhouse as I have sitting down to read. Word has it that Emma Goldman once uttered, "When things are bad, scrub floors." I'm down with the spirit of that—when I'm feeling down and out, I start pouring water. It almost never fails to reignite my energy and increase my appreciation for all the great food and very fine people I get to work with everyday. It's one of the best moves I've made over the years. I'm not sure what the parallel to water pouring is in your work, but it's worth giving it some thought. What follows, I'm fairly sure, is not a subject that's being taught in any school in the country. But maybe it will be one day.

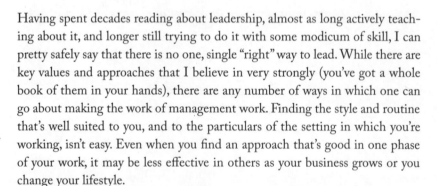

Having spent decades reading about leadership, almost as long actively teaching about it, and longer still trying to do it with some modicum of skill, I can pretty safely say that there is no one, single "right" way to lead. While there are key values and approaches that I believe in very strongly (you've got a whole book of them in your hands), there are any number of ways in which one can go about making the work of management work. Finding the style and routine that's well suited to you, and to the particulars of the setting in which you're working, isn't easy. Even when you find an approach that's good in one phase of your work, it may be less effective in others as your business grows or you change your lifestyle.

What follows is a technique that's been successful for me in a particular part of my work for the last few years. It's not the only one I use, and it's certainly not ideal for every manager or every business setting. Essentially it's my take on what has long been taught as "managing by walking around." But in this case—everyone here at Zingerman's will laugh—it's called "Managing by Pouring Water." I'll abbreviate it down to "MbPW" to save space.

The way that MbPW works has developed rather organically at Zingerman's Roadhouse, the full service, 180-seat, sit-down restaurant that we opened eight years ago. Since each of the Zingerman's businesses is different in terms of size, scale, scope, and experience of the managing partners who run it every day, the way that I work within and with each one is different. I try to adjust the style I use as the businesses mature and their needs change. At the time this all got going, the Roadhouse was at a different, younger stage of development than our other businesses, and it's a sit-down restaurant, not a retail shop, mail-order call center, or production setting. I found myself searching for ways to be active and present, to see what was going on and contribute to things without trying (and inevitably failing if I had) to do everything myself.

The name "Managing by Pouring Water" came from a regular customer who'd watched me do it many a night. Aside from eating our food regularly, she's achieved quite a lot in business herself and has done a fair bit of organizational consulting as well. Anyway, one night when I was working her table, she suggested with a smile that "Managing by Pouring Water" should be the title of my next book. As you can see, it didn't quite make it that far, but I figured at least it was worth an essay. Like I said, they don't teach this stuff in school, but it sure has had a lot of positive outcomes over here.

The whole thing happened because one busy day, purely in the interest of helping out on a busy dinner rush, I picked up the ice water pitcher to fill customers' nearly empty glasses. I did it as anyone else would have, going table to table, filling glasses and doing whatever else needed to be done. In the moment it was really just practical. In truth, it was a simple form of Servant Leadership in action—someone needed water and I was trying to be helpful. Once I had the water in hand, I kept going around the dining room. And pretty quickly, I realized that without intending to, I'd come upon a really effective routine, one that had some hugely positive pieces to it.

The routine is just what it sounds like. I grab a water pitcher and start going around the dining room with it. When people need water, I fill their glasses. Actually pouring water is really just the most superficial, if nevertheless totally practical, element of the benefits of MbPW. The much bigger work is what happens in, around, and after all the water pouring.

Ultimately, MbPW is just about being in the business where the action, people, and product are. It is a fairly obvious idea to those of us who do it. But there is something special, something about this particular process that's worked really well in this particular setting. It's weird to say, but it's almost like some magical management thing. The cool part, I think, is that anyone, anywhere, can do it. While the details of what I'm doing are specific to the Roadhouse, I think a similar regimen could be done at the Deli where customers come up and order at the counter, and we deliver food to them at their table. I've never done it for long periods of time, but my sense is that I might gain similar benefits by standing at the end of a cash line and bagging groceries. I used to do something similar at our Mail Order by checking orders for accuracy. And, way back when, I used to bag orders for customers at the cash register at the Deli. Same idea, same good outcomes. I hope that sharing this system stimulates a creative approach in your business, one that will reap you as many rewards as this happy accident has for me.

I know that others have come up with similar routines. Vikram Vij, who runs one of my favorite restaurants—Vij's—up in Vancouver, accomplishes much the same thing by personally taking the dinner order at each and every table. He's not the server, nor does he do everything that each table needs himself. But he's created a system in which he plays one key role and through that personal interaction he greets each guest, hears what they're looking to have for dinner, and knows what to watch out for at every table. I'm sure as the restaurant has grown Vikram might not be visiting each and every table himself. But I'll bet he still gets to a lot of them—it's only one piece of the puzzle that ends up being a very special restaurant, but it's a good one. If I get tired of pouring water, maybe I'll start taking orders again.

Twelve Ways to Win by Pouring Water

1. It Allows for a Practical Entrée into the Dining Room

It didn't take me all that long to realize that there was a lot more to be gained from pouring water than I'd ever have thought. In the moment, maybe the biggest short-term win was that it allowed me to be active in the dining room while actually doing work that needed doing. Now I know that in many restaurant settings, managers seem to circulate through the dining room and do a fine job of it. And maybe it's just me, but as a customer, I've never really loved when a manager walks empty-handed from table to table and asks the standard, "How was everything tonight?" question that we've all been asked so many times. Mind you, it's not a bad question and I'm glad that they're asking. But while the question can be asked in a meaningful, engaged way, it rarely is. Usually it comes across to me as a well-intended, functional but fairly formulaic query. To which, when I'm a customer, I usually give a pleasant but not very in-depth or particularly detailed response, usually along the lines of, "Everything is fine, thank you." Pouring water was the opposite—it gave me a way to do all that other stuff that dining room managers everywhere are supposed to be doing, but to do it all while contributing something concrete to the cause.

It was really like a great management gift someone had given me. Pouring water provided an in-the-moment reason to interact with customers which was both hands-on and of very practical value. In hindsight, it's a rather obvious entrée; every customer drinks water and water always needs to be refilled, and that work needs to happen from the time the guests sit down to the moment they get up to leave. People like water, and no one likes to be left with an empty water glass. Which means that when I visit the table, I'm not just an extraneous body in the way—I'm actually contributing something that's of value to customers and to servers who otherwise would need to make sure that they're "watering" their own tables. What I found fairly quickly was that there were a lot of less obvious, but ultimately much more meaningful, things that came from walking around filling water glasses. It's all about being conscious of what one sees, hears, smells, touches, and tastes. But if you pay close attention, all this stuff is out there—there's a lot of interesting information available that can help us run our business better.

Finding Your Version of MbPW

Management by Pouring Water happens to work for me at the Roadhouse. But I think the basic principles are probably applicable in many management settings. Here are the things I'd look for in creating a workable way to do the same things in your work setting:

- Identify a practical way to contribute to the work at hand, something that's needed so you're not hovering needlessly near the action.

- Find a place to work that's not obtrusive, but that allows you to be positioned (or moving) around customers, staff, and product.

- Determine a contributing role in which you're not totally tied to the schedule—you want something that allows you to provide support when needed but then exit gracefully when not. One of the great things about MbPW is that the position doesn't really exist. All the work I'm doing is actually broken out into various pieces owned by others. And because nothing I'm doing is "required" of me, the system is in place and can function well whether I'm standing there or not. It's not all about me—others can, and are also responsible to, pour the water, both literally and figuratively.

- Do it in a way that allows customers and staff who want to engage you to engage, while others can let you go about your business without stopping their own conversations or work.

2. Watch Customer Buying Patterns Firsthand

When I'm working the tables—even if it's only for an hour or so—I quickly see which customers go for the exotic fish and meat dishes and which are more conservative. I can catch their eating patterns, spot any trends tied to age groups, watch how out-of-towners order differently from locals, stay conscious of how business people's purchasing patterns are different from families. I see what kids want, what items people have heard they should order from their friends. In the process, I can contribute better to the more effective management of our menu, see what's hot in the market and what's not, identify opportunities to offer new items, etc. I've never tracked the ratio of really good insights I glean per pitcher of water poured, but maybe it'd be a good stat to start watching.

3. Get a Real Time Feel for On-Time Delivery

I can keep an eye on timing and delivery of the food. By moving through the dining rooms constantly, I have a mental picture of where most every table is in its eating sequence. That helps me know which servers are on top of their timing, how the kitchen's doing, etc.

4. Get Close to Your Customer's Consumption

Getting data from afar can be a great help to any leader. But it's not the same as being able to watch customers consume your product in real time and real life. MbPW allows me to watch how people are eating their food, i.e., how they're "using our product." I can see what gets consumed quickly, what dishes people are oohing and aahing over, which items get pushed to the side of the plate and are rarely eaten. I notice things that you can't see from the kitchen, customer feedback forms or, really, anywhere else. Like the homemade pork rinds we use as a garnish on our barbecue dinner—they're delicious. But after seeing 75 percent of them left on the plate, it dawned on me that hardly any of our customers had a clue what they were. Up here in the North pork rinds are not the everyday item they are in the South. Most of our customers haven't ever eaten them. And if they have, they've been pork rinds out of the plastic package that you get at a gas station. Homemade pork rinds from free-running, heirloom pigs like we serve at the Roadhouse aren't exactly something your average Ann Arborite has ever thought of, let alone been able to identify. Understandably, when they get an odd-shaped, flattish, brown thing sticking out of their mashed potatoes, they politely move it to the side of their plate and leave it there. Which means that instead of enjoying this really nice homemade crackling, something you won't get in any other place in town, we're all missing out. Seeing that pattern repeated plate after plate, it didn't take me all that long to realize that we needed to actually tell every guest who orders the barbecue dinner plate about the homemade pork rind. For no real extra effort, telling them what it is adds a small bit of value to their meal and makes for something special in our presentation; more customers try the pork rind and most really like it. Some customers now ask for extras! But I'd never have noticed it without being up close to the tables on a regular basis.

5. Provide Quick Response Time to Customer Queries

MbPW means that, when appropriate, I can constructively contribute to the dialogue that servers are having with the guest. Often I'll stop to pour water at a table that a staff member is interacting with. Most of the time I just keep my mouth shut and fill the glasses. But sometimes a question will come up that the server doesn't know the answer to, in which case I can quickly chime in. I give on-the-spot support and on-shift training, and in the process we help the guest's experience as well.

6. Manage Moments of Truth

Moments of truth, as we define the term here, are those situations where a customer isn't complaining, but where something is about to happen (or has already happened) that is likely to lose us a guest for life. Conversely, if we catch it and handle it well, we can make them a long-time and loyal promoter of our business.

One of the biggest benefits of MbPW is that it allows me the opportunity to monitor—and then help alter for the better—the course of each table's experience. In theory, of course, every service person on staff is going to be able to give a great experience to every guest. Most folks here do it really well most of the time. The more experienced servers are really great at it. But let's face reality. When you get into the complexities of service, there are a million little nuances that are hard to pick up, a myriad of small signs that years of experience and high attention to detail allow you to read; things that someone who's been on staff for six weeks—no matter how good they are—probably won't notice. MbPW allows the staff member to do their work and do it well, while allowing me the opportunity to identify customers who clearly—to me at least—need some extra attention. Mind you, 90 percent of the time the customers haven't asked for it, nor are they knowingly unhappy, nor have they actively complained about anything. I can just tell—as would the best of our other service providers—that they need something extra.

Sometimes that "extra" means doing things that violate all the rules of service that we teach. I'm laughing now, but the other night I came upon an elderly guest who just wasn't happy with her meal. The server had offered to replace it but she refused anything else. I happened to go by the table where she again registered her unhappiness. I also offered to replace the item. "No," she said shaking her head. "I looked at the menu and this is the only thing that interested me." That may not mean much until I tell you that the Roadhouse menu has about a hundred items on it, in addition to ten or twelve daily specials, along with the fact that we'll custom make most anything a customer asks for. Even her friend tried to suggest alternatives but she refused to have any replacement. "I'll just eat this," she said shaking her head. Now, straight service as we teach it would have meant continuing to apologize. But she was reminding me more and more of my grandmother, and I decided I'd try reversing gears and dealing with it as we did in my family, instead of the way we teach it in all of our service classes. I told her how guilty I was feeling about our failure to get her a good meal. And, since she wouldn't take anything in replacement, I offered dessert. She said, "I shouldn't eat dessert." I said, "I didn't ask you if you *should* eat it—only if you *would* eat it." She shook her head side to side, then said resignedly, "I'll have to walk around the block three times if I do." This had become a game of guilt-chess. Fortunately, I was raised playing that game. I parried with the fact that I'm a runner and that, although I'd already done my sixty-minute jog that afternoon, I'd change shoes and go out with her again if she wanted. She said it was too late in the evening and she'd have to wait 'til daylight. I told her I'd give her my cell phone number so she could call me the next morning and I'd come over. Anyway, . . . you get the idea: eventually I won her over. This sort of service interaction isn't something a new staff member is going to be able to pull off. But because I'd been out there with my plastic water pitcher, I had the chance to intervene and, amazingly, the guest and her friends left smiling and laughing after all that!

7. SHOW STRONG ON-SITE OWNERSHIP PRESENCE

While I never set out to pour water regularly, the funny thing is that the customers who know who I am seem amazed to see it. While it is exceptionally normal to me that I would be doing this work, customers just seem to love the fact that an owner of a business is pouring water. They like to tease me about it: "Maybe if you're good you'll get a promotion one day!" is a pretty common Roadhouse refrain. Some stop to tell their friends who I am. Others suggest I ask for a raise. Some tell me I work too hard. Many regulars feel good because they're in the know—they get to introduce their friends to an owner. And the better the regular customers feel, the more positive word of mouth they send about us into the community. Others make fun of my history degree. Some take it very seriously. One woman told me how shocked her twenty-something son was to see me pouring water and how she used it to point out what one has to do to be successful in life. I have no idea whether the message got across to her son, but she loved telling me the story, so that alone makes it worth it. Pouring water became a discussion point for her family and a metaphor they may well come back to many times in the future.

8. BUILD BETTER CUSTOMER RELATIONSHIPS

Through MbPW I get to meet a lot of customers I'd never otherwise talk to. Sometimes they know or find out I'm the owner and they say something. That gives me an opening to introduce myself and welcome them to our business. And it's a chance to bond personally with them in a way that most of our competitors won't. It's proven in many cases to be the beginning of long-term customer relationships that benefit us enormously.

9. PROVIDE A CHANCE TO PRAISE THE STAFF IN PUBLIC

By getting so close to the customers and staff, I can give servers compliments in front of the guests. We have a lot of great staff members. Complimenting them in front of their guests—and I don't do it unless I mean it—helps them feel better about their work. And it helps the customer feel calmer and more confident that they're going to have a great experience. These two things then work in tandem to create that more positive experience, an improvement from which all involved benefit. I also make a point of introducing new staff members to longtime customers—they all feel a bit more special, and I love that we can create positive bonds between people who might otherwise wait on one another but never really talk.

10. HEAR WHAT OTHERWISE GOES UNSAID (TO US!)

Because a lot of customers know who I am, MbPW allows them a chance to chat with an owner without feeling like they're intruding into other things I'm doing. And let's face it, lots of customers like to talk to owners, and for good reason—it's one of our biggest edges on the mass market and franchise folks we compete with. We're on site; they're not. We listen; they probably never hear 98 percent of what their customers might be saying. And believe me, I hear a whole lot more from these casual, unplanned interactions than I'd ever get sitting in an office away from the guests.

Additionally, MbPW gives me the chance to catch customer comments that I'd never hear if I were getting them through others. I hear a lot of feedback anyway, but when you're pouring water at the table you hear a whole lot more—with body language, nuances in tone of voice, etc.—than you do scanning customer surveys. Because not everyone knows who I am, they say things they'd never say otherwise. I don't hide who I am—but I don't announce it either.

All of this means that I hear what people are saying to each other. Which in turn tells me a lot about what they want, what we're doing well, where we're falling short, and where we can proactively pick up our pace to preempt a problem. More often than not, I don't actually do what needs to be done myself, but I can relay the information to a staff member who in turn can take care of the situation and look downright heroic to the customer for having been able to figure out so smoothly what was needed.

11. BE IN POSITION TO HELP IN A HURRY

Let's face it. This is the food business—the only thing you can really count on every day is that something is going to happen that you didn't count on happening. On a busy shift, MbPW means that I'm there when something crops up at the last second, making it easier for me to support the staff, help fix problems when needed, etc. When I am really needed because it got exceptionally busy or whatever, I'm there. I'm in sight, able to help at short notice.

12. Make It Easy to Teach the Little Things

In part, I guess the teaching takes place simply by setting a good example in all these areas. Being out there and doing all of the above in front of the staff certainly makes it easier to model the behaviors that we're looking for in our service work.

But ultimately, *the most important part* is that MbPW allows me a wealth of teaching opportunities. Servers—whether in a restaurant or in most retail settings—are really operating on their own a great deal of the time. Unless we're standing near them it's very hard to be able to share some of the subtleties and nuances, to show them the small touches of how to read a guest, how to gamble on service in a good way, how to give positive reinforcement to customers, how to preempt problems. A skilled new staff member will have finished their formal initial training period, but they still have years' worth of subtle stuff to pick up while they're "out in the field." And using the old-school methods, the only way we have to know if they fall short is if a customer complains. By getting closer to the table in a constructive way, MbPW allows me to see, hear, and watch what they're doing. Please understand, this is *not* an attempt to catch them doing something wrong. To the contrary: I want to catch them doing things right and compliment them on those. There are so many opportunities to teach them about small but meaningful pieces of their service work.

What Pouring Water Isn't

Please note that none of what I'm saying here should imply that we don't need carefully thought-out systems, very good staff training work, effective delegation, or regular reviews of key data. Nor is it intended to say that leaders have to do everything themselves. The point is merely that Management by Pouring Water (or whatever version of it you have in your business) is a way to enhance all the other good things you're already doing, a way to gain great return on relatively small investments of our time. When it's done well, everyone—staff, customer, organization, and the community—has a better experience, and we're building a more sustainable, more engaged, and more responsive organization in the process. I don't know what the corollary would be in your company, but I'm confident there is one. If it's half as helpful to you as MbPW has been for me, it'll be a hugely positive investment of time, energy, and resources.

Concluding Thoughts: Good to the Last Drop

In reflecting on this whole thing, I have to sort of chuckle. So much of what our leadership work is based on, and so much of what's in this book, came from studying the insightful and elegant teachings of others—the contributions of Anese Cavanaugh, Robert Greenleaf, Peter Block, Emma Goldman, Gustav Landauer, and all the others are woven throughout our work. In its own down-to-earth, easily ignored way, MbPW sort of weaves them all together into one workable, easily implemented routine. If I do it well, the role is all about effective energy management—me being on the floor sets the tone and, for better or for worse, the leader's presence can get things effectively recalibrated fairly quickly. It's also all about Servant Leadership—the bulk of the work is about helping the frontline staff in the restaurant be more successful. And although I don't really give it much of a thought myself, I know that others marvel at the CEO being on the floor on Friday night (or whenever) doing what they consider to be "lowly" tasks without any fanfare. It's also in synch with Stewardship—it's not like I never ask anyone working on the floor to do anything. I'm still the CEO. But when I do it, I work hard to give a clear exchange of purpose, to share clear expectations, and to negotiate (quickly of course—it's a busy restaurant). I don't abdicate or stand by passively if problems come up. And after all that, I try to hold my tongue and let the staff go about getting great results without me telling them exactly how to do every little thing. In return I'm pretty confident that we get a very high level of conscious commitment from the crew—their energy is solid, they're mostly there because they want to be, they take initiative, and they take their responsibilities to customers, co-workers, and the restaurant seriously.

The final thought here goes to a guest who sent me this email. It's from a food service professional who had brought his management team into the Roadhouse for dinner. I'm including it only to show how much positive impact an hour or two of pouring water can have.

"Hi, Ari. Let me tell you something—after you were at our table the other night talking to us (and filling up water glasses)—one of our younger chefs leaned over to me and asked, 'What was the deal with that whole conversation you guys were having with the busboy pouring the water?'" I know he was laughing when he hit send on the email, and I was laughing out loud long after I opened it. "I think," he continued, "that totally exemplifies why you guys are as good as you are, your great culture and values, and the positive, trickle-down effect you have on your entire staff and organization. Really amazing."

The Inside Scoop on Working Here at Zingerman's

Sharon Kramer, Server, Zingerman's Roadhouse

From day number one here I noticed a difference from my past employers. Everyone seems to care, from the dishwashers to the managers. Ari may bend down to pick up a scrap of paper that has fallen on the floor, and in the process two or three of us may try to pick it up first. Not because Ari can't pick it up, but because *we* should have picked it up first. That's the thing—it makes us all want to be better. Because if your manager is willing to do it, you should be willing to do it as well."

an ancient olive grove in southern italy

Beekeeping and Leadership

*A Really Good Metaphor
for Effective Management*

I know this beekeeping metaphor may sound odd, but it's helped any number of folks here in our own organization, so it seemed silly not to share it. The metaphor alone won't make you the world's best manager, but every little bit helps! As author Michael Gerber writes in E-Myth Mastery, *"The technician goes to work in his business. The entrepreneur goes to work on his business." He has the right idea. While Managing by Pouring Water is, essentially, a way to make working in your business for a couple of hours particularly productive, what follows is all about the work we can and need to do on it. The idea of being the beekeeper might be the small bit of a mental boost that could help keep a couple of well-meaning managers and business owners from working solely in the business. So, go on, be the beekeeper!*

Early in the first day of ZingTrain's two-day Leading with Zing seminar, we ask all the attendees to take a few minutes to reflect on and write down how they spend their work time. We suggest that they break their week into three categories. The first is what we call *working in your business,* i.e., doing the day-to-day, hour-to-hour tasks that make up the bulk of the routine activity any organization does. It could include working the counter, packing boxes, placing orders, taking orders, paying bills, or maybe doing the schedule. It's important activity that most certainly needs to get done if the business is going to operate.

The second area we ask them to consider is what we refer to as *working on your business.* That means time spent on stuff like reviewing and improving production processes, redoing a performance review system for staff, designing new (or redesigning old) training, coming up with better ways to market your business, etc. The third area we refer to in the exercise is *working on yourself—* time spent on self-development and any activity that's focused on improving one's own skills as a leader. That could include reading, attending seminars, listening to audio books, time spent learning from a coach or mentor, even time spent reflecting or journaling.

We ask people to assign an estimated percentage to their week. In the interest of making this essay interactive, I'll ask you to do the same here. Don't worry about being perfectly accurate—your first gut response is probably pretty right on. Go ahead and write your numbers right here in the book.

	Working *in* Your Business	Working *on* Your Business	Working on Yourself as a Leader
% of the Week			

Got some numbers down? Good. While all three areas are important, it's actually the second column that I want to concentrate on. For most of us, setting aside time to work *on* the business requires a lot more self-discipline to make it happen. While the work we do *in* our businesses can often feel absolutely critical ("If I don't help with the lunch counter customers are going to start leaving!" is a normal and reasonable thought), working *on* the business is rarely urgent. Without question it's an area that's easily ignored in the day-to-day of our lives.

Having taught the Leading with Zing seminar for ten years, I'm certain that this exercise makes it easier for attendees to get their minds around the importance of the "on" work. But in my experience, awareness alone isn't enough. The pull to dive into the nuts and bolts activities that make up the work we do *in* the business is so strong that, before we know it, our entire week is almost gone and we've gotten next to nothing done other than running around to take care of crises. In a brand-new, small startup that's probably not an inappropriate approach. But as our organizations grow, we're going to start sliding into frustration if we're focusing only on the day-to-day. Falling into this pattern for any length of time—and I don't think anyone intends it—is a recipe for long-term organizational disaster.

I don't mean to imply that working *in* the business isn't an important part of what we do. I'm very hands-on and I'm all about being present on your version of "the floor." But while the day-to-day work is obviously critical, the truth is that the work *on* the business is of equal import. It's just harder to see its value if you're not looking for it. Although our systems, recipes, and organizational processes may be in need of redesign, the systems aren't ever going to rise up off the computer screen or come alive from the pages of the staff handbook to initiate the work. The organizational systems and processes never call you to complain, they don't send automatic renewal notices, and they don't overtly ask for help!

The sad truth is that the more our systems are in need of improvement, the more ineffective our work tends to be. Which, in turn, means there's less time in our day to work *on* the business, making things run less and less efficiently, leaving less time and less money to allow us the resources to work *on* the business. This is (obviously) not a good cycle to get stuck in.

I know this cycle so well because I've unwittingly lived it more times than I'd like to admit. I've never done it on purpose; it's just way too easy to slip into it, even when one's intentions are really good. There's always— *always!*—pressure from customers and staff to go to the front lines. And there's usually comparable pressure from within and without to get home to be with friends or family. But there's rarely in-the-moment pressure from anyone to be working *on* the business, to tackle stuff like training program development, the writing of a new long-term vision, or implementing open-book finance. At least, not until it's almost too late.

All of this is usually made worse because so many of us are so comfortable doing the day-to-day work *in* the business. It's where we got our start. It's work we can do almost without thinking about it. It's also what we tend to get the most immediate gratification from—customers and staff like it when we're in there working with them, we feel good about the quality of our work, and all of that combines to create a pretty compelling, if not consciously considered, list of reasons to *not* have time.

There are certainly ways to make sure that we stay on task and don't get sucked back into the day-to-day. Hiring a coach, someone who can hold your feet to the organizational fire, to make sure you don't fritter away all your time each week without getting to these all-important tasks of working on your business is one way to go. It's a serious investment, but with the right person it can be well worth it. Realistically, most leaders may not be ready—or have the resources—to make that happen. And with that in mind, working *on* the business becomes mostly about self-management.

One way to make it work is, simply, to schedule the time. Devote two hours a week (or whatever amount of time you think best) to working *on* the business. Hold tight to that time the way you would to any other major commitment you make, like going to your kid's soccer game, or showing up at the board meeting. Even still, in my experience, many leaders start down this road with good intentions but quickly slip back. I don't have a magic solution. But I do have a valuable mental model about this subject, one that's already proven helpful to me and other folks I've shared it with at Zingerman's.

The paragraphs that follow may seem something of a side road en route to the metaphor. They are, I suppose, akin to the less than glamorous work bees do to make the honey. If you'd prefer to skip the thought process and push straight through to the finished product, make a beeline to page 193. On the other hand, if you're interested in ideas and their progression, keep reading—bees may travel the shortest distance between two points, but ideas, initiatives, or concepts rarely go from insight through to successful implementation in a straightforward way.

Beekeepers, Bees, and SUVs

Before I go any further, please know that I realize that beekeeping is not the absolute be-all and end-all analogy for management. You only have to consider the concept for about a minute and a half to understand that some of the core elements of effective leadership (by my standards at least) just don't work in the context of keepers and the winged "beings" they work with—"leading by example" is a pretty laughable idea in this context. And no matter how skilled the beekeeper may be, he's going to have high annual "staff turnover" by HR department standards—pretty much 100 percent every few months. (Six weeks is the typical lifespan for drones, while worker bees live for somewhere from six weeks to six months depending on time of year. Queens are as good as it gets and can live from two to six years.)

So, you might reasonably wonder, how did I come up with this rather odd idea of comparing the work of beekeeping with effective leadership? It hit me while sitting in the back seat of an SUV driving around Chile.

I was traveling with Paulina Peñaloza and Roberto Manieu, with whom we'd been working to bring traditional, sustainably produced Chilean products to Ann Arbor. We'd just been to visit Enrique, from whom Paulina and Roberto buy the amazing Ulmo blossom honey we buy from them. As we embarked on the highway, I started to put my thoughts down on paper before I lost them. I remember writing something about Enrique, and his being "the man who makes the Ulmo honey." But I quickly realized there was something seriously mistaken about what I'd written.

It was, I think, my rather extreme self-awareness about language that got me going. Although I (and others) frequently refer to the beekeepers as being the ones who "make the honey," it's obvious that that's a wholly inaccurate statement. Everyone knows that it's the creatures with the wings and not the tall bipeds standing alongside the hives that make the actual honey. While people play an integral role in the human world of getting the honey from the hive to our homes, they themselves make nary a spoonful of the sweet stuff. And so the idea of beekeeping and business came into my mind.

The beauty of journaling is that I just write down ideas even if they seem totally silly, stupid, absurd, or slightly insane. Later I look back a bit, and if they seem sound at all, I still have them on hand to draw from. That's what happened in this case. I tripped on the idea, I put it away for a day, I came back to it later, and since I still sort of liked it, I started doing a quick list of ways that the concept seemed to work. The next day, I still liked the metaphor, so I added a bit more to my list.

Feeling slightly silly—beekeeping and leadership are not generally bound together in management magazines—I sat on it for a while. About a month after I got back to Ann Arbor, still having never shared the idea with anyone else, I still liked it. So I figured I should find a safe space in which to unveil it. That space, I decided one day in mid-March, was in the leadership workshop I run a couple times a year here at Zingerman's. It's a semester-long course that folks apply to for acceptance. For each group, I take six or seven people from various parts of the organization, mixing things up to get a variety of experience levels, positions, etc., to end with a diverse group. I've been running the workshop for probably ten years now, and in its own distinct way, each group has been really great to learn with and from. The group works together over a couple of months in discussion about various leadership learnings and the struggles that go with trying to put them into practice. Each group member does reading and also a work-related project in their business or department. All the group sessions are confidential in order to create a safe spot for folks to share difficult challenges, uncertainties, frustrations, and new ideas. There are always a thousand reasons not to make time to run these workshops—the pull to go to customers, answer emails, or return phone calls is always high. But, in essence, because they're all about developing leaders in the organization, they are very much working *on* our organization.

In the workshop that winter, I figured I could model what we teach here about taking risks and putting uncertain thoughts out in a safe space by bringing the beginnings of my metaphor to them to see what their reaction would be. By the end of the three-hour session in which I first shared the idea, they were kidding each other about not sliding right back into working *in* their business. "Come on, be the beekeeper!" came up more than once that day! Others emailed me later in the week with stories and examples of how I might add to the analogy.

That experience gave me the confidence to carry the concept forward to the next level; I decided I'd make my public debut of it at the ZingTrain Leading with Zing seminar. I figured even if they laughed at me, people might appreciate getting to hear a new idea.

So I sketched out my bullet points about beekeeping and business, waited until near the end of the seminar (the big stuff comes up five minutes before the end of the therapy session, right?), and then shared my concept. Despite my trepidation, most everyone in the room seemed to love it. A number of them shared thoughts on how the metaphor worked for them, and how I might enhance it even further. Two attendees actually came up to tell me to turn the beekeeping model into a book. I haven't made it that far yet, but it is now, officially, in this book. If the concept comes together for you, run with it. Share the model. Start the buzz. The improvement in work effectiveness ("the honey," so to speak) will come soon thereafter.

The Secret Life of Beekeepers

I've come to believe that the idea of being a beekeeper can assist us in staying in the mental space we need to be in, to resist that unintentional slide back into the more comfortable day-to-day duties that beckon so strongly. If we are beekeepers, then *leading by example* by getting in there and doing it ourselves—making the honey—is way out of the question. That's what makes the metaphor so marvelous for the most hands-on, heads-down, stubborn, I-can-do-it-better-myself leaders among us.

To really drive home the importance of working *on* your business and not *in* it—I want you to think for a moment about your role as a leader being akin to that of a beekeeper. Imagine that within minutes of your arrival to work one day, you find the bees in the hive aren't performing the way you'd like them to. Think about how incredibly frustrating it can be to watch from the sideline when you know you could just knock out the work yourself in no time. Get into that familiar (for me at least) feeling where the frustration gets so intense that you feel almost compelled to just get in there and do it yourself. Been there? I have—a few billion times.

When you've got that image going good, and you've evoked all the intensity of emotion that goes with it, think next about trying to squeeze your big ol' human body through one of those tiny little openings through which the bees enter and exit the hive. Or if that won't work, channel all that dissonant energy and all your well-intended desire to fix everything firsthand, and try to just take off and fly to the flowers yourself. Go gather that nectar the way it's *supposed* to be done, setting a good example throughout, and then make a very efficient beeline right back to the hive to drop it off and help get production levels back on track.

Won't work? Bummer. Well, at least the point is made. And with that impossible image in mind, and without further ado, let me share with you the details behind this rather curious construct.

Be the Beekeeper!

Thinking of beekeepers as the bosses, here are fifteen reasons why beekeeping is a beautiful image to help us all stay focused on effectively working *on* our organizations.

1. The Leaders Don't Make the Raw Material

We're all limited to some degree by what nature offers us. If we want honey from the hive, try as we might, we have to rely on the worker bees to fly to the flowers, bring nectar back to the hive, and then make even the tiniest drop of honey. All the beekeeper can do is work *on* the hive, managing the space and the systems and supplying the resources the bees need. Then he stands aside and hopes that the insects and the weather will cooperate, knowing that if they do, the honey will come and the business will work well, too.

2. Good Beekeeping Means That Everyone Wins

In our model of business here at Zingerman's, it's always about working towards win-win outcomes, a mutually beneficial, preferred future that all involved contribute to and gain from. And that's absolutely the way it is in the world of apiculture. The better the bees are doing, the bigger the benefit to the beekeeper, the more the plants are getting pollinated, and the better and more plentiful the honey we all have to eat. (Beekeepers often pay rent for the use of the land as a percentage of the honey produced. Enrique hands over a kilo per hive.) In beekeeping and in business, the best protection against competitors or outside attacks is a healthy organization. As Amina Harris, co-owner of MoonShine Trading, one of this country's best honey merchants, said on the subject, "The best defense against pests is maintaining a strong colony."

3. Exploitation May Get Short-Term Results, but in the End It Isn't Sustainable

While the beekeeper can basically bankrupt the hive to get a bit more honey in the moment, it's only a matter of time before that hive is "out of business."

Without some honey, the bees can't survive. For the hive to work well over the long haul, the beekeeper needs to be sure to share the wealth—if the bees eat their fair share, they work all the harder to make the hive efficient. The same problem, I'd say, is found in the old-school business model. Many bosses focus only on getting as much out of their workers as they possibly can and are essentially unconcerned with much of anything that has to do with quality of life for the staff. But we know now that won't work in the modern world. The effective manager, like the best beekeepers, needs to make sure that everyone in the business, regardless of rank, gets something meaningful out of their work. Similarly, if we exploit the employees and give them next to nothing for their work, everyone will suffer; staff who aren't able to live a sustainable life are unlikely to bring positive energy to work every day.

4. Working Together Means Working Better

When leaders and frontline workers are in alignment and all treat each other respectfully, everyone is likely to fully benefit from each other's efforts. Same goes for the bees. I'm not a beekeeper, but I know enough to know that every successful apiarist treats the bees with respect. It's actually pretty amazing to see the passion and care they put into it. What I've come to realize is that being near the bees in a gentle and caring way, as beekeepers are, is a lot like great leadership work. Being able to get workably close in respectful, meaningful ways to both bees and human beings without confining or even restricting them in their work is a big piece of what makes good beekeeping and good leadership.

Applied to apiculture, I can't imagine that a fear of the bees would ever make for particularly good honey or good yields. Rather, it's akin to the sort of stuff that I typically would ascribe to old-school, hierarchically oriented leaders, who often seem to hide from their employees by getting behind big desks, corporate assistants, and fifteenth-floor offices, and who fail to connect on a personal and meaningful level.

I think, too, it's not just about being at peace with the bees—good beekeepers are also at peace with themselves. If they're not, the bees pick up on their fear and uncertainty, get stressed, the yields go down, and hive management gets a whole lot harder than it has to be. I'll always remember the day I met Joan Piñol, a Catalan beekeeper with nearly five decades of work with the hives. "Do the bees ever bother you?" I asked him. He smiled, looked at me with this great calm energy in his eyes, and then said serenely, "I would sleep with the bees."

5A. IF WE FIGHT WITH THE WORKERS, WE GET STUNG

Here at Zingerman's, we've long believed that effective leadership is about aligning everyone's energies to go towards the shared vision of the future that we've agreed upon. By contrast, when we're in big conflict with the crew—when one falls back into the old, "win-lose," "us versus them" model —the business just won't work well. In beekeeping and in the workplace as we know it, fighting against—as opposed to aligning *with*—the crew is pretty much sure to get us stung, often when we're not looking and all too often in really unpleasant places. Most of the time, when a bee stings us it's because it's caught off-guard and reacts reflexively without forethought or malice. And I'd posit the same is generally true for even the most cynical of staff. While the stings rarely cause long-term hardship, they hurt like hell in the moment—stress is high, trust is low, communication is increasingly ineffective, no one is having fun, and the organization isn't working well at all.

5B. IF WE FIGHT HARDER, IT GETS EVEN WORSE

I've never lived this one but it's pretty much common knowledge: the harder people fight back at bees by swatting and swearing at them the worse it gets. I've watched it on the patio at the Deli for years. At the height of summer we have a fair number of bees that come down to feed on the scraps of food that fall on the ground, or the leftover bits of sweetened beverages. Some customers seem barely distracted, sit quietly, and move the bees away with a gentle, nonaggressive wave of their hand. For the most part, the bees cooperate and the whole situation stays calm. The people who are most afraid swat and run around to escape the bees. The bees, of course, are far faster, and once they fix on the person, they seem to lock on and won't let go. The more the people persist, the more aggressive the bees get. Some folks go at it so furiously they get stung or end up fleeing to the tables inside. The same is true in organizational life as well; leaders who "swat furiously" at their staff members don't do really well in business. The more the bosses argue, the more the staff gets angry, the more isolated the leaders get, and the worse the problem becomes.

6. IF WE SPRAY THE WORKERS TO STOP THEM, WE GET MOMENTARY RELIEF

With employees and bees, if we get mad enough, we can knock 'em out or knock 'em down. Some aggressive bosses get sick of swatting and pull out the "bug spray." When we do it, we may look big and strong for a bit, and we've certainly shown 'em who's boss. But the truth is that while we win in the moment, the game is pretty much over. Granted, we get the honey that's left at the time, but we aren't going to be getting any more unless we go out and bring in an entirely new crew. I guess this works in a way, but this "smash and burn" approach isn't really sustainable, nor is it very rewarding for beekeepers, bosses, bees, or anyone working in the business.

7. You Can't Make the Bees Do Anything

When it comes to bees, no one will really argue with this statement. While we know much of what influences their behavior, there's no way to sit a bee down to have a serious conversation about job performance. But it's easy to argue the opposite in the context of one's company—"We're paying them," "I'm the boss," and all that. The truth of the matter is that managers have as much chance of making employees do something as beekeepers have of forcing the insects to make honey. Both staff and bees do what they do only by choice. With that in mind, here at Zingerman's, we long ago arrived at the approach that we treat our staff as if they were volunteers. As I've said a number of times in earlier essays, we definitely can't *make* them do anything.

I love the bee analogy on this one because with staff we can still easily slide into the old illusion that since we're paying people, we have "control," or they somehow "have to" do what we ask. When others argue that way (as they often do), I almost always immediately state firmly what I believe to be true— "It's all out of control; all we have are varying degrees of influence." Great beekeepers and great leaders alike know this and act accordingly.

Honey Time!

If you aren't familiar with them, great varietal honeys are truly delicious. Even after all the increase in attention to great food we've had in this country in the last couple of decades, they're still really almost unknown outside select circles of honey aficionados. With that in mind, I think it's safe to say that this essay will be more enjoyable if you open a jar of a great varietal honey and eat it straight from the spoon (as I often do), on toast, or with a bit of good cheese. Or do as Enrique, the man who "makes" the Ulmo honey, does every morning in Chile and drink a big glass of steamed milk with just an espresso-shot's worth of coffee and a whole bunch of his honey mixed into it.

8. Sometimes the Bees Don't Behave

Given that all behavior is somewhat out of control, let me state what I'm sure you already know. No matter how good the beekeeper, no matter how much we want good outcomes, no matter how at peace the beekeeper is with the bees or herself, no matter anything . . . sometimes the bees ignore all the beekeeper's best efforts. While I haven't kept bees myself, I have managed a lot of people. And, sometimes, even when I've *done everything I can,* things go awry anyway. Projects fail, people I trusted trip up, folks who promised they were going to work with us for years up and leave with no notice. It's incredibly frustrating when those things happen, but sometimes that's just the way it is. And when that's the case, the sooner we make peace with the reality of that fact, the less stressed-out we'll be, the more likely we are to reverse the trend, and slowly but surely start to get better results down the road.

9. Even the Kindest Beekeepers Still Get Stung

Like it or not (personally, I don't), even when one is really respectful to the workers or bees, there still aren't any guarantees—sometimes they sting you anyway even when you haven't done anything to deserve it. Inexperienced apiarists get angry and fight back, insistent on proving their point. I've certainly done it too many times. By contrast, experienced beekeepers know all too well that acting in anger only makes things worse. While I'm sure they still don't really like it, they just get used to the occasional sting. They learn to absorb the blow, stay centered, and quickly get re-focused on what needs to be done. Getting stung is most certainly not the fun part of the work, but it happens, and there's not a whole lot any of us can do to totally prevent it, other than get a new job.

10. You Can Find Ways to Manage the Response to the Stings

If you *do* get stung, there are things you can do to take care of yourself; you can ice it, you can take Benadryl, or, as Enrique showed me when I got stung while we were out by the Ulmo trees, you can rub a cut clove of garlic on the sting. Similarly, we as leaders are going to get stung, but having support around us—good people, caring colleagues, folks who will listen and offer good insight and help us unload our stress—is a huge help.

(By the way, this is wholly applicable to people like me who are allergic. Knowing one's weak points or vulnerabilities as a leader and being able to prepare in advance by lining up effective ways to manage our reactivity is really quite critical to long-term success. If we know where we're particularly vulnerable, we're far more likely to manage effectively than we are when we're in denial about what's going on inside us.)

11. THE SYSTEMS WE DESIGN ARE ABSOLUTELY ESSENTIAL

This is where I realized that the "working on" model gets particularly interesting—because, ultimately, the biggest factors in quantity and quality of honey are nature and the way the beekeeper manages the location, size, and scale of the hives. Even the biggest control freaks among us know that nature is *not* in our control. We can and must adapt to it or we'll get next to nothing done. The skilled beekeeper makes adjustments based on sun, rain, wind, etc. How high the beekeeper stacks the hives, how large he leaves the openings for the bees, where he places the hives in the first place, and a hundred other little things will have a big impact on productivity.

For instance, in 1851 the Reverend Lorenzo Lorraine Langstroth of Philadelphia discovered what's known today as "bee space," meaning that when a one-centimeter gap was left between the panels in the hive, bees would leave that space free from comb. All modern hives are built with that measure in mind. (If you'd like to read more on the subject, find a copy of Langstroth's 1853 *The Hive and the Honey-Bee.*) Another simple but helpful technique is to make the various stacks of bee boxes from different-colored woods so that the bees can find their own hive more easily. Leaders can do simple things to help create a more productive workplace.

The construction and management of sound structures and smoothly running systems is the bulk of both a beekeeper's and a leader's work. She should work *on* her business to create systems and structures in which the workers will do well, and then to position the workplace and the workers in a spot where they'll have a very high likelihood of success.

12. EFFECTIVE BEEKEEPERS EMBRACE DIVERSITY

If all the beekeeper has to work with is a single bee, he'll have no honey, nor even a hive. It takes a range of contributors—the queen, the drones, the worker bees—for the whole thing to function. It also takes a range of blossoms to make for a financially sound hive—beekeepers move the hives mindfully through the months in order to get the sort of honey they want in the region. Clearly, the same is true for us as leaders in the modern world. Peppe Avola, a very skilled, very smart, now-retired Sicilian beekeeper whom I met years ago, told me that "Every bee is like a cell of a single body. Its work changes as it gets older. When it's born, it cleans in the hive. Then it makes royal jelly. Then it feeds the royal jelly to the queen. Then it makes the wax. Then it defends the nest. The last thing it gets to do is collect pollen for honey making." Peppe's fascination with his crew and his ability to manage them as they develop and do their different jobs and get great honey fascinate me. The leader has to learn to handle and enhance the work of wholly different types of people to bring the business to greatness.

13. Better Beekeepers Bring Out Better Honey

While less skilled beekeepers might get good yields in any given year, over time the most rewarding results come from those who practice the most sustainable styles year in and year out. Most of us start out with uncertainty, a bit of fear, less-than-great decision-making, and overuse of tactics that feel safer in the moment. As Amina Harris related, it may take time to settle in. "I (and many others) started out in my beekeeping fearful, using the smoker a lot to keep the bees pacified. But the best way is to learn to work with the hive and use the smoker only when you really need to." (The smoker basically works against nature to interrupt the normal flow of action and interaction in the hive. It's another example of how a boss can force his or her way into the flow and get short-term results, but in the long run the unnatural intervention actually creates negative consequences.) The leaders and beekeepers (like Amina) who continue to build their knowledge grow more at peace with themselves, with the bees, and with nature. They make small, subtle, meaningful changes to the way they work—enhancing their results even more with each passing year. For whatever seemingly-hard-to-explain reasons, the flavor of the honey these artisans get from the hive is more interesting and the yields are generally higher.

14. There Aren't Any Guarantees

Despite all we do, and all I've written up to here, we all know that there aren't any guarantees in life, or work, or in beekeeping. Sometimes we do all the stuff we're supposed to do, but things just don't work out; it's frustrating, not fair at all, but nevertheless true. The year I visited Enrique's Ulmo honey production, it looked like it was going to come in at about two tons. The previous year, it had surpassed seventy. What happened? "This has been one of the driest years ever," he said. "In December [remember the seasons are reversed down there], we had 31°C (that's over 90°F), and we've never had that. Usually it might be 25°C or 26°C at the most." High heat, global warming, hardly any blossoms, and almost no nectar result in lower honey yields. Same thing can happen when the economy suddenly goes south, snowstorms arrive on significant days, construction workers accidentally cut power cables, customers cancel big catering events. Not fair, but there's not really anything a beekeeper or business owner can do other than take a deep breath and go back to work with a positive belief in the future, a great crew, and good beekeeping techniques in hand.

15. BEEKEEPING IS REALLY HARD WORK, BUT IT WORKS!

Although we as consumers mostly just think about—and enjoy—the sweetness of the end product, the reality is that beekeeping is very hard work and hardly very glamorous. While anyone *could* do it, it takes a lot of focus, enormous attention to detail, and a lot of small day-to-day work to add up to superior product. As per Natural Law 7, "Successful businesses [or in this case, beekeepers] do the things that others know they should do but generally don't." While most leaders know what they ought to do, for whatever combination of internal reasons and external pressures, they sometimes choose the easier path and settle for similar, if not equal, results by staying with the mainstream of the market.

That said, most every single skilled beekeeper I've met *loves* what he or she does. Their passion is high. They all take great pride in their craft and seem endlessly fascinated with the blending of science, passion, and art that goes into it. Amina Harris noted that most will pause regularly to "admire the bees' handiwork." That reminded me of something I heard from Peppe, who said to me with obvious wonderment, "I'm completely fascinated by the honey and the bees." For Peppe and for most of the other men and women who do this work, it feels to me very much like they have a vocation, a passion, a lifelong way to learn and feel alive while finding a way to make a living doing it. I can relate, because I truly feel the same way about what I do with food and leadership. And that's pretty much true for most every great leader I've ever encountered.

Final Thoughts

The thing I really like about this comparison between beekeeping and working *on* your business is that it's just so black and white. Quite simply, the beekeeper only works *on* the business of the hive, the bees only work *in* it; and the better the former does his work, the more likely it is that the latter will bring us good results. We all know that a) even if the beekeeper wants to fly, he can't; b) no matter how hard he tries he'll never fit his big body into the bee box; and c) he can forage for flowers all he wants, but despite his best efforts and outstandingly good intentions, the eventual results will not be honey.

With both beehives and businesses, the reality is that the best "beekeepers" work most effectively *on* the hive, not *in* it. For those of us who are prone to just dive in and start *doing*, rather than stepping back, assessing things, and then working *on* the organization by adjusting systems and styles to get the better outcomes we want, the metaphor works pretty darned well.

So the next time you start to feel that old familiar feeling, the almost innate desire most of us have to just get in there and do it ourselves, I want to encourage you to pull your mind back from that old instinct and put your energy into assessing what's going on. Start looking at ways to improve systems and inputs to enhance results. Ultimately, I think that's our work. The better we do it, the better for all. Because better beekeepers almost always bring out better-tasting honey—and more of it. Over time, everyone wins from our self-discipline and big-picture outlook. And just think of how good it's going to taste! When the pressure's at its highest, then more than ever try to recall the mantra: "Come on! Be the beekeeper!"

In, On, and On Yourself, Take 2

Now that you've got the idea of beekeeping and the import of working on your business in your mind, it's worth revisiting your time allocations to see if you want to do anything differently. The key is to work towards rough ratios (it's all in flux anyway) that get you and your organization the most rewarding results possible and help all involved be better able to find the flowers, as well as make and then eat and appreciate the honey!

	Working *in* Your Business	Working *on* Your Business	Working on Yourself as a Leader
% of the week as I've been doing it			
% of the week as it will be three months from now			

P.S.: Keep the Honey Jar Handy

To help them stay focused on being the beekeeper, a few folks who've heard this whole theory have started to keep a jar of really good varietal honey on their desks. The honey helps them by serving as a visual reminder to avoid the tendency to unconsciously revert to simply doing more *in* the business and that the real key is their ability to devote the time and creativity needed to working *on* it. Plus when the day gets long, stress gets high, and the bees don't behave, a quick, healthy, and delicious spoonful of great honey serves as a sweet reminder of why we work so darned hard every day.

The Inside Scoop on Working Here at Zingerman's

Valerie Neff-Rasmussen, Service Star, Zingerman's Mail Order

I wanted to thank you for giving me the opportunity to attend the ZingTrain seminar today and tomorrow. I think it's easy to sometimes get caught up in the day-to-day minutiae and lose sight of the bigger picture. Zingerman's is a truly remarkable place. Talking in detail about the Natural Laws of Business only further instills what I see around me every day, but it's also provoking ideas of where we (and I) could do even better. Chatting with outside attendees who are just starting to think about implementing some of these practices really reinforces to me what a special place this is, and how fortunate I am to be a part of it. Thank you for working so hard for so long to create and foster an environment that is such a pleasure to be a part of. I feel so, so lucky to have the opportunity to work, learn, and grow here, and to be a part of making Zingerman's great.

coffee company managing partner aLLen Leibowitz at the test roaster

The Entrepreneurial Approach to Management

Applying the Free Market to Our Work as Managers

The little scenario that follows is something I put down on paper one day long ago. I remember being incredibly frustrated hearing managers complaining about how their staff continued to not come through for them over and over again. I was reminded of something I'd heard from my friend Richard Kempter many years ago. "Most of us," he told me, "love our problems so much that we'll usually do almost anything not to let go of them." With this, as with so many other things I learned from him, I think Richard was right on. Though he's never been in business, his wisdom and teaching is, in truth, all over this book. As I felt myself getting more and more frustrated with this repetitive rant about employees behaving badly, I tried to keep Richard's maxim in mind. Fairly quickly, I realized that most of what our managers were frustrated with, while very real, was also very much a problem they were choosing. Whether they knew it or not, it was clear that they were comfortable complaining and they weren't anywhere near ready to let go and move on to a new (and better, as per Natural Law 9) set of problems.

I also knew that it didn't have to be that difficult. I started to look at the situation less as a manager and more as the free market businessperson that I am most of the time. Changing lenses worked beautifully. Out of frustration with what felt to me like the same, staid, old-school-bureaucratic approach to management, the Entrepreneurial Approach was born. It is applying the same sort of creative, compelling, fun, energy-building approaches in our leadership that we'd so long ago started to apply in our merchandising and sales work.

The Entrepreneurial Approach flows quite naturally from what you might (likely) have read earlier in this book. Instead of getting all serious and bureaucratic, it brings fun and positive energy into employee management. If, as per Servant Leadership, the staff are our customers, this approach is all about selling them on what we believe is best. If our work with Stewardship says that we want to encourage people to make conscious choices to commit to what we're doing, the Entrepreneurial Approach is guaranteed to raise the odds of that happening. And if everyone's a leader, then anyone here can kick the approach into action. It works far better than old-school stuff that orders staff to behave.

―――――

The Entrepreneurial Approach is about a different, more creative way to run a business. But before I get into the details, let me do a little bit of workplace docudrama with you. In truth, I know the scene below so well because I've lived it myself (way too) many times. Putting it in writing has helped me stay clear on how I—knowingly or not—contribute to the situations that I'm simultaneously complaining about and also struggling to solve. There are, of course, answers to the issues below in much of what's preceded this piece in the book, but the specific solution to this scenario follows.

The New Blue Shirt Case Study

So, if you can, forget all this uplifting leadership stuff I've been going on about and transport yourself for a few minutes back into a more mainstream, status quo management setting. Let's just say, for story's sake, you're the manager at Scoop, a new ice cream shop. After much discussion, we've decided to implement a new dress code. As of Monday, all the staff have been asked to start wearing the new blue shirts we've picked out. At the moment, though, it's still Sunday afternoon. The day shift is getting ready to go home. Thinking that tomorrow is the big day, you decide to help out one of your longtime employees, Sue, by reminding her about the shirt switch.

"Sue, don't forget about the new dress code, ok?"
"Oh, sure," she says smiling, "no problem. See you tomorrow!"

Next day, she shows up for work but, unfortunately, not wearing the new uniform. You sigh, take a deep breath, and head over to where she's working.

"Sue, you told me you were going to wear the new blue shirt. What happened?"
"Oh, man, I am so sorry. I just plum forgot all about it."
"Well, try to remember for tomorrow, ok?"
"Oh yeah. Definitely. I promise."

Next day, sadly, still no blue shirt.

"Sue, what's the deal? Where's the blue shirt?"
"Jeez, I feel so bad. You know, I asked my mom to wash that one. And she thought I said *not* to wash it because last week she'd washed the wrong stuff and all my best clothes got faded. I'll try to get it done for tomorrow."
"OK, it's really important, Sue, so don't forget, OK?"
"Don't worry. I won't. Really. It's all good!"

Meanwhile, Laura, the general manager—your boss—stops you in the hall.

"Hey, I notice Sue hasn't been wearing the new blue shirts. What's up? This has been going on for over a week already. You're really gonna have to do something here. Or pretty soon, if she doesn't get with the program, she's just gonna have to go."

You think for a minute, then decide to get the real issue out on the table.

"I hear you, Laura. You're right. But the problem is that I can't really afford to let her go. I mean, there are only so many shifts I can cover on my own. Other than this shirt thing, she's a great employee. She cares, she's here on time, and she's great with the customers. You know she stays late to help when we need it and she never complains about it. And we do have those big football weekends coming up."

"Well, all right," she says with a sigh, "but you'd better get her in line pretty soon."

Back down to the floor. Next day, guess what? Your employee Sue shows up again, but still no blue shirt. (Is this sounding at all familiar?)

"Sue, this is really going overboard. I'm the manager. I need you to wear that blue shirt or there's going to be some really serious consequences."

"I'm sorry. I'm really sorry. I feel terrible about it. I promise I'll have it. I'll get right on it as soon as I get home today. You know I really love working here. It's just been a rough week. You can count on me."

"All right," you say. "But I'm not messing around here anymore."

Monday morning arrives. Sue shows up in the blue shirt. You breathe a super big sigh of relief. Finally!

"Thanks, Sue, I really appreciate it."
"Oh, no problem. I told you that you could count on me."
"Thanks, Sue!"

You smile. A small but arguably significant achievement. Unfortunately, it's short-lived. Next day, no blue shirt. Your stress level shoots way up again.

"Sue, what's up? Where's the shirt?"
"Oh, I'm sorry. Do we really have to wear 'em every day? I

thought it was sort of just a good idea on the weekends, you know, when it's really busy? During the week the regular customers all know who we are anyway so I figured we didn't need to wear 'em."

"No, Sue. It's *every* day. Can I count on you to wear it tomorrow? (This is when we get really stressed and pull out the "other parent" card.) This is really important. Laura's my boss and she's gonna kill me if you don't get this together. You're making me look really bad!"

"No problem," she says sternly, "I'll have it on."

Breaking character, let me move into a more analytical mindset. So . . . is this sounding at all familiar? I could probably take this scenario out another two or three paragraphs without exaggerating much, if at all. It is, unfortunately, all too often the way things work in most of our organizations. Ultimately Sue either a) gives in and actually wears the shirt, b) the new dress code fizzles out, or c) she gets fired. The last two, obviously, are not our desired outcomes. And, I would argue, although the first option is a bit better, it's not great either. What we want to attain is commitment and conscious free choice (see page 269 for more on this). And Sue's "giving in" may be better than her getting fired, but it's still not optimal.

In theory, as effective leaders we've negotiated agreement on the new program before we implement it. But unfortunately, in Sue's case, that alone isn't working. And, while the scenario above is playing out, there's another big problem in the making, *one that may actually have bigger negative implications.* So, switching back into the land of the blue shirts . . .

Through this whole two weeks, Jamie, one of our best staff members, has been diligently wearing the new blue shirts as requested. From day one, she's been on top of it. She went out and bought five of the new shirts so she'd have enough to wear—clean and ironed—every day. When you open the front door in the morning, there she is, ready to work in a new blue shirt. You smile. But then, right there next to her, is Sue, who as we know, is *not* wearing one. Day after day after day.

By the end of a few weeks of this discrepancy, how would you imagine Jamie would be feeling? I'd guess some combination of angry, frustrated, unappreciated, and disenchanted. Why? We aren't holding Sue to the new expectations. But these are the exact same expectations Jamie is diligently meeting. As a result, our integrity rating is taking a big beating in the eyes of one of our best staff members. And we're trapped—we don't think firing Sue is a good move. Yet the new dress code is important. Think on it. What messages are we sending to Jamie, who's been coming through for us every day? I believe that the implicit message is: you really *don't* make a difference. And you can pretty much ignore what we ask you to do if you don't like it because we're going to let you do what you want anyway.

Jamie did what we asked her to do. Sue agrees to do it, but doesn't. Yet I'll bet you that they still make roughly the same money and work roughly the same shifts. It's just that Jamie is stressed out, taking all this seriously, and then dressing appropriately. Sue, on the other hand, isn't coming through at all. Granted, if this drags on long enough Sue might actually get fired for failing to come dressed in the proper uniform. But we all know that firing, if it ever comes, is still probably weeks or months away.

And what, you might wonder, is the upside for wearing the new shirts here at Scoop? Not much, actually. Maybe some praise en route, but probably no more than once or twice in the first few weeks and then not at all. Assuming that Jamie is a really good employee, she might eventually get a small raise. But that's about it.

Problem made clear? This isn't entrepreneurial. It's more like some sort of ineffective, old-school, Stalinist socialism (the anarchists and communists were not on good terms—the former was about freedom, the latter about control). Our integrity is suffering; we aren't firing the offender because it's not "that big a deal" and "we really need people to work." And, en route, one of our best employees is increasingly less motivated to excel.

So what do we do about it? Certainly, we need to make sure that we've been very clear about our expectations. And throughout this situation, we need to be certain to focus on performance results, not on intentions. Sure, it's nice that Sue is *trying* to wear the blue shirt, but the reality is, *she still isn't actually wearing one.* Which still leaves us stuck with the choice of continued ineffective nagging, letting her get away with it, or ultimately letting her go. My belief is that none of these are great options by which to operate.

What would work more effectively? Be entrepreneurial! *Imagine, in this new scenario, that the staff are your customers and that you are selling them on wearing the new blue shirts to work.* No more bugging them and threatening them (you don't use those techniques to get customers to buy, do you?). Just creative, free-market selling in action. To do it, you simply apply all the same techniques to selling them on the new dress code as you would to selling your customers on a new dessert. That, in a nutshell, is what the Entrepreneurial Approach to Management is all about. Read on for the full recipe.

The End of Bureaucracy, or Why Selling Beats Nagging Any Day of the Week

As you may already know from reading Secret 23, one of the key tenets of our application of Servant Leadership here at Zingerman's is that we treat our staff as our customers. The Entrepreneurial Approach below follows directly from that supposition; if the staff are our customers, then the idea here is to *apply the same sort of creative, engaging, entertaining, and effective approaches we use in selling and serving them as we would put into play when dealing with paying customers.* With that in mind, the Entrepreneurial Approach brings free-market forces—in the caring, Anarcho-Capitalist, and sustainable ways we work them—and well-practiced merchandising and marketing techniques (all based on our well-founded belief in the food we sell and our efforts to be financially successful in the free market) into our work as leaders.

The old-school model of management is, all too often, using authoritarian or bureaucratic approaches (or in some cases, the two in tandem). In either of those old models the way one would generally initiate change would be to command it to happen from the top of the organization. Bosses are there to be brilliant, to be responsible for what happens, and to reap the rewards when things work well. Employees, by contrast, come to work to do what they're told, to get paid, and to start saving for retirement. Obviously, not all organizations are like that, but there are still many where that mindset is the norm. In more progressive, courtesy-centered companies, we may well make our demands more politely, thanking people en route for their support, but still not really asking them what they think or how they'd suggest that we have them participate. Polite though it may be, management in this style is still essentially done by one or two methods (sometimes both): sending out emails and memos from headquarters or calling meetings and giving directives.

Unfortunately, despite even the best of intentions, the most inspiring of meetings and the most well written of memos rarely seem to bring about the desired changes. When our memos and meetings are ineffective, we begin working to bring the sources of resistance—our critics, foot draggers, and even opponents—on board. When the pace of change lags, we may try to persuade; sometimes that works, often it doesn't. Sometimes we simply turn a blind eye and hope the problems go away, but we all know that's not an effective answer either.

Almost inevitably, we then fall into using what I've taken to calling "The Four Horsemen of Ineffective Management": cajoling, begging, nagging, and, finally, threatening termination. To my view, these are the unspoken but predominant techniques in play in the old-school style of bureaucratic management. I hate them all, but I know I can fall into them, too, if I'm not careful.

Although it's all too common, this bureaucratic approach, I'd argue, is rarely effective. At least I've never seen it work very well. Even when things get done in the near term, the energy underlying the surface-level achievements gets worse by the week. Over time, the energy erodes to the point where we end up with the sort of energy crisis in the workplace I outlined back in Secret 19. We can order people to do things, but the reality is that more often than not, they don't really do what we tell them to. The old model creates a slew of significant struggles, but there are a few that seem particularly poignant in the context of this essay:

> **a. We need our staff more than they need us.** Although the general wisdom is that employees are dependent on us, I think that's short-sighted and naive. Many may act needy, and others truly are deeply dependent on their employer while the economy is in suboptimal shape. But, at least in our industry, if our staff want to leave tomorrow, they can probably go find a few new jobs within a week or two. And we need a lot more from them than just showing up and going through the motions. To do great things we need everyone's full energy engaged in the pursuit of excellence pretty much all the time. Even if they feel like they need us, and they need the work, most people know how to put on a game face well enough to keep things going, all the while working at far less than fantastic levels. In the big picture, if the people in the organization aren't giving it their all, the likelihood of us as leaders being successful is very small.

> **b. Our staff know how to get us off their back without necessarily doing what needs to be done.** I call this the "no problem" problem. Most of us have been "trained" all too well as children in the art of nodding our heads and saying "sure, no problem," but then going right on doing what we want to do anyway. This is certainly

how many of us learned to "manage" our parents and other authority figures while we were growing up.

c. Rewards frequently fail to match up with what we say we want. Although nearly every organization says that it rewards its top performers at the highest levels, in practice many don't. Far more often than not, there is little, if any, difference in reward and recognition between those who are buying in and implementing the new changes and programs and those who aren't.

All of these things create what I think is an unsustainable system. We give orders, then most of our staff either avoid the issues, go along to keep us quiet, or do only enough to make it seem like there's some motion. It's anything but adult to adult, and it's hardly creative or constructive. It's actually a lot like what I remember of being twelve, and I don't think that was much fun for me, my parents, or anyone else who came too close. Which I guess then makes clear why, when this stuff happens, most managers revert to those old parental tactics, the previously mentioned Four Horsemen. In my experience, these tactics are about as ineffective for us now as they were back when our parents were using them on us. In management, it usually goes something along the lines of what I scripted out in the New Blue Shirt Case Study.

Why Use the Entrepreneurial Approach?

In a nutshell, the Entrepreneurial Approach is more fun, it's more creative, and it's in synch with the free-market philosophy we're all supposed to believe in. The old model may still kind of work, but I think it's out of touch with the realities of the world in which we live. If the staff are essentially our customers, we need to treat them as such, not just pay lip service to the concept. The Entrepreneurial Approach does that really well. It also makes it easier to make organizational change happen. And anything we can do to help the cause of positive change—as long as it's ethical and up-front—is going to reduce management, staff, and organizational stress. With the free market in mind, if we truly believe in the changes, values, visions, and programs that we're trying to put in place, then we need to actively solicit support from people in the organization. That support will help us to make it as rewarding as possible for people to buy into the changes and ideas we're "selling" and, at the same time, to make it more appealing to get on board. And, in the end, the Entrepreneurial Approach is about 80 times more effective (and fun!) than begging, nagging, cajoling, and threatening termination.

When we use it well, our Entrepreneurial Approach to Management puts a wide range of new tools into our leadership toolbox. Conceptually, it's really just putting the same free-market, sustainable, respect-for-all-involved principles into play in management that we comfortably use all day long with customers who come in to buy our food and our services. Selling something you believe in is just way better than sending out reprimand slips.

Can selling ideas and new programs or products to staff really be so much like selling to customers? Sure can. In case you're not convinced, let me do some suggestive, scenario-based selling. Let's say we wanted to increase restaurant sales at off-peak hours, maybe on Tuesday evenings. If we were at a ZingTrain seminar, I'd have you brainstorm and we'd write all your suggestions up on the white boards. Having done that before, here's a likely list of what you all would (appropriately) come up with:

- create some sort of special promotion to run on Tuesday evenings to make dining more fun than at other times of the week
- create incentives for customers to buy more on Tuesdays: discounts, special Tuesday price packages, early bird specials, etc.
- reward frequent Tuesday buyers with something extra like free desserts
- get testimonials from others who come on Tuesdays and like it
- run ads
- send out personal appeals to customers who we know come in on Tuesdays
- talk about how great Tuesdays are for shopping in one-on-one conversations
- solicit support from our suppliers
- create disincentives to come at peak times by raising prices during our busiest hours like weekends or lunch rushes in order to make it more appealing for Tuesday evening buyers
- run staff contests for sales
- put up posters to promote it
- do samplings or tastings
- teach classes to the staff
- write about it in our newsletter

Note what's missing from this list? That's right. There are *no memos and no meetings*. Memos and meetings, used as the primary tools to make a change happen, really don't work very well. If anyone out there wants to argue that they're really great tools to help get people to change their behavior, imagine for a minute that we decided to go after increased Tuesday evening sales by writing a really nice email memo to our customers. You know, politely telling them to get their acts together and start coming in more. In this economy, we can't really afford to have any off nights and we need our customers to come in more often! Weekends are all well and good, but we need traffic on Tuesday, our off night. This mythical memo (no, I did not actually send something like this) might be something along the lines of the following:

Subject: TUESDAY EVENING SALES AT ZINGERMAN'S

Dear Zingerman's Customer,

Greetings. As of last week we've noticed that our Tuesday evening sales are lagging behind annual projections. In order to get back on track, we're asking that each of you—our valued customers—increase the frequency of your Tuesday evening purchases by roughly ten percent per month. While this will only be a small inconvenience for you, it will really help the company. And in the end we'll all be better off for it. We know you can do it. We really appreciate your support and look forward to seeing those increased sales we all know are possible.

Sincerely,
Your Zingerman's Management Team

If you want to make it really real, you can leave in all that stuff that shows up in emails now about privacy, legal rights, and lawsuits. What do you think most customers would do with this politely written note? Laugh? Wonder if we'd gone crazy? Toss it in the trash? Hit "delete"? All of the above?

I know this scenario seems a little ludicrous. But my belief is that *sending notes to our staff about improving, say, service performance would be almost as ineffective as sending this memo to paying customers to get them to increase purchases.* In fact, an email of this sort to the staff is likely to get pretty much the same results: laughter, amazement, and a quick flick of the wrist to send it to the (virtual or veritable) trash can. Unfortunately, there's way too much truth in this scenario. I know I addressed it to customers, but you could of course plug in "employee" and change the subject to be about wearing the new blue shirts (as one example). Show your draft to managers anywhere for feedback, and all but a few would do little more than offer a few nice suggestions for grammatical improvement.

The Entrepreneurial Approach in Action

The good news is that if you're up for a little creative, free-market-minded fun, it doesn't have to be this way. We can relegate the memos to what they really ought to be—one small tool in a very big and creative management tool box, one that's definitely not the first thing we pull out when we need to kick off a change. As per what I'll call Emile DeFelice's "law of opposites" (where we are pretty likely do the opposite of what the mass market does—see page 13 for details), the Entrepreneurial Approach is basically the inverse of the bureaucratic methods of memos and meetings. If you can sell whatever product or service you already sell to make a living, then I'm sure you can successfully use this approach in your organization.

1. SELL OUR IDEAS AND BELIEFS TO OUR STAFF

As leaders, more than anything else, we are selling a belief system, a set of values, a vision of the future, a belief that a contribution to our organization is meaningful. If we want to improve food quality, we have to start by selling that improvement to people in the organization. Similarly, if we want to make service better, we need to get the people who work with us to "buy" the concept of better service. The same goes for improving the quality of our workplace, a new product, more profit, etc. *Whatever it is, if we're trying to make positive change happen, we need to start out by successfully selling that belief or idea to the people we work with.*

We do that, quite simply, by using all the same techniques we'd use to merchandise, promote, and sell to a customer. Put up posters, run promotions, make it fun, run specials, do demos, etc. Effective merchandising, in our experience, requires that it's not just enough to say something once. We have to repeat our main message often enough that it actually registers and is not just emitted into the ether. How often? Twenty-seven times. No joke. That's the number we use when we want to effectively merchandise a product to our customers, and it's no different in selling to our staff. More background on this bit in a future edition of *Zingerman's Guide to Good Leading*, but in a nutshell, data has shown that you need to repeat your message nine times before the customer hears it. Other data demonstrates that customers generally hear only one out of every three messages we may send. Using my most basic math skills, I stuck the two together, multiplied 9 by 3 and got 27.

While I'm hardly the world's best salesperson, I have gotten pretty good at it. Above and beyond all else, though, I have a big advantage over most of the market—*I only sell stuff I believe in.* That's true of bacon, barbecue, brownies, or bottles of olive oil. And it's also true of what we're trying to do organizationally. (Sure, there are some things I've sold that I'm not 100 percent, totally behind in the moment. But I'm still maybe 80 or 90 percent of the way there, and those are all short-term exceptions that I believe are headed back to the 100 percent point in the near future.) That belief, alone, gives me far more solid ground from which to start selling. That ground is firmed up even further because we always guarantee what we're selling—if someone doesn't like something we sold them, we just replace it or refund their money.

In essence, Servant Leadership sets the table for the Entrepreneurial Approach—it's also about treating staff like customers in a caring and supportive way. With that sort of solid, belief-based, values-driven approach as a foundation, it allows you to go after what you believe in and have fun in the process. The way we do it, though, it's a productive and creative piece of work; the most effective salespeople are, of course, those who can effectively adapt their selling to the style in which the customer is most comfortable buying. Different people learn in different ways, so the more you can mix up formal and informal, visual and verbal, serious and humorous, the more effective your selling will be. And the most successful managers are usually those who will sell their concepts and principles to the staff in the way the staff would like, rather than the way we want to sell to them.

Remember, too, that every prospective buyer—in this case, every staff member—wants to know "What's in it for me?" How will implementing the change at hand make their lives better? It could be, simply, that they'll be able to feel good about their contribution to the organization. It might be that we're a socially responsible organization. It may be that they'll have fun. Maybe they'll make some extra money. Maybe they'll be held in high esteem in the organization. Conversely, if we can't tell them what's in it for them, it's not very likely that we're going to get them to "buy."

Note that names and language are as important here as they are in merchandising work on a store level. Every major initiative you take will do better if it's got a catchy name. If you can, come up with something that fits your culture and your look and feel. At Zingerman's, as you already know, we call our approach to training "Bottom-Line Training," which, let's face it, is a lot easier to remember than "SOP 173," or "that stuff we do when we have to train someone new." So just as you'd think about how to name a new product you were bringing on line, come up with fun, creative names for the beliefs and values that you're selling.

2. USE FREE-MARKET CONCEPTS TO REWARD WHAT YOU REALLY WANT

Almost every company says it rewards the people who are meeting or exceeding expectations. I suppose that's true with commission-based salespeople. But beyond that, few companies actually do it well when it comes to other, culturally important—even if not directly sales-related—work. In practice we rarely do the rewarding anywhere near as well with staff as we do with customers. With the public, if we want more early evening business, we run "Early Bird Specials." But internally, when we need weekend dishwashers, we generally just complain about how hard they are to find. The Entrepreneurial Approach encourages us to be more creative. Instead of complaining, why not just pay dishwashers more to work on Saturday nights than on Tuesdays? Better still, how about just doing it for the first four Saturdays to get your "promo" off the ground, then go back to regular rates?

Trying to get service improvements? Which do you think is more likely to get the staff's attention? An offer to send the first three departments in the organization who demonstrate a meaningful and measurable service improvement a free trip to the local amusement park? Or maybe a nice, long, not-so-juicy memo? The bottom line here is . . . the bottom line. When I talk about this idea of free-market-based rewards, managers often object that they "don't have the budget to pay for extra rewards." But my response is that if we really believe the initiative in question is going to pay such big dividends to the organization, shouldn't we put our money where our mouth is by investing in our desired outcomes? If we want to get the results, then let's compensate those who deliver them. If money is tight, we can give time—offer to go cook dinner for the staff, or clean the houses of successful staff members. Don't have time, either? Maybe other local businesses will trade gift certificates with you. Or maybe suppliers will donate their products or logo-wear to fund staff contests. What if you offer a reward and nobody "buys"? Well, what if you ran a $30 olive oil on special for $29? Not likely to get much response, right? The amount of the discount isn't enough to get the attention of the customer. Offer a drawing of a free trip to Italy with each purchase, or buy two get one free, and you know you're going to see a much better buy-in.

Take our dress code example in the New Blue Shirt Case Study. Truthfully, what's in it for staff if they wear the new blue shirt as requested? Doesn't seem like there's much, to me. So why not just jump-start our new program with a nice reward? Maybe every time you wear the new shirt for the first month you get an entry into a drawing to win a $100 gift certificate to a local clothing store. Or if you wear the new shirt twenty straight shifts you get a free shirt. Better still, consider group rewards—more on that in a minute, but let's just say if we hit a group goal of 100 percent participation in the first five days, everyone gets something small but enjoyable, such as movie tickets, a massage, or whatever would work in your business.

When I explain this at our training seminars, one or two managers in the group will inevitably object, saying something along the lines of the following:

a. "Why do I have to reward them when that's what we're paying them to do already?"

My response—based on the scenario in the case study—is that, in practice, you aren't paying them to do it. In fact, in Sue's case, she keeps showing up without the shirt, and we keep right on paying her. So if you think about it, in that all-too-common scenario, we're actually paying people *not* to do what's being asked of them.

b. "I can't afford to reward everybody for everything."

No, you can't. But the point isn't to reward everyone for everything in perpetuity. You wouldn't run every product in your store on special every day for three years straight, would you? Yet you do keep running specials, right?

The idea, in either case, is to pick a "product" or two that you think is important and then to find some way to help build organizational momentum towards their implementation. Can't afford to reward it? Then why is it worth doing? If there's no tangible return on the investment we're going to make on the dress code changing, why are we bothering to do it? And if it is truly a big issue for you—even if it's just an emotional one—then do something to find a way to reward what you'd like to see. And if it's not important, why are you stressing out over it? Remember: the rewards alone will accomplish little. You still need effective leadership, a motivated staff, competitive benefits, etc. But the point of these rewards is to use them to improve the effectiveness of our organization by helping to jump-start the change program we're trying to put in place.

What if by offering an incentive you got two of the four people who were borderline on the new blue shirts to actually wear them? That's got to save you twenty or thirty minutes a week that you'd most certainly have wasted cajoling, begging, and nagging them to wear the shirts. And if you had that twenty or thirty minutes, maybe you could invest it in spending some time where it's more important and more effective—with your best staff members, instead of with the ones who aren't performing!

What do you do if you aren't sure what will get your staff members excited? What would you do if customers weren't buying? Share your story— with the New Blue Shirt Case Study it would have made sense to actually tell staff the story behind the new shirts: why they're important, why we want people to wear them, how that will impact the business, etc. Then maybe try some survey work—ask staff what they'd like. Hold customer roundtables and try the same with staff. They'll be happy to tell you what will get them excited. And remember, it's not always money. We've often had far more excitement and interest from offering limited edition t-shirts than we have cash. Better yet, give them the budget and let them design the rewards for you! You'll be getting buy-in before the work even starts.

3. ROTATE REWARDS TO MAINTAIN HIGH YIELDS

Effective rewards need to be approached in the same way we do sustainable agriculture. What happens if you plant the same exact crop year after year? The soil gets tired, your yields go down, and you have problems with erosion. So what do you do? You can start with crop rotation. While it does require more near-term work by the grower, it keeps the soil vital and yields high. The same approach will work with reward programs. Keep them fresh. *I recommend that all reward programs come with an expiration date.* That way you help keep the rewards from becoming an entitlement and give yourself the freedom to alter the rewards regularly to meet the changing needs of your business.

The worst case is that you decide to continue a given reward program for another month or year or whatever. Maybe you didn't have time to review it.

Or maybe you liked the way it worked and you want to keep it going. But if you forget to deal with it or you aren't sure how to proceed, the program comes to an end at a given point in time. The default is to no program rather than letting one go on and on in perpetuity.

4. USE CREATIVE CONSEQUENCES

This is probably the most difficult part of the Entrepreneurial Approach to implement. *And it's not the place to start using it.* When I teach this in ZingTrain seminars I ask attendees to promise me that they'll lead with rewards no matter how excited they get about creative consequences. I firmly recommend that you *begin with creative, effective, free-market promotion and appropriate creative rewards* before you move into this realm. Used well, creative consequences can be an extremely effective management tool.

Creative consequences can reduce the frequency of use of those Four Horsemen of Ineffective Management. Cajoling, begging, and nagging are about as innovative and attention-getting as a sleepy, late-night CNN broadcast of a Senate farm bill filibuster. You and I both know they almost never work. And threatening termination is so extreme that we hardly ever act on it. So can't we come up with some stuff that's somewhere in between fretting and firing? There have got to be less extreme outcomes than outright termination. And better yet, how about some stuff that kicks into place without us having to be the ones to make it happen?

6 Elements of the Entrepreneurial Approach

1. Sell our ideas and beliefs to our staff.
2. Use free-market concepts to reward what you really want.
3. Rotate rewards to maintain high yields.
4. Use creative consequences.
5. Try group rewards and consequences.
6. Use the Entrepreneurial Approach in all directions.

What's a creative consequence? It's a meaningful, but not life- (or job-) threatening consequence that comes into play when an agreed-upon action isn't taken. Creative consequences are not punishment and they're not random or vindictive. The way we use them, they have to be *agreed upon in advance* by all involved and applied uniformly throughout the *entire* group. What are some examples of creative consequences that we've used? The management team at the Bakehouse ran a game to get caught up on staff performance reviews and agreed that if they weren't done on time, they'd all spend a Sunday afternoon washing staff members' cars. For our regular session of our Partner's Group (where all the managing partners of our organization meet every other week), we have a self-imposed, five-dollar fine for being late. While it's hard to imagine that five bucks would make a big difference to partner-level professionals, before we implemented the creative consequence it was pretty standard that one or two or more people would be late to the meeting. Their arrival was inevitably frustrating for those who were there on time, holding up or interfering with everyone else's work. But, somehow, that seemingly silly little consequence changed our whole culture. We reached—and stayed at—a point where, to this day, hardly anyone ever comes late. And when they do, they merely walk past the chairman and drop off their five dollars without much tension or comment from anyone else. The meeting always starts on time, those who are there on time benefit, those who are late—for whatever reason—just pay up and we all move on effectively.

Creative consequences are not for everything. In my experience they're most effective when used in seemingly bureaucratic, repetitive problems: the things we all commit to doing but realistically will fall short on at some point. In baseball, it's things like not running out a ground ball. In business, it's attendance, promptness, filing reports, timeliness, etc. Usually not critical in the moment, but things that will inevitably cause a slide down to ineffectiveness when we don't stick to doing them as we said we would. Winning teams don't become losing teams overnight—while talent may seem tantamount, there's a lot to be said for diligently watching the details.

To be clear, *it's very important that creative consequences should be constructive;* when they're put into place they should contribute positively back to the group or the organization at large. It could be work that's not all that desirable but clearly needs to be done anyway—cleaning bathrooms, garbage cans, dumpsters, or washing dishes on the weekend. It could be something that adds a little boost to the day of the staff, like buying cappuccino for the rest of the crew. It could be a donation to the community (which is what we do with the fines from late arrival at Partner's Group). But it needs to create some constructive interaction.

How serious do they have to be? Enough to get people to pay attention but not so intense that they really adversely affect anyone in the scheme of life. If they aren't at all meaningful (e.g., pay a penny to the community chest), then they don't get anyone's attention. On the other hand, if they're too extreme, we're creating an ethical conflict for ourselves (e.g., lose a week's pay every time you forget to wear your new blue shirt).

So why use creative consequences? For openers, because consequences are natural; when we fail to do certain things, consequences result. And when we make the consequences creative—things that return positively to the organization and the community—we're turning what's normally perceived as a negative into a win. It is, in essence, energy management recycling—we can take a loss, let people down easy, and recycle the otherwise wasted energy into a constructive use. When we don't use them, I believe that the consequences are there anyway. They're just not the consequences we intend. Even worse, these unplanned, unacknowledged consequences are usually being borne by *the very people whom we say we want to reward!*

Think back to our theoretical scenario about Sue, Jamie, and the new dress code. Who actually absorbs the stress for Sue's failure to wear the new shirt? Well, you can start with Jamie. One of our best employees, she's paid out extra cash to have more shirts on hand, she spends extra time doing laundry to have them ready, and she's losing that all-important belief in our organization that helps keeps her motivated day in and day out.

Then there are our customers—they bear the consequences too, because they get an inconsistent message from us. And then our organizational integrity pays the price. We speak the words, "wear the shirt," but our actions say, "wear whatever you want because nothing's really going to happen anyway."

What consequence does Sue bear for not wearing the new shirt? All she has to do is smile, nod, bow, and scrape her way through the old cajoling, begging, nagging, and, finally, threatened termination. In fact she sort of benefits from not wearing the new uniform; by not wearing the shirt she gets extra attention. And the more time we spend talking to her about the dress code, the less work she has to do because we keep pulling her off the line to review the situation. (Not to mention the fact that she's getting paid to have all those discussions.) Which in turn means additional consequences for poor Jamie, who's left on the line to cover while we bug Sue some more.

On the other hand, well-designed creative consequences make for a more appropriate distribution of stress in the organization. Going back to our dress code example, let's say that when you don't wear the new shirt you have to take a weekend dish shift. By the time we're done, Sue will be covering every weekend for two months! Seeing that there's some consequence for not wearing the new shirts, Jamie can relax. She sure won't be doing any dishwashing. And Laura, our general manager, can cope a little better since it'll be Sue in the dish room, not her.

What's the difference between creative consequences and punishment? To me, punishment is an action we decide to take *after the fact*. It's usually done in anger. It's not logically connected to the issue at hand. It's arbitrary and, in my belief, ineffective, unless you want everyone living in fear of random retribution. *Creative consequences*, on the other hand, *are agreed to before performance has fallen short*. They become the agreed-upon rules of the game of working in our organization. When you come to work here we tell you about them up front. They're part of our expectations. And you can say no or propose and get agreement around an alternative. But if you choose to work with us this is what we do.

Who resists implementing creative consequences? I have to laugh. I'll tell you flat out, it's almost never the people who consistently do what they say they're going to do. To a detail- and achievement-oriented person, creative consequences are usually perceived as helpful. At worst, they're neutral. Why worry what the consequences are for something you said you're going to do, when you already do it anyway? In my experience, many high achievers actually welcome the implementation of creative consequences. Why? First, because high achievers hate falling short—creative consequences give them one more reason to finish things in a timely and efficient manner. Additionally, when achievers do fall short, being able to put creative consequences into play allows them to feel right with the world: "I forgot to bring my shirt today, but I've bought the requisite cappuccino for the rest of the crew, so I've got that one off my back." (Pun actually not intended, but present nevertheless.)

So, again, who resists implementing creative consequences? Try it and see for yourself. I'll bet you dollars to bread dough that the ones who fight you most are almost always the people who are notorious for not meeting their commitments. Check it out. They'll inevitably tell you "we don't need that kind of stupid stuff." Or "people should just do these things because they're committed to them." Or "that's treating people like children." Their objections sound so sincere that we often let them off the hook. (I know, because I've fallen for these lines way too many times!) And guess what happens then? They don't come through. And we're right back to cajoling, begging, nagging, and, finally, threatening termination.

The other objection that comes up is along the lines of "Billy tried so hard to do it right, so there shouldn't be a consequence. It's not his fault." But at the end of the day, the problem is that *effort does not equal results*. What if Billy didn't try and didn't get results? Then it's not okay? How do we measure effort? What if we tried to get a customer their holiday order on time but didn't? We pay a consequence to the customer—we refund their money. In our dress code example, "trying" to wear the new blue shirt just doesn't cut it. While we all would love to get both results and effort, which one are you really paying for? What would you rather have? A staff member who "tried" to wear the new shirt but failed eight days in a row? Or another one who couldn't care less about wearing it but shows up in uniform day after day? Honestly, I'd go with the latter. (By the way, if we have a staff member who has failed to meet the commitment for understandable reasons, I have the option—and I've used it many times—of bearing the consequence *for them* so they don't have to. That respects the consequence the group has agreed to and sends the message that I take it seriously, but lets the well-intended staff member not have to pay the price this one time.)

5. TRY GROUP REWARDS AND CONSEQUENCES

At Zingerman's we focus more on the "we" at every level; it's way more about the group's success than about what any of us achieve as individuals. In truth, group rewards are almost always where I'd look first. They encourage teamwork, build collaboration, and get colleagues looking out for each other and for the organization at the same time. They also teach the reality of life—some of us will fall short, but it's the job of the rest of us to pick up the pace to get our whole group to success. Since each of us will slip up in certain situations but not in others, the diversity of the group brings more resilience and long-term success. People learn that powering through *together*—not as isolated individuals—is most often the best way to get to meaningful, sustainable success.

Done well, group rewards can get the whole of the organization focused on the same goal. Having taught (and also having read) a lot about team-building techniques, the truth is that most of those exercises are ultimately ineffective. People feel better for a few days, and then fairly quickly slide right back to where they were before the training. By contrast, getting people focused on results, where they have to work as a team to really win, is a far more effective approach. People learn to work together because without it they can't win. People like winning. And once they get used to winning, almost no one wants to go back to losing.

Group rewards, and the achievements that accrue from them, help organizations avoid the sort of infighting that can come from solo contests when what we'd rather encourage is teamwork. They help bring peer pressure into play to get the group going. They encourage people to really work together. Similarly, group consequences can get the higher-achieving team members to help mentor and guide the work of the poorer performers. In either case, you're effectively turning peer pressure from your best staff members onto those least likely to succeed. And that pressure will often be far more effective a tool than anything you or I can do "commanding" from "above."

6. Use the Entrepreneurial Approach in All Directions

Remember that although our organizational chart may show any number of staff members reporting to you, you really need to manage everyone you come into contact with—your boss, your peers, your customers, yourself. In this context, all of the information outlined here about our Entrepreneurial Approach to Management is applicable in all of these directions. Propose creative rewards and consequences with your peers; use them to get yourself to do what needs to be done and to reward yourself for taking on a long-running challenge; propose entrepreneurial (ad)ventures to your boss; market your new approaches to your peers to get early buy-in, etc.

The driving issue for me is *not* about some manipulative form of motivation. I think this method is the opposite of manipulation. The Entrepreneurial Approach encourages free, mindful choice, and respects the free market in a constructive, up-front, nondiscriminatory, team-oriented way. If we offer a reward, it ought to be because a particular result or behavior is actually worth more to us. In the same way that a great handmade cheese costs more to make and sells for more on the market, effectively delivered service takes more careful consideration and is worth more in the workplace. *Collaboration and group achievement are worth even more still.* If we use the Entrepreneurial Approach, we can clearly encourage, support, and assist everyone we work with to go that route—in the end getting better results all the way around. In the process, we can do a lot to undercut the old passive-aggressive reliance on authority, hierarchy, and people's habit of going along rather than making waves.

The old model, I would argue, is the opposite—manipulative, parental, ineffective, and not much fun. While I still slip on occasion, for the most part I'm done with it. And, I might add, very happily so. Selling stuff you believe in beats the heck out of nagging any day of the week.

Successful Free Market Management

Just to be clear, the Entrepreneurial Approach isn't going to remake your organization overnight. If people are used to the old model, they're not going to get all that excited about entrepreneurial activity inside the organization the first time you try it. Meaningful organizational change takes time; to make the Entrepreneurial Approach work, you have to stick with it consistently while you and those around you get comfortable with it. Using the metaphor of our organization as a sustainable small farm, you can't make change happen overnight—if you want to convert from conventional farming to organic, the minimum legal requirement is three years—you have to have time for poisons to be purged from the soil before new, organic, heirloom seeds will really grow. Once the soil in your organization has been reenergized, new ideas—like the Entrepreneurial Approach—will generally take more quickly. Change, as we've already discussed at length, isn't easy, and there's always resistance. After all, it's almost always easier to stay with the same old problems we've gotten so used to complaining about. But aren't you tired of those same old problems? Carrying an inordinate share of stress on your shoulders? Being mad at people around you who don't do the things that they've said they're going to do? The Entrepreneurial Approach is one tool that can help you get out of this old, tired reality into a new, more invigorating, more rewarding reality of your own choosing.

One of the best byproducts of using the Entrepreneurial Approach is that it helps us to develop business people, instead of just "training employees." When we get managers and staff to use it, we're helping them to learn how business works in the real world. In small but manageable ways, they're getting the chance to see how the free market functions, how you can be creative and have fun in business and in management instead of being bureaucratic. It gets you out of the old, parental, "what's fair" model and into the real world in which we operate as business people every day. And it helps us leave the Four Horsemen—cajoling, begging, nagging, and, finally, threatening termination—far behind, and shift to a far more sustainable, productive, positive, peer-to-peer approach to work.

Use the Entrepreneurial Approach to let people own and enjoy successes; let them taste the bitterness of failure and enjoy the wealth of success for themselves. Help them find a way to go forward. Help them learn how the business world works, because that's how they're going to be successful: by thinking more like positive, creative, proactive business people and less like employees.

notes from the back dock

The Inside Scoop on Working Here at Zingerman's

Jessica Fishwick, Retail Counter Person, Zingerman's Bakeshop

Working at Zingerman's has completely redefined my understanding of community and service. It's simple, but it's about genuinely supporting those around you.

I like to give the example of when I went to Zingerman's Roadhouse one night with a good friend who was in town. There I ran into my mom, dad, and brother, who were seated in the same room as us. I also saw some of the other ZCoB partners, and a frequent customer I serve at the Bakeshop. Ari was pouring water for folks, and when I introduced myself to our server I learned she was one of my boss's daughters. I realized I knew eleven people in the dining room, and I thought it was all a funny coincidence until I reflected on it further and realized it was no coincidence at all; it's community!

We learn in our early orientation classes at Zingerman's that it is 100 percent the responsibility of the managers to train the new employees. But it's also 100 percent the responsibility of the new employees to take control of their training. This analogy can be made between a business and its customers, too. It's usual to think of servers at a restaurant as serving the customers, but at a place like Zingerman's—and I imagine many other successful businesses—the opposite is true as well. The customers really, truly serve the business. It's a 100 percent/100 percent service exchange.

It's pretty amazing to think about the millions of people worldwide who are affected by what Zingerman's does. But it's almost even more amazing to think about the core thousands of customers who regularly frequent the businesses, who go to as many Zingerman's events as they can, who make efforts to get to know the employees and other regulars, who truly identify the business (maybe not even consciously) as an important part of their life, and who rely on it as much as the business relies on them (like the eleven people I knew at the Roadhouse that night). They support the business, and the business supports them. And along these lines, as an employee, it's highly unlikely that I will ever buy a baguette or cream cheese from anywhere else, because I want to support the businesses that directly or indirectly write my paycheck and support my lifestyle. And that's community!

jenny tucker, roadhouse butcher from heLL (heLL, michigan, that is)

Moving Your Organization from V to A

18 Do's and Don'ts of Better Management

Here is a list of basic, but important, small things that leaders can (and by all rights ought to) do to be effective in their work. Unlike most of this book, what follows aren't even remotely "secrets"—it's all been said many times before. The radical thing would be to actually do them every day! If you believe, as I do, that the little things make all the difference, then this "secret" is a great place to start your leadership work. Following through, being consistent, and acting in caring and considerate ways are simple and old-fashioned, but, ultimately, they're incredibly effective ways to raise energy and build a better business.

＿＿＿＿＿

While I was winding up the work on this book, I had coffee with a good friend. She was telling me her frustrations of working for a boss who was, shall we say, not exactly the sort of leader I've been writing about here. It's safe to say that Servant Leadership, Stewardship, and the Entrepreneurial Approach were not part of his portfolio. The conversation with my friend was a combination of her incredible irritation and annoyance over the obvious absurdity of the way her boss was behaving, blended with the simultaneous acceptance that's come from years of learning to effectively work with—and around—him. Other than a coup d'état or quitting, there really isn't much she can do—the organization is successful, she has a good job that she really likes, and she believes passionately in her product. Her boss isn't a bad guy; he's just a bad boss.

Her story is all too incredibly common. There are millions of smart, caring people stuck in similar situations all over the country. You might be one or, more likely, know someone who's in the same sort of spot. Most learn, as my friend has, to work around it; they know their boss isn't going to change, so they simply try to steer clear and make positive change happen where they can anyway. I know my friend has come up with a range of creative ways to get things done in spite of the strange and unproductive stuff that swirls around her. In reality, she's pretty much made peace with the problem—it's hardly the end of the world and, although she's regularly frustrated, coup d'états and quitting aren't good options for anyone with a house payment and a couple of kids to raise, especially when she likes a lot about her job.

There's not really any big story to blow the cover off here; what's wrong in corporate America's everyday existence was already immortalized long ago in stuff like Dilbert, and I've already given you my sense of things in the essay on the energy crisis back on page 35. As my friend was sharing her story it dawned on me that with all my high-spirited, service-oriented, and abundantly positive approaches to leadership, I might have missed out on some of the more basic issues of management. Hence, the appearance of what follows—a long list of the basic do's and don'ts of business leadership: fairly straightforward, simple to agree to, hard to live up to, little things that contribute (or not, as the case might be) towards helping anyone who's interested in being a better boss. What got me thinking was the unglamorous, yet all-too-common, spirit-killing nature of it all when it's not done well.

When you get right down to it, nothing on this list is particularly creative, innovative, or controversial; in fact, it's fairly likely to be stuff that anyone who aspires to leadership greatness, anywhere, and in any era, would want to do. Autocrats, anarchists, assistant managers, entrepreneurs, and eighth-grade teachers would all, I believe, benefit from doing all the do's and foregoing the don'ts that follow. Really, anyone who's interested could be good at them.

I don't take credit for inventing anything that's on this list. For better or for worse (probably both) it's all been done many times before. I'm quite sure that all the positives here have been written about two thousand times elsewhere. Every tip on the list has, I'm confident, been covered in classes and essays by everyone from Stephen Covey to Jim Collins, Peter Drucker to Peter Kropotkin. It's hardly shocking material—stuff like showing up on time, saying thank you, and being supportive of your staff isn't at all innovative. But in the context of this book I want to lay it out here. Managing your energy well is great, but if you don't answer emails from staff, your effectiveness is inevitably undercut. Thinking of staff as customers is a key component of Servant Leadership, but belief in the concept without coming through on what you committed to delivering isn't going to win many staff members over to your cause.

Because some of us learn better by playing off the positive, while others do better being warned about what's wrong, I decided to write my list both ways. It is like an upside-down book of management. The A list is the positive side of the coin. In my case, the *A* might stand for Anarcho-Capitalism, but it's just the right thing to do and would probably fit perfectly into any caring, thoughtful philosophy. It's a list of positive, energy-building, courtesy-based behaviors that are guaranteed to make anyone a more effective boss, regardless of industry, ideology, ability to innovate, or anything else. For those who are already living the list effectively every day, it'll probably seem overly obvious; feel free, in that case, to skim through it quickly and then just cut and paste it somewhere so that it can be of service to new staff to whom this stuff might be somewhat less obvious than it is to you.

By contrast, the other list is made up of all the things I'd recommend that any leader attempting to perform at an above-average level would most definitely want to avoid doing. I feel a bit funny putting them down on paper—I can't imagine any manager *tries* to be bad. But any hope I had that my friend's struggle was a one-off experience was dashed by showing this essay to others I know. I don't think anyone's yet teaching Bad Management 101, but the stuff on the list happens so frequently that it might well have been sent out from Washington as some all-American-business standard operating procedure. It's all too clear that this stuff can happen pretty much anywhere—in organizations of every size, with any set of values, political orientation, for-profit or not-for-profit, in any industry, and in any part of the country.

It is the sort of screwed up, unnecessary behavior by bosses that my friend was so frustrated about. As I've said, she's not alone—by the time I'd shown the list to six or eight people I knew around the country, it was clear that they'd been through this bad manager wringer so many times that they were actually laughing out loud as they went through the list. "Oh yeah. My boss definitely does that!" "Oh, yeah, and he does that, too," they'd add as they went down the list. Then they'd laugh sort of an eerie, slightly strange laugh and add, "And that one, oh, yeah, he definitely does that one too!" Granted it was a rather, shall we say, bitter, biting bit of humor—they were laughing at what is clearly so endemic that they probably really wanted to cry but knew there was no longer any point. If tears could turn things around, North America would be on a huge economic high. Others clearly were still very close to it all—folks who are still trying to find a way to survive in this sometimes sordid, sometimes silly, reality didn't see much humor in it all.

If the A list is the stuff we all aspire to, I was going to call the second, don't-do, side of things the B list. But as I worked on all of this, I realized that perhaps the more appropriate letter to use was a V. Which, in this case, stands for "victim." The behaviors on the V list are things that ineffective leaders—intentions actually unknown—do that create a culture in which victims rule. Quite simply, it's all the stuff I'd suggest one would want to avoid. It's odd, actually; I know that no one writes a long-term organizational vision in which victims play the starring role, but somehow managers do all this stuff anyway. Bosses behave badly, they believe the worst, they act arbitrarily, angrily, and inconsiderately. They unwittingly (or maybe wittingly) work over their own staff by undercutting them, underpreparing them, and embarrassing them in public, by claiming to have said things they've never said, then denying claims they made a month earlier. One week they act like autocrats, the next week they're inclusive, and in the third they're neither—"just following the rules sent down from corporate."

One outcome of all that not-so-admirable activity is that we end up with a plethora of organizations overloaded with victims. It's what early 20th-century anarchist Gustav Landauer referred to as "a spirit of resignation that delights in replacing action with permanent and meaningless complaint." While many folks (like my friend) who work in these situations figure out how to make good things happen in spite of their boss's behavior, all too many simply slide into being victims: nothing they can do, they're not in charge, they're not on the board, they're not the one who hired the boss, and no one asked their opinion anyway. All of which, I'm all too certain, contributes mightily to the energy crisis in the workplace; while you wouldn't know it from reading the front page of the papers or watching TV talk shows, common courtesy isn't tied to corporate tax rates.

To be clear, I doubt that anyone actually goes home and decides to intentionally initiate any of the things on the V list. I don't imagine that even the most mean-spirited managers actually want to screw up their staff; they just, clearly if incoherently, do it anyway. Please know that I didn't put these lists together in order to embarrass anyone. We're all human and we all have habits and instinctive responses that aren't really in synch with what we believe. Speaking of which, I'm hardly immune from doing these things. I've slipped, I'm very sure, and done all of them at one point or another. The V list is here just to help raise our awareness; if acceptance is the first step towards recovery, then knowing that this stuff is happening is a very solid step in the right direction. From there the simple act of consciously deciding not to do them can only help make your business—and really, the whole world—a better place! It is, after all, all about free choice. Me, I'm gonna try to get on the A team.

1. ALWAYS BE CONSIDERATE

A LIST As I told a classroom full of K-4 kids a few years ago, "Kindness is free." A gentle hand, a welcoming tone, and a caring question are almost always appreciated. Thinking of things from someone else's perspective, having empathy, and looking at a task from the point of view of a new employee are always helpful. Used rotely, polite words are pretty much meaningless; but saying them when you mean them, truly thinking kindly and considerately of others, means the world. If nothing else, you exude good energy, which surely will get you good energy in return, and get your entire organization going in the right direction.

1. BE RUDE

I don't know if this is so stupidly obvious as to make it unworthy of appearing here, but rudely riding over others, cutting people off midsentence, yelling unnecessarily, and, basically, just being a jerk are never helpful behaviors. Behaving this way **V LIST** helps no one, least of all the leader who's doing it. To quote early 20th-century Italian anarchist, Errico Malatesta, "Hate does not produce love, and by hate one cannot remake the world." What it does do is sow seeds of victimhood—when people can't get heard, when no one cares what they think, when they're shut down and shut off before they've even finished sharing their thoughts, then starting to think and feel like a victim comes naturally. What else can you do?

2. BE CONSISTENT

A LIST Whatever style you choose for yourself as a leader, one key is to keep living it as consistently as possible every day. One of the most important roles for any leader is to create confidence; and that confidence is, in part (though certainly not fully), based on consistency. People want to know what they can count on—the more consistent we are, the less they're worrying about the random wackiness we're going to do or say next. If you want to be strict, that's fine—just be strict all the time. If you want to keep things loose, that's lovely—just do that all the time. The point is just to be consistent with your energy, your personality, your decision style, your . . . everything.

2. Be All over the Place

By contrast, the most frustrating bosses to be engaged with are all over the place: open to input and appreciative on one day, then distant and dictatorial on the next. Sure, I'm an anarchist, but I'm not at all about being unprofessional. People can learn to cope with most anything; even undesirable behaviors done daily are probably less stressful to adjust to than a manager who's mellow on Monday, tough on Tuesday, wimpy on Wednesday, thorough on Thursday, fun loving on Friday, scattered on Saturday, and sensitive and supportive on Sunday. This scattershot style is only productive if you're out to produce a victim mindset in your staff. When bosses are predictable only in their unpredictability, people on the front lines don't go for greatness, they just look for cover. No sane frontline person wants to step up and take a leadership role on a shift when they don't know what role the leaders will be playing until they show up for work.

3. Be Reasonable

While it's true that we're not on Planet Fair (see *Zingerman's Guide to Giving Great Service* for details on that one), it's way easier to work with, and for, a manager who's reasonable and who consistently and effectively explains their reasoning. Look, even the most spoiled souls among us know that we're not going to get our way every single time. What everyone does want is to know that, whatever decision is delivered, there was a fair process behind it. I'm not necessarily talking about Solomon-like wisdom or breathtaking leadership brilliance—just some balanced, reasonable, ethically oriented thinking and decisions that are explicable without expletives. Whether your organizational orientation is anarchistic, autocratic, or anywhere in between, pretty much all adults like to know why we're doing what we're doing and why we're asking them to do what we're asking them to do.

3. Be Arbitrary

By contrast, managers whose comebacks to questions about their decisions include things like, "That's the way it is," "Just take care of it," "I'm in charge here," or " I don't want to talk about it—just get it done," are anything but effective. While

I know there's something going on in those managers' minds, from the outside it sure seems like their decisions are random, driven more by mood or electrical disconnects than by depth, deference, and attention to detail. Arbitrary action at the top leads verily towards victimhood as well. When reason, reality, and what's right have little to do with what the bigwigs decide, it's hard not to feel like one's future is completely out of control. Frontline folks are, literally, at the mercy of the way the management winds happen to blow on any given day. And when frontline people start basing their actions on the mood of the manager, you can be sure that the business is not benefiting.

4. BRING GOOD ENERGY

Effective leaders, without question, will bring positive energy to the workplace almost every day. Through thick and thin, profit and painful loss, successes and shortfalls, the best bosses stay positive pretty much all the time. While none of us are perfect, the ability to bring a good game face every day is a huge help. Everything, after all, starts with us, and if our presence is positive, calm, and focused, it's far more likely that everyone else around us will show up in a similar style. All of which means better decisions, better teamwork, and better business.

4. BRING BAD ENERGY TO WORK

Bad energy from the boss can break down an organization's culture far more effectively than any frontline cynics ever will. Remember, whether you intend it or not, for better and for worse, everyone around you will pick up your energy. When the energy at the top is bad or erratic, everyone knows it in an instant. The best possible scenario in this situation is that people still believe in the "cause" and learn to lay low—they want to, and will do, good work in spite of consistently poor leadership. At worst they take bad energy as the everyday norm, in which case they, knowingly or not, start to replicate it. Before long your entire organization will be sending bad vibes out into the universe. The connection between the energy crisis in the American workplace and the economy is exceptionally clear. You can laugh if you like, but I'll tell you flat out that it's only a matter of time before bad energy leads to bad bottom-line results.

Victims thrive on bad energy the way vampires feast on blood. Under cover of organizational darkness, they'll sink their teeth into the necks of negatively oriented managers and then carry that bad juju throughout the rest of the organization in no time flat. Flipping that otherworldly analogy around, I'll posit that positive energy is to victims what mirrors are to the vampires—put it in front of them and they'll flee the room forthwith. Good energy, at the end of the day, is a victim killer—they can't stand to be around it for any length of time.

5. Be Humble and Share the Credit

 Effective leaders, I think, always share the success—emotionally, financially, and otherwise—with the group. Generosity of spirit and pretty much everything else as well can only help. Effective leaders are also pretty humble. They don't brag, they don't bullshit, and they're always deferential. No matter what they've achieved, they'll almost always tell you that others did most of the work, that it can all be done better down the road, and that they have a whole lot yet to learn. And, actually, no matter how much they've achieved, that statement is still very accurate. Constantly affirming—assuming you mean it—your desire to keep learning and improving sets the right tone for the rest of the team.

If you've done a lot to lead the way, don't worry; everyone will know without you having to tell them how great you are. Ultimately, it's really all about the group anyway, and giving credit liberally and consistently to others will almost inevitably raise the effectiveness of the entire group. For effective leaders, it's pretty literally always about the team. Jim Collins, in his classic book, *Good to Great*, laid out five levels of leadership. The highest, L5, is marked by a blend of humility and will. "The central dimension for Level 5 is a leader who is ambitious first and foremost for the cause, for the company, for the work, not for himself or herself, and has an absolutely terrifying iron will to make good on that ambition. It is that combination, the fact that it is not about them, it's not first and foremost for them, it is for the company and its long-term interests, of which they are just a part."

5. Brag, Get Cocky, and Grab All the Attention

Yeah, I know that there are bosses who pull this off and are somehow seen by society as big successes. But there are also thieves who make off with lots of other people's money and live to tell the tale; that doesn't mean anyone else needs to aspire to replicate their unethical activity. The need to be the center of attention can be somewhat endearing at the age of seven, but in a CEO it's anything but. Bragging by the boss rarely achieves anything good; cockiness, I suppose, somewhere, must have its place—maybe it works when you're about to play in the Super Bowl, but best I can tell that's about it. No one who works for any of those people will ever speak up—why risk it? But don't let the lack of frustration being expressed fool you; I can't believe that anyone actually likes being around a bragging boss. Even if it works for a while, it's anything but sustainable. Victims fit in very well with self-centered CEO types; when the boss is busy bragging, the cynics can have lots of fun finding all of his or her faults from the safety of the sideline. And since the spotlight is pretty much permanently fixed on the boss, it's easy to complain regularly from the corners of the corporate culture without risk of anyone really noticing.

6. Take Responsibility

There's really nothing fancy or insightful about this one—people like to be led by people who are quick to own responsibility for everything around them. I don't mean over-functioning and letting others off the hook. I just mean that blaming, deflecting, or disappearing when the problems come up and the pressure's on is never a good idea. It makes little or no difference what line of work you're in, how big your organization is, what your politics are, or when you plan to retire: effective leaders are always up for taking responsibility. Even if it's something that we ourselves didn't do wrong, even if it's something that we actually asked others not to do, even if we weren't here when it happened or didn't have a chance to properly input: at the end of the day, the issue still lands on our—the leader's—plate. It's simple, really—if it happened while we're in charge, we're responsible. Which means that, while we want to share credit liberally (what's the risk?), we also want to be quick to own any errors that might have occurred. As per our 5 Steps to Handling a Complaint and our belief in Servant Leadership, we can start correcting course by acknowledging the problem and then apologizing (for more on that see page 127). Extenuating circumstances and creative excuses are all well and good, but we remain responsible nevertheless.

6. ABDICATE, DENY RESPONSIBILITY, OR ACT LIKE YOU DIDN'T KNOW (ESPECIALLY IF EVERYONE KNOWS YOU DID)

In honesty, most all of us will have slipped and done one or all of these. But when they become a regular routine, most everything good about the organization starts to erode. Leaders who blame others aren't likely to earn the respect of the organization. If we act helpless and unempowered, it's pretty safe to say that the rest of the organization will soon follow suit. Worse still, if we act like we knew nothing about something, when everyone else knows we did (via email, in meetings, conversations, etc.), our organizational integrity, effectiveness, and energy will all steadily start to decline. Victims, of course, love this approach from their leaders; in a setting in which even those at the top refuse to own the issues at hand, it's all the easier for anyone else who wants to avoid taking responsibility for anything. After a while, the whole experience starts to feel a bit like Alice in Wonderland. Responsibility means nothing. Reality never happened. Quite simply, we'll never get to greatness if what we say is not what we do.

7. SHOW YOUR BELIEF IN THOSE AROUND YOU

The more we believe in the abilities, creativity, and commitment of the people we have with us, the more likely they are to perform at ever higher levels. Belief isn't a magic pill that guarantees great performance, but it sure increases the odds. I've come to see belief, basically, as a modifier—it can enhance whatever natural abilities anyone has, or, when the leader doesn't believe, it will work in reverse, making everyone worse than they would have probably been left to their own devices. A bit of belief costs nothing and will go a long ways towards making wonderful things happen.

7. CONVEY CONSTANT CRITICISM, DISBELIEF, AND DISTRUST

Those three, without a huge infusion of positive belief to counterbalance them, are a recipe for certain failure. When the leader acts like others have nothing to offer, I will forecast with high confidence that will be your collective future. The staff will perform poorly, and the leader will lament ever hiring them. Each on its own is undesirable; together, the three create instability, uncertainty, and ineffectiveness, the only reward for which is that the negative leaders get to be right about how awful everyone around them is. Talk about alignment—this is the near-perfect breeding ground for victims and cynics. They thrive on believing the worst, so what more could they ask for than a boss who actively shares that worldview.

8. FOLLOW THROUGH!

This entry on the A list is surprisingly uncommon, as basic as it is. I've already mentioned this back in Secret 23, but it's so shocking to me that I'm going to repeat it again: Data says that American executives complete only 50 percent of what they commit to doing. Batting .500 in baseball is beyond-belief good; in leadership, it's embarrassingly horrific. How can we expect anyone else to do well when we only do half of what we say we're going to do? We are, after all, the bar by which everyone else will likely measure their performance. Following through is not fancy—if you get a phone call or an email or a letter, just respond. If you say you're going to be at a meeting, it's good to actually show up as you said you would. And if, for whatever reason, you realize that you aren't going to get to it, just apologize and let everyone know in advance. It's no different than what we'd expect from a staff member who was thinking of calling in sick.

I know that we all mess up. I've certainly dropped the ball any number of times. But when our stack of misses is as high as our successes, something's seriously wrong. Winning teams don't make a lot of silly mistakes; great organizations get the little things done; and leaders of winning organizations, both large and small, know that it all starts with them. The way I see it, it's our bar to set, but the higher the rate of follow through we can deliver, regardless of all else, the better the rest of the company's going to run.

8. Drop the Ball Regularly

I don't really know any great way to say this. It's so simple, but really, all too shockingly common. If all managers did was return phone calls promptly and answer emails in a reasonable time frame, organizations could improve their effectiveness about eighteen times in a mere ten days. I actually made those stats up (in honor of the late, great, Moose Millard, former Southwest Airlines pilot and presenter on leadership, who once fired off in front of an audience of about 400 that "46 percent of statistics are made up on the spot!"), but they're probably not all that far off. Answering email, showing up for scheduled training sessions, and returning phone calls are the free-throw shooting, the foundation laying, or whatever analogy you want to use, of organizational life. If you don't do them well, it won't really matter how well you do all the more glamorous work—no matter what else you create, no matter how great your highlight films look, the edges of everything will always be fraying. By the way, ball dropping and a record of "incompletes" at the top creates an ideal work environment for victims—if no one is doing what they're supposed to do, how can they possibly be held responsible for anything?

9. Listen Well

I've gone on at length on this subject in the essay on Servant Leadership. Robert Greenleaf writes, "I believe that the first step in good communication, anywhere, is listening." He goes on to explain, "Everyone who aspires to strength should consciously practice listening, regularly. Every week, set aside an hour to listen to somebody who might have something to say that will be of interest. It should be conscious practice in which all of the impulses to argue, inform, judge, and 'straighten out' the other person are denied. Every response should be calculated to reflect interest, understanding, seeking for more knowledge. You can practice listening for brief periods, too. Just thirty seconds of concentrated listening may make the difference between understanding and not understanding something important." I like what Greenleaf says—if you create even a limited slot for adding active listening to your weekly routines, it's safe to say that the quality of your leadership work will improve. Have you had listening practice yet today?

Brenda Ueland and the "Fine Art of Listening"

Lord knows how many business books I've read over the years. But if you asked me to tell you which ten or twelve pages changed my leadership work more than any other, I'd probably say that it was an essay by Brenda Ueland. "Tell Me More: On the Fine Art of Listening" is, I'm sure, never referenced in business schools nor, for all I know, in any school anywhere. Yet it probably should be required reading for first-year MBA candidates, if not everyone in the country. It was published first in her Twin Cities newspaper column in the middle of the 20th century, then reprinted in 1992 (seven years after her death at the age of ninety-three) in *Strength to Your Sword Arm,* a collection of her essays.

Given all that I've read, it might be hard to imagine, but it's true—those ten pages totally changed the way I come to work. I suppose, in a sense, I was ready to listen to what Brenda had to say. I'd read her book *If You Want to Write* a year or two earlier and that, too, had a huge impact on me. Writing became a whole lot more fun, and probably entirely more effective, after I found Brenda! On top of which, I was in a learning mode in my life—particularly reflective and especially open to insight—when I read the essay. "When the student is ready, the teacher will appear" is certainly both apropos and accurate. But in this case it's Brenda, not me, who should get the credit. She brought the wisdom. All I did was listen.

It's not like I didn't know that listening was important before I read her essay. Everyone knows it. The hard part is doing it. Like everything, good listening is a whole lot easier said than it ever is done. To do it, to really do it, in the engaged, interested, meaningful, emotionally connected way that Brenda Ueland writes about, you need to have a sense of what listening really is. You need—or at least I did—to do it from your core.

Coming back to my world, I suppose listening is not unlike tasting. Everyone eats, and consequently, most consider themselves fully qualified to critique food. But there's a difference between personal opinion and meaningful professional culinary assessment. Anyone can do the former any time, but tasting as a professional entails noticing all the nuance and complexity that's actually present in the food; while anyone is able, very few actually take the time and pay enough attention to do it well. The biggest key, I think, is merely just slowing down, paying attention, and taking it all in, studying the subtleties in the same way that anyone who loves anything pays close attention to it.

The same, I learned from Brenda Ueland, is also true of listening. Everyone hears, and everyone talks, which makes most people think that they're immediately and eminently qualified as expert listeners. But the truth is that few of us take the time and energy to really listen in a way that I would equate with professional food assessment. It's worth the effort to boost our abilities. I know it changed the way I work. As Brenda writes, "[L]istening is a magnetic and strange thing, a creative force."

Paul, my partner, is a natural. He was already doing this sort of high-skill listening stuff when we started the Deli in the early '80s. I, on the other hand, probably sucked. I'm not a natural, which means that I have to really work at it. Brenda's essay got me going. If you listen, you learn. A lot. And if you listen, really listen to the nuance—the same way I and others around me taste a new cheese that just showed up from some farm in southern Wisconsin—perhaps, more than any other single thing you or I can do, our leadership skills will soar.

Not yet convinced? Try it for a day, or at the least maybe two hours, and see what happens. To get myself going I often take notes to help me stay focused and keep my mouth shut and my mind open. I will 100 percent guarantee that, truly, only good things can come of it—the people around you, the folks you are paying, partnering with, leading, and learning to appreciate, will only benefit from your listening work. And that doesn't even count what good things will come from careful listening to customers! To quote Brenda, "When we are listened to, it creates us, makes us unfold and expand. Ideas actually begin to grow within us and come to life."

If what's in this book prompts you to read one thing, I say, make it Brenda's essay. The truth is, it helped me so much I want to reprint the whole thing here. You can read it online right now, or, better still, buy a copy of *Strength to Your Sword Arm*. If it helps you half as much as it did me, it could be the best ten pages you've ever read.

9. TUNE OUT

There's a fine line between high levels of focus that lead to greatness and totally tuning out the struggles, hopes, and dreams of others around you. I love the book *Ignore Everybody*, but author Hugh MacLeod makes clear that he doesn't mean those words literally. He's writing about going after your dreams and passions. In his context, "ignoring everybody" means going for greatness (as you define it for yourself) and not succumbing to the stagnation of the status quo. But he's not suggesting that we should literally just stop being sensitive. Caring and connection pay big dividends; but being uncaring and callous and tuning out what's going on in the lives (at work and at home) of your staff members leads to a large emotional deficit. Really, if you want to alienate anyone you work with, you could start simply and effectively ignoring whatever they say. Victims, of course, totally love this scenario since their entire worldview works off their belief that no one is listening to them anyway. Please understand that I'm not suggesting you start taking orders from the new short-order cook—listening doesn't mean you have to do what the person who's speaking is suggesting you do, just that you truly hear what they have to say, both in spirit and in substance.

10. BE REAL

For much more on this subject, see Secret 29 on Anarcho-Capitalism. But for the moment, let me just suggest that effective leaders learn to consistently share their feelings in inoffensive, meaningful ways that allow others to hear what they're saying but still not feel completely put upon or instantly buried under someone else's inappropriate emotional avalanche. People like to know that the people they work for are people, too. As long as it's done in an appropriate and timely way, sharing that you're anxious, angry, unsure, etc., is usually perfectly fine. Don't confuse being real with being really weak. Showing uncertainty at times does not have to mean you're indecisive or incompetent. To the contrary, when you've asked people's input to improve the outcomes, when you're making mindful and meaningful decisions, when they know you had your doubts but decided in a considered and caring way to go forward anyway, I think they're far more likely to get behind you. To pig farmer

Emile DeFelice's point (see page 13), we pretty much do everything the opposite of how it's done in the mainstream work world. The old school says that sharing uncertainty is weak and a sure way to fail; I say it's a sign of strength and a certain way to increase the odds of winning!

10. Fake It

No one of any ability wants to be around someone who's not authentic. Everyone knows that leaders are human; acting like we have no feelings, or are infallible, only focuses everyone on finding our flaws. Which, of course, they'll have little trouble doing since we all have problems aplenty. I know many management books out there that argue "Leaders should never show fear," but I can't fathom how that can work in the real world. Expressing that you have some fear is a far cry from acting out of fear, or letting panic take over in your organization. Of course, the paradox is that neither I nor anyone else can really coach you on how to do it. By definition, authenticity has to emerge from within. As Simon Synek says in his book, *Start with Why*, "You can't ask others what you have to do to be more authentic. Being authentic means that you already know." Take note that the more dysfunctionally we deal with the world, the more inauthentic everything becomes. In a setting in which everyone is slightly off center, victims generally prosper. It's like living in one of those fun houses: when everyone and everything is different than they seem, no one has time to worry about warding off the passive-aggressive power of the victims.

11. Honor the Way Others Feel

Simply seeing others for who they are, acknowledging the way they feel and think, treating them with respect, getting to know where people are at, is all hugely important work. Add in a little empathy and appreciation and you're really on a roll. Remember, just because you honor them as human beings doesn't mean you're obligated to do what they want you to do—it just means you're not regularly beating on them to be someone other than who they are. You can honor others' feelings and then still constructively and caringly encourage them to go well beyond their comfort zone in the interest of personal growth and organizational success. By the way, the biggest cause of burnout, I believe, is people going to work in a setting not in synch with their values. By contrast, when people feel respected and appreciated, and when they feel their values are in alignment with those of the organization, their commitment goes up, their energy increases, and all our outcomes improve. Everyone's ability to be real with themselves and with each other increases as well.

11. DENY PEOPLE'S FEELINGS

Telling someone not to feel the way that they feel is a pretty surefire way towards a leadership shortfall. There's simply no good outcome from it—either frontline staff accept your inaccurate views, in which case they start to deny their feelings, even to themselves; or, equally undesirable, they learn not to be vulnerable in your presence, and they simply hide how they really feel about things. Denying reality leads, very surely and steadily, to a dysfunctional world in which "up" starts to be "down," "a" starts to mean "b," and "yes" means "no." If you really want to live on the other side of the looking glass, I guess you can go for it. It's so confusing that everything takes far longer, energy falls rapidly, and less and less gets done every day. What's a well-ensconced victim to do?

12. DON'T HOLD GRUDGES

Look, everyone in the world, sooner or later, will fall short on something. Most of us mess up a couple things most every day. Although I know that one can argue otherwise, I'd suggest that hardly any of those mistakes are made mindfully. And even if they are, holding grudges, getting back at someone for behaving badly, punishing people over and over again for an error that occurred eight or nine years ago just isn't helpful. Sure, it makes sense to be incensed by others' shortfalls but acting on the anger, being vindictive, is never a good move. By contrast, the spirit of understanding and generosity, letting go of what's long since done, can only create positive energy in your organization.

12. Be as Vindictive as You Can Be

Not really much to say here—it's all in the history books. Read up on the Hatfields and McCoys, watch any of the Godfather films on late-night cable, or read the Congressional transcripts from health care or tax code issues. Vendettas make for great novels but they're never helpful in building a great business.

13. Never Act in Anger

I'm not saying don't be angry. Others may have done things that reasonably triggered your anger. I'm not suggesting that you don't let people know that you are angry. I'm just saying that other than in an exceptional emergency situation where the sky is literally, or figuratively, falling, making a decision in the moment, while you're angry, is always a bad move. Quite simply, nothing good can come of it. When I'm having a really bad day, the best thing I can usually do is go for a run—it's my adult version of a "time out." Know what works for you. To the same point, someone shared with me a saying from the Persian philosopher Rumi that goes something like this: "When you're drunk and near a cliff, sit down." Enough said?

13. Act in Anger

If your primary intent is to relieve your own stress, and secondarily to prove a point to people who should have known better in the first place, acting in anger is a great way to kill both of those bad business birds with one deadly decision stone. Seriously, if you start firing off decisions when discomfort is high and your anger is building, you may feel better for the first five minutes, but after that you're pretty much guaranteed to get yourself and, unfortunately, your firm in trouble. I haven't acted in anger often, but every time I have I spend days—and on occasion weeks or months—making it all right again. If you have nothing better to do with your time and you want to bring some emotional sadomasochism into your management work, I guess you can go for it. Personally, I try to remind myself of the time when I was eight and got so angry I broke my own toy truck to prove a point. Then I was *really* upset—with myself. I wanted my toy back, but what can you do? The point I'd made wasn't the one I was after, but that really bad, stupid feeling imprinted so deeply on my mind that I can usually keep myself from slipping up too badly.

14. BE APPRECIATIVE

A LIST I've already said this many times elsewhere, but I don't think I can say it enough, so here it is again. Better leaders pretty much always say thanks! They say it with feeling and they say it a lot! Appreciating others, both in the moment and also when it's least expected, is an excellent way to get any business going in the right direction. I'm probably saying this as much for my own self-discipline as anything else—if I'm not careful, I, like so many overachievers, can slide into acting as if I don't appreciate much of anything at all. The good news is showing appreciation is easy, and like kindness, it's free; learning to be actively and effectively appreciate is not rocket science, and it's far simpler than almost anything else one would do to run a business. You can start by just saying thanks at the end of every shift. You can follow that by thanking people—individually and in groups—for whatever it is they've achieved. You can thank customers, suppliers, your payroll person, your regular dishwashers, and your tech team. In fact, there's an entire essay on this in *Part 1* in Secret 13: "Creating a culture of positive appreciation." The risk is really low (so low, literally, as to probably be less than zero) and the upside is enormous. People like to know you notice!

14. ACT AS IF YOU NEVER CARED

Going on every day as if you have everything coming to you, as if the little things that people work so hard to deliver on all day are a given, as if people are lucky that you're giving them the chance to work for you is likely to eliminate any loyalty anyone **V LIST** might ever have had for the organization. I will guarantee (there I go again) that when we at the top don't act appreciatively, the little things will slowly but surely stop getting done. And, even worse, the attitude we bring to all this will surely be handed on down the line—new people learn that no one appreciates what they do, which means the drive to do well diminishes every day. This approach is a particularly positive one for victims. They already feel unappreciated, and in this case, they really are. I'd say take your lead from that story about the husband and wife on their tenth anniversary. Realizing that she hadn't heard her husband profess his passions for her for a long time, she asked him whether he still loved her. "Look," he replied rather brusquely, "I told you I loved you when we got married, and if anything changes, I'll be sure to let you know."

15. Live the Standards You Set

 Whether it's values we've documented, systems we've set up, guidelines we've got going, or ethical standards we've established, it's both common courtesy and common sense to stick to what we, the leaders, set up. Now, please understand, I'm a rule breaker from way back. I'm well in line with Thoreau's oft-repeated line: "It is not desirable to cultivate a respect for law, so much as a respect for right." I'm a big believer that rules do need to be broken and that tying creative people down with unnecessary bureaucracy is really bad business. But if we're going to make rules for everyone else, the whole thing will work way better if we actually follow them, too. Like the rest of this stuff, sticking to our own standards is not neurosurgery. If you put yourself on the schedule, show up on time. If you're not sure when you're going to show up, just don't put yourself on the schedule and then get there when you want. But it's tough to be tough on frontline staff for not showing up on time when we don't do the same ourselves. I could give you about 8,000 other examples, but I'm sure you get the idea. If we're going to break all our rules regularly, then in the interest of consistency (see 2A above) it would be far better if we allow others to adhere to them as inconsistently as we do. At the least, let's be consistent in our inconsistency.

15. Randomly Ignore Your Own Systems

Look, I know I've slipped on this myself many times—none of us are perfect—but, honestly, it's never a great move to get a guideline going and then turn right around and act as if it didn't exist. The ol' "do as I say, not as I do" is an awfully dif- ficult line to lead with if you're trying to actually accomplish anything other than alienating everyone on your staff. It is, however, a really easy way to have your credibility go to crap and people's faith in you drop fifty points in a hurry. Almost needless to say, the old inverted relationship between rule following and hierarchy—the higher you go the less you follow the agreed-upon guidelines—is a great way to go nowhere.

16. SHARE INFORMATION LAVISHLY

A LIST You can be as old school as you like, but still, sharing information effectively and often can only help everyone you hire to do a better job. Although I haven't been in it, I'd guess that's as equally true in the Army as it is in an anarchist organization—no one can make good decisions without good information. People need to know what you want, why you want it, where you're going, what you believe, and what you're thinking if you want them to do well. If for some good reason (privacy, respect for those involved, etc.) you don't want to share information, then at the least take time to explain to folks that you aren't going to and why you aren't in this particular case.

16. KEEP SECRETS AND MAKE SURE EVERYONE KNOWS YOU'RE KEEPING THEM

I have a fair few friends who've told me that the management team in their organization meets regularly but that no one else is allowed to know what the leaders worked on. Mind you, none of these people work for the CIA, the Supreme Court, **V LIST** or some secret society, so I don't think that what's going on behind those tightly closed doors is truly a life-and-death issue. Certainly there are matters that require privacy, but I wouldn't really recommend promoting the fact that others aren't allowed any input. Exclusion can only exacerbate pre-existing problems—when you keep people in the dark, they start to assume the worst; trust drops, rumors spread, and pretty soon your office starts to resemble the Kremlin, circa 1977. (If you want to really whip things up, a good bit of inaccurate gossip can get a whole company going in no time flat!) This sort of communication vacuum is also a veritable windfall for victims. In place of the truth, they get to mold reality to fit their own, darkly cynical sort of worldview. It's also a great insurance policy for them—even if they actually took action, should it fail, they can always just say they were acting on the insufficient bit of info they'd been given. What else can they do, right?

17. Make Sure People Have the Tools They Need

 This is hardly a shocking statement—you can see it spelled out everywhere from the Gallup-research-based book *First, Break all the Rules* to the U.S. Army handbook. If you're going to send someone in to do a job, run a project, or solve a problem, please, I pray, be sure to provide them with the resources they need to do the work well. Sure, there's a lot to be said for pushing people to sort stuff out on their own that they've not yet dealt with before—a good leader is always moving the bar a bit higher so that staff achieve at a level that's commensurate with their capabilities and are not just stuck in the status quo. But sending them to build a bridge with a box of Popsicle sticks, some glue, and a nasty glare isn't going to get anything good to happen.

17. Let Them Figure It Out on Their Own

I suppose you could say that proving oneself this way as a frontline staffer is something akin to Navy Seal survival training. In which case it would make total sense to assign someone to a big project, give them none of what they need in order to succeed, and then get mad at them later for making a mess of things. To make matters worse, I've heard tell of some supervisors who actually get angry at their people when they have the nerve to actually ask for assistance because they're worried that the work won't be done on time. Stuff like this brings bad energy, excessive anger, and pretty much every bad thing you can imagine into the workplace. Victims are probably the only ones who can find some solace in it—they knew it was all a set-up from the start.

18. Study Hard

I don't mean to sound old school, seriously, but you gotta study if you want to have any serious shot at success. Studying and applying what you learn by working on yourself and on your business aren't guarantees of success. But they sure do help. I've been out in the world a long time now, and I've never yet met anyone, of any age, in any field, who was really great at what they did who didn't seriously work really hard to get there. Scientist, sax player, sandwich maker, or shooting guard for the Celtics, the people at the top generally get where they are for a reason, and that reason is not (I'm pretty sure) random intervention from on high. The drive to do more, to study and practice, is a prerequisite for mastering whatever it is that you're interested in. While we have a commitment here to help those who may be operating with some significant social disadvantages, high achievement is generally not an accident. To quote Hugh MacLeod in *Ignore Everybody*, "If somebody in your industry is more successful than you, it's probably because he works harder at it than you do. Sure, maybe he's more inherently talented, more adept at networking, but I don't consider that an excuse. Over time, that advantage counts for less and less. Which is why," he adds quite accurately, "the world is full of highly talented, network-savvy, failed mediocrities."

Just working hard at something may not make you the best, but as Rodger Bowser, one of the managing partners at the Deli, once said, "The world is run by people who show up." That means both literally—showing up for meetings, planning sessions, and other such stuff—and it means participating intellectually. To be succinct about it, if you don't study, stay engaged, and on the cutting edge, you're very simply a lot less likely to succeed. I don't mean you shouldn't take time off, go to your kid's soccer game, or have hobbies. I just mean that failure to study, failure to work hard, or holding back instead of giving your all aren't likely to get you all that far.

18. Slack Now

This one, I think, is the victim-clincher. The surest way to make sure you don't get to success is to slack. Mind you, laying back on learning isn't a bad thing if you're good with the status quo—there's a lot to be said for goofing off and having a good time. But if you aspire to higher (whatever that means) levels of achievement, a steady diet of slacking is pretty sure to lead to perpetual frustration, serious bouts of anger, and a solid base for a cynical worldview. It's a pretty sure bet—if the boss is slacking, problems are sure to follow. If you want to increase your odds of failure, and accomplish the same for all those you're leading, then really, don't bother reading books, going to seminars, listening to public radio, or benchmarking with others in your industry. Don't ever stay late to get something done, don't go out of your way for guests, staff, or colleagues. As Hugh MacLeod laid out in *Ignore Everybody*, "Being good at anything is like figure skating—the definition of being good at it is being able to make it look easy. But it never is easy. Ever. That's what the stupidly wrong people conveniently forget." Of course, if we at the top start things off by slacking, you can only imagine how wonderful and nurturing an environment that creates for newly developing victims—if we're not working particularly hard, it's hard to really get on others for not working hard, either.

Solidifying the Shift from V to A

The focus in frustrating situations like the one my friend is working in, understandably, goes towards what wrongs have been done to the frontline staff, but it's not enjoyable for those at the top who are handling things in less than wonderful ways either. While they may acquire status, stuff, and a place at the podium from which they can look down on others, the reality is that it's not a very rewarding way to work for anyone. Bosses who behave badly generally don't feel good either.

Let me restate that there's nothing on the A list that is overly complicated or probably at all shocking to anyone who's truly given the quality of their leadership work even the slightest bit of consideration. While it's hard to hold true to everything I've mentioned a hundred percent of the time—I know it is for me at least, and we're obviously all human—nothing on the list is actually all that tough to take on. The hard parts, I'd posit, are a) consistently holding ourselves to these commitments and keeping on course when all the world's wackiness seems like it's working to knock you off center; and b) teaching it all effectively to everyone else in our organizations. While I won't guarantee that living the A list religiously is guaranteed to get you into heaven or even to getting the greatest results in the history of your industry, I will say that it will keep you squarely, spiritually, and, at the least, solidly in the game. How well you do once you're on the court (field, stage, or whatever other metaphor you like to use) is up to you. But at least you're in good playing shape when the game gets going. And once you're in shape, it's a lot easier to stay that way.

By contrast, moving an ineffective, angry organization from V to A isn't an easy, nor is it an overnight, activity. Starting to fully live this small stuff effectively every day is a good way to start. Creating the kind of positive, caring culture of responsibility that comes from living this A list, one where baseline trust is the reality, gives the victims of the world very little to work with. While victims can be voracious in their appetite for eating up positive organizational energy, most exit A list organizations for more fertile, messed up, victim-friendly fields elsewhere. Conversely, consistently living the A list makes your business much more attractive to others who like to live it too, which creates a stronger, more responsible culture, which can't help but contribute effectively to organizational success. None of this stuff is elaborate, but it sure is effective. It won't ever get headlines, but it'll definitely help you make headway! Have fun. And remember, if all else fails, even when things are bad, it's always better to be considerate.

While it would be easy to blame the bosses, that's a bit too easy and victim-like for my taste. After all, if we're all leaders, then really, it's incumbent on all of us equally to take the lead and live the A list wherever we can. Reacting in kind kills our own spirit more than it does those at the top who are acting arbitrarily and ineffectively. Everyone who's stuck serving a boss who manages from that V list gets my empathy and support; I wish I could make it better. But in the meantime, I encourage everyone, as many already do, to (as my partner Paul always says) try to work on the higher spiritual plane; do the right thing. It's not at all fair, but living the A list makes life more positive, even if those above you on the org chart choose to act as if it didn't exist.

notes from the
back dock

The Inside Scoop on Working Here at Zingerman's

Ally Hurst, Wholesale Salesperson, Zingerman's Bakehouse

Thank you for sharing your V to A essay with me. Now that I've had a chance to read and reflect, I noticed a theme. When I asked the Bakehouse staff about what makes a good manager, over half of the employees first gave me the "what-not-to-do answer" and were quite vehement about it. Usually what followed was "I had this boss who would..." At first I thought, jeez, that was two or three jobs ago, why hold on to the bitterness? And then I thought about the rancor in my voice when I've talked about bosses past. And then while reading your essay, it occurred to me how many times in the past I acted like the victim. And how hypocritical it was to be mad at those who display that mentality, when I spent my fair share of time in the "victim camp." I guess it's like that old saying: "You hate in others what you hate in yourself." Coming to that realization has inspired me to let go of those past experiences and focus on being a better version of me: someone who's up front, supportive, and certainly not a victim. Thank you again for the springboard.

robert greenleaf and emma goldman, sitting in front of the deli discussing the zingerman's experience

Twelve Tenets of Anarcho-Capitalism

How to Make Money without Getting Hung Up on Hierarchy

In the spirit of freedom, reader's choice, and limited time, the twelve tenets are listed below. Like any of the "secrets" in the book, you can skip from tenet to tenet without reading them in order. While I (obviously) like all twelve, you can pick and choose from the list as you like—this is an à la carte menu of Anarcho-Capitalism.

Over the years we've done a great deal to craft what we at Zingerman's call "organizational recipes"—clearly documented formulas that allow us to teach our approaches to pretty much every subject. We've got 4 Elements of an Effective Vision, 3 Steps to Great Service, 5 Steps to Handling a Complaint, and more. Secret 3 in Zingerman's Guide to Good Leading, Part 1 *will give you an in-depth look at the thought process we use to design the recipes. In most every case, the process was mapped out in an after-the-fact effort to clarify what we were already doing in practice. We didn't start giving great service after we wrote the recipe—the 3 Steps were just a written version of what Paul and I were already doing. Documenting them helped us bring greater clarity, gave free-thinking, smart staff members a better shot at being successful, encouraged everyone here to use their innate intelligence and creativity, and made it much easier to teach and train more effectively. Same goes for the essay that follows. The structure and the subheads are new, but the twelve tenets that follow are all things that Paul and I and others have had in our minds for most of the thirty years we've been in business.*

While the content was well used, the image of Zingerman's as an anarcho-capitalist organization came to me, out of the blue, as I was working on the first volume of this series. In the moment, I threw it down into my draft to see what would happen. Six months later, Part 1 *went to print with the idea intact, at which point I guess we officially became Anarcho-Capitalists.*

<hr/>

There are so many misconceptions about anarchism that before I dive into my own modern-day, Zingerman's interpretation, I should share a small bit of background on what the anarchists' work was all about. Or maybe I'd do better to lead with what it is *not*. In fact, I'll just show you what early 20th-century anarchist Alexander (Sasha) Berkman said on the subject: "I must tell you, first of all, what Anarchism is not. It is not bombs, disorder, or chaos. It is not robbery and murder. It is not a war of each against all. It is not a return to barbarism or to the wild state of man. Anarchism is the very opposite of all that."

So what *is* anarchism then? Well, not surprisingly, there are many definitions. The most overt element of anarchist activity over the centuries has been its focus on getting rid of government. I stopped worrying about that a long time ago—I don't have a better suggestion. But there was far, far more to what the anarchists were about than just eliminating the state.

My views on the subject are fully in synch with those of early 20th-century German anarchist Gustav Landauer. Rather than tearing down the state, Landauer looked for ways to build up positive community and support the individuals within it. His solution wasn't to fight the state, but to ignore it, and to create caring, free communities in its place. "The state," he said, "is a social relationship, a certain way of people relating to one another. It can be destroyed by creating new social relationships, i.e., by people relating to one another differently." His view is all about the local, the positive, and the possible. This theme of Landauer's runs through most everything I've written on organizations. *Stop worrying so much about what others are doing wrong and take the initiative: dream big, do good things, and start going for greatness right here!*

The message is a consistent one—it's up to us to claim our own freedom, not by arguing about it, but by living it, in a caring and community-minded way. As Landauer pointed out, "We who have imprisoned ourselves in the absolute state must realize the truth: *we are the state!* And we will be the state as long as we are nothing different, as long as we have not yet created the institutions necessary for a true community and a true society of human beings." Take out "state" and plug in "big business" and the same situation still exists today. We can blame the corporate world for what we don't like, but it's up to us to create the kind of workplace we want.

Landauer went on, "[Anarchism] is first and foremost a movement of spirit. [I]t can only emerge," he explained, "from the spirit of freedom and of voluntary union; it can only arise within the individuals and their communities." In essence, what he's saying is, this is all about energy. The better, more positive, freely given energy we all bring to the workplace, the better things are going to work. It's up to each of us to go out and make a difference. People, Landauer said, "must not think of what others can do for them. They must think of what they themselves can do. They must think what they really think. They must be what they really are."

What he's describing, and what we're doing, is creating a community in which each individual is alive and energized, and where the group is better off for it. I agree with Emma Goldman, who wrote, "Anarchism insists that the center of gravity in society is the individual—that he must think for himself, act freely, and live fully. The aim of anarchism is that every individual in the world shall be able to do this." Additionally, she said, "More than any other idea, it is helping to do away with the wrong and foolish; more than any other idea, it is building and sustaining new life." For a more modern take, look to Liz Highleyman, writing for the Black Rose Collective in Boston back in 1995. "The basic tenet of anarchism," she says, "is that hierarchical authority . . . is not only unnecessary, but is inherently detrimental to the maximization of human potential. Anarchists generally believe that human beings are capable of managing their own affairs on the basis of creativity, cooperation, and mutual respect."

What Goldman, Berkman, Landauer, and Highleyman had to say is all in synch with my own views on the subject. Other anarchists, of course, had their own view of things. But in that regard, I'll align myself, again, with Gustav Landauer, who wrote, "These anarchists are not anarchic enough for me." Anarchism for me is *not* about tearing down, destroying, nay-saying, or selfish individualism. For me, it's about free thinking, mutual respect, and the freedom to find your own way in the belief that working that way would most surely create a caring and collaborative community.

As with Anese Cavanaugh's approach to energy (Secret 20), Robert Greenleaf's suppositions about Servant Leadership (Secret 23), and Peter Block's beliefs about Stewardship (Secret 24), what follows is my effort to take these inspiring anarchist ideals and turn them into a way to move beyond the concept into action. It might resonate. As one customer who'd read *Part 1* of this series yelled to me across the aisle at the farmer's market, "Hey! I loved your book. You really brought out the old anarchist in me!" See what you think—maybe there's a little anarchist in you, too.

1. All for One—Bringing Out the Best in Each and Every Individual in the Organization

So much of society is organized around externally assigned identities, pre-conceived images, stereotypes, prejudices, and all the problems that go with them. Biases, we know, abound. You can fill in about as many blanks as you have time or interest to come up with: "Young people today just don't have a good work ethic." "Old people are out of touch." "Kids these days don't care." "Black people . . ." "White people . . ." "Women . . ." "Men . . ." Add to that all the standard corporate stuff about hierarchies: "Bosses look down on their subordinates." "Frontline folks have no patience for people in power." "Capitalists are crooks." "Customers are crazy." While there are probably a handful of people in the world who actually fit some of these stereotypes, there are a whole lot more who don't. I've never really understood the need to stereotype that way. *It is an absolutely essential element of our approach here that we treat everyone as an equal,* and help them all to succeed by building on whatever skills they bring to the workplace.

Honestly, I don't think we do away with the stereotypes just because it's the right thing to do. Nor is it just some do-good, golden-rule kind of thing our grandmothers threw at us when we were young. We treat everyone respectfully because, quite simply, they deserve it. When it comes to the basic elements of humanity, everyone—regardless of background, business skill, or position—is on par. For whatever reason of reality, randomness, upbringing, anarchist orientation, or long-ingrained ethics, Paul and I (and hundreds of other good folks around here) have always operated with the mindset that it makes absolutely no difference what someone's spot on an org chart is, what college they went to, what their background, religion, race, or sexual orientation is, how fancy their resume might look, or what football team they root for. Sure, we know that some folks are smarter, some have more power, others more education, a few may have more physical ability and others still have more money, more moxie, or fancier titles. None of that makes them better people. They're just people who have more of . . . whatever it is they have. Everyone, always, deserves a shot, a bit of belief in their ability to grow, learn, improve, and contribute.

Saying that we treat everyone as an equal seems so simple, so straightforwardly obvious, but I've come to realize that this approach is not one that's been adopted in most workplaces. People in the corporate world seem, all too often, caught up in tying self-worth to so-called titles and salary levels. Here, in our little crazy community, it's the opposite—while, I'm sure, we fall short about every six minutes, the aim of all our interactions is simply to treat everyone respectfully: *to accept, and actively support, everyone in being the unique, creative, thinking, caring, and contributing individual they are.* Treating them otherwise goes against nature.

On a more professional level, it's bad business—leave out everyone on the "lower levels" and you can't but miss out on good ideas and good input. As modern day eco-anarchist author Murray Bookchin makes clear in his book, *Remaking Society,* "There was no need in these (old) organic societies to 'achieve' equality, for what (already) existed was an absolute respect for man, for all individuals apart from any personal traits." Or to quote Gustav Landauer, "No one lacks the ability, the disposition, the potential." All of which, then, is why our work as an organization is to help bring out the best in everyone we work with: to help each person (including customers and suppliers) to go after their dreams, to be true to themselves, to pursue their passions, and to help bring those passions into their daily lives.

I'm with Emma Goldman, who said a century or so ago, "I will accept an anarchist organization on just one condition: that it be based on the absolute respect for all individual initiatives and not obstruct their development or evolution." Our work is to encourage everyone here (you and me included!) to be true to ourselves, to respectfully acknowledge that we're each going to have our own ways of thinking, being, and breathing. In the process, we create safety and support, helping to make each of us ever more . . . ourselves. To quote

Emma's Italian anarchist compatriot, Errico Malatesta, "That which frees the individual, that which allows him to develop all his faculties, is not solitude, but association." A great organization brings out the best of everyone in it. Treating everyone with respect also means that we respect ourselves as individuals. What this comes down to is that the best leaders are almost always the people who work hard on themselves. They treat themselves as they'd like to be treated by others, are the most self-reflective, and consistently work for meaningful self-improvement. As the Taoist saying goes, "A violent man dies a violent death." The way we treat ourselves is going to come through in our interactions with others. I believe, as anarchist Max Baginski writes, that "Individualism . . . means working for inner mental liberation of the individual while organization means association between conscious individuals with a goal to reach or for an economic need to satisfy." It all starts with the work we do on ourselves. As Michigan anarchist Voltairine de Cleyre construed a hundred years or so ago, "The free and spontaneous inner life of the individual the Anarchists have regarded as the source of greatest pleasure and also of progress itself, or as some would prefer to say, social change."

These same themes come up equally often in the work of progressive, modern-day, business writers. Robert Greenleaf, who worked forty-some years for AT&T and whose writing about Servant Leadership is a core element of what we do here (see page 113), sounded a lot like Emma Goldman when he wrote about business back in 1979 that "Superficially, the [modern-day] freedom revolution . . . is at heart a struggle for meaning and significance in individual lives. . . . The aim of all this is not to motivate people. Motivation ceases to be what is done to people. Motivation becomes what people generate for themselves when they experience growth." Lay that alongside Emma's early 20th-century elucidation: "[Anarchism's] goal is the freest possible expression of all the latent powers of the individual." Or Gustav Landauer's line about how in an anarchist society "[h]umans have the capacity to freely and independently create a life that is their own." Hmm . . . you can see where this concept of caring and constructive Anarcho-Capitalism came from.

Treating co-workers as the smart, insightful, creative people they are is a good way to get your business going in the right direction. "I have always wondered," Roadhouse hostess Kristin Beckett told me, "what it is about my job that makes it something that I choose to do rather than invest in a different work specialty that would perhaps pay me more or require that I become good at only one thing. It's because, in my role as hostess, every talent and all knowledge can be applied in a useful manner. I suppose that could be true at any job, if you are someone who incorporates everyday knowledge into all aspects of your life. But very few organizations I have worked for in the past have been such a collection of amazing, intelligent people who realize that we all benefit from helping one another, and then actually *do* it. We are not perfect, by any means, but we are *aware!"*

A company can only do better when people feel respected and valued—when their voice is as important as anyone else's. They know they may not get their way on every issue, but the fact that they're being treated as intelligent adults and listened to respectfully, rather than looked down on and dismissed as slightly better than dumb, makes a difference. Gussie Denenberg (quoted in *Anarchist Voices,* an oral history done by Professor Paul Avrich) said a century or so ago, "Anarchism is a way of life, no matter what your view is of human nature. No authority over you, no slaves under you—that's the anarchist life. So when I think of Voltairine de Cleyre, when I think of [Alexander] Sasha [Berkman] and Emma [Goldman], that's what I think of. That was their way of life, a revolt against injustice and inhumanity."

Please don't pick up this first tenet and pay it lip service only. Whether we want them to or not, our beliefs will bleed through into the energy we bring to work—*this approach absolutely will not work unless you believe it to be true.* Saying you respect someone is not the same as respecting them, and any employee who's paying attention will feel the difference between the real thing and any superficial attempt at it. It all starts with us. If we don't truly respect the people we work with as equals, then they aren't likely to respect themselves, their contributions, us, the organization, the world, or much of anything else.

This issue of beliefs, the way we think about ourselves in relation to those around us, carries through into all aspects of our lives. My friend Heather Porter Engwall made the point that, to work well, this belief about equality and respect has to flow throughout a leader's whole life. While many managers will have heard talk of equality and respect at work, *at home* many also may still feel themselves to be hierarchically positioned above everyone else. While sitting atop a family hierarchy hardly makes them bad people, it does mean that, as Heather pointed out, they're going to have a hard time pulling off a "treat everyone as an equal" approach when they get to work. That hierarchically oriented energy will, inevitably, be felt by, and impact, others around them.

Goethe said it well a century ago: "I have come to the frightening conclusion that I am the decisive element. It is my personal approach that creates the climate. It is my daily mood that makes the weather. I possess tremendous power to make life miserable or joyous. I can be a tool of torture or an instrument of inspiration; I can humiliate or humor, hurt or heal. In all situations, it is my response that decides whether a crisis is escalated or de-escalated, and a person is humanized or de-humanized. If we treat people as they are, we make them worse. If we treat people as they ought to be, we help them become what they are capable of becoming."

The bottom line on this is simple: the organization exists to meaningfully help everyone here develop into who and what they can, and want, to be; our work as leaders is to help make that happen. Is there really a viable alternative? I don't think so. Do the math—the less of themselves everyone brings to work, the worse we're going to do as an organization. How many teams are you familiar with that won championships without everyone contributing fully?

2. One for All—Individual Responsibility for the Organization's Success

If the first tenet of Anarcho-Capitalism is about our belief in everyone's ability and a commitment to helping them get to greatness for themselves, the flip side, Tenet 2, is that we all take constructive responsibility for the success of the entire organization.

At Zingerman's we all recognize that our work impacts everyone around us. Everyone understands that every seemingly infinitesimal action makes a difference in how the organization performs. In this sense we've moved past the passive and still essentially parental notion of empowerment. What we're talking about goes beyond just having the chance to chime in or take action if you happen to feel inspired to do so. Instead, we expect everyone in the ZCoB to actively participate in running the business.

Organizations are only as good as the people who are part of them. You simply cannot build a great business out of a group of people whose desire is to do as little as possible and who are focused primarily on their own self-interest. If people don't care, the company will inevitably do poorly. Max Baginski made this clear at the 1907 International Anarchist Conference in Amsterdam: "An organization in the true sense cannot result from the combination of mere nonentities." In other words, you aren't going to get a great, sustainable business by hiring a superstar boss and surrounding her or him with a so-so support team. "It must," he continued, "be composed of self-conscious intelligent individualities. Indeed, the total of the possibilities and activities of an organization is represented by the expression of individual energies. We must not, however, forget that a revolutionary organization requires particularly energetic and conscious individuals." He went on, "It therefore logically follows that the greater the number of self-conscious personalities in an organization the lesser the danger of stagnation and the more intense its life-element."

Please note that this isn't only about managers and owners being "nice" to folks further down the org chart—it means that each of us needs to understand and embrace the influence that we have on the organization. Not being hung up on hierarchy works in *all* directions. Just because a manager messed up doesn't make everyone else less responsible for success! If frontline folks don't respect the people they work for or with, that, too, will poison the organization's energy. While we start with Servant Leadership, passively tolerating poor leadership is never a good way to get to greatness. The whole point is that we're all in this together. One of the earliest anarchists, the twenty-two-year-old Frenchman Étienne de La Boétie, wrote in his mid-16th century "Discourse on Voluntary Servitude," "It is . . . the inhabitants themselves who permit, or, rather, bring about, their own subjection."

This construct does not leave a lot of room for passivity, and even less so for a victim mentality. While these tendencies do still turn up, the people who evince them generally don't last long. Most everything we teach is about living actively and collaboratively, all the while mindfully making the business better in the process. That mindset is right there in our mission statement (see page 366)—everyone here knows that they're fully responsible for bringing a great Zingerman's Experience to every customer, co-worker, supplier, and neighbor that we come into contact with. All Zingerman's-wide decisions are made by consensus of all the managing partners. The same is true in our work groups—while members certainly can and should share the perspective of their colleagues or co-workers, at decision-making time they focus on "what's best for Zingerman's overall." It's a big part of the way we do open-book finance— all our "huddles" are open, most anyone who really wants to "own a line" and be responsible for a set of numbers (and the story behind them) can do that, and anyone who doesn't like the way things are going can come and speak up. It's in our service "recipes"—each of us takes full responsibility for making every customer happy, and everyone is authorized to do whatever they need to do to make that happen. In fact, it's in the primary message we put out there to our crew—"You really *can* make a difference." If everyone's not going for greatness for the group, we aren't going to get there.

3. Frame Everything in Free Choice

Everything in this Anarcho-Capitalist way of working is built onto a foundation of freely made, mindful choices. Quite simply, as a few of my friends are probably sick of me saying, none of us *have* to do anything. Whatever we do, we do—mindfully or not—because we choose to do it, not because someone else "made us." As Benjamin Tucker, early 20th-century American anarchist, said, "There is, in one sense, plenty of bossing to be done in this world but not against the will or desire of even the humblest person." Acknowledging our power to make choices in everything we do very literally changes lives. For better or for worse, you'll feel the impact in the organization's energy. When people feel free, when they collaborate willingly to get group greatness, the energy is almost always going to be really positive.

Honoring free choice in business is a big change—although almost all the buzzwords in the political world are about this being a free country, it's amazing how little free choice is supported and rewarded in the workplace. Bosses, in the old school at least, generally operate in the belief that they can order others around; while they're all for free choice in the voting booth, employees are expected to basically do what they've been told when they come to work. I don't want to get too political about this. My point is just that everything works better when we encourage everyone around us to take ownership of their own conscious and considered decisions. As Gustav Landauer wrote, "[T]here can be only one monarch: the inner being of each individual. If our situation is to improve, it is this monarch who must claim his rule and point us in the right direction."

That doesn't mean everyone's going to just do whatever they want, whenever they want. We each bear the consequences for our actions, just as we take responsibility for our freely made decisions. Remember, we're talking Anarcho-Capitalism here, not complete chaos—there are systems and structures that we've all chosen to be accountable to (see Tenet 11). In our world at least, our work is never about giving orders. It's about asking people to do what needs to be done and explaining why it's important; getting clear about expectations and allowing for dialogue whenever possible. It means getting clear consequences in advance so that everyone knows what the ramifications are of their decisions. The work still has to get done and leaders still have to lead; but those who follow do so by choice, not because they're forced. And anyone can step up to lead when they need or want to.

Framing everything in free choice is not just about the way leaders work with staff; it's about everyone in the organization understanding that they're making free choices and owning the consequences of those decisions. It is most definitely a two-way street. While few frontliners actually enjoy being lorded over, most will still sit back and wait for those in charge to give orders before they take action anyway. The average American employee—this is my opinion only—acts as if he or she is being compelled to do what they do. The mindset is so pervasive that few people even realize they're thinking that way. This sense of compulsion pervades our everyday language. Take ten minutes at your next meeting and count how many times someone says, "I have to," "I can't," or "I should." There's a lot of power floating around those tables, but when we're talking like that, I can tell you from personal experience, the power is noticeably not inside of us. I'll tell you first-hand, feeling "forced" to do something is never a good feeling. No person or organization is going to get to greatness unless each of us reclaims our power with and exercises our right to free choice in a grounded, caring, and responsible way.

I've come to view this commitment to free choice as a personal, internal declaration of independence. Other than through the use of force and in other very extreme circumstances, we all make our own choices. Anarcho-Capitalism acknowledges this and asks that we make mindful decisions all day long. Internally, most of us would feel freer and more fulfilled if we would just own that all day long we are *actively* making choices. No one makes us do what we do—we choose to do it. We choose to move quickly or not; to be in a good mood or bad; to smile or look sullen; to pick up trash off the street or walk past it as we've probably done two thousand times before. Personally speaking, I will say that my life became a whole lot more fun and a lot less stressful after I realized that everything I did started with a decision I had made.

On the flip side, we also need to respect that others will then make choices we won't particularly like. This is inherent in encouraging people to be themselves and telling them to speak up for what they believe. The traditional work world operates on the belief that "we're paying these people, of course they're going to do what we tell them to." The idea of letting staff say "no" in a constructive manner, where they're not immediately stomped on for saying so, is not the norm in most places. Performance may be poor, discussions may be difficult, and employment may ultimately end anyway, but dialogue, respect, and fair treatment never need to go away because someone opted not to do what we would have liked them to.

Making the mental shifts that underlie this approach is not easy work, but the payoff is huge. If we each acknowledge that we're making free choices, there's very little room for people to act like victims. The organization's obligation is to make it reasonably safe for anyone who wants to speak up to do so. It will probably always be awkward to raise tough issues, even if someone has created a space that's safe for speaking out. We just have to take a deep breath and raise them regardless. If someone chooses to stay silent anyway, that is their choice. If we don't go after what we want, we're unlikely to get it. And if we're waiting for the bosses to fix things for us, it's likely to be a long wait.

Mind you, free choice doesn't mean choice free from influence or free of consequence. Both are great fantasies, but, best I can tell, there's just no such thing. Often this means that we need to find effective, positive, and uplifting ways to work together even when we aren't in agreement. Stewardship (Secret 24) is a key part of this—it teaches us how to communicate using an adult-to-adult, peer-to-peer approach, through which we encourage openness, collaboration, and conscious commitment. It's a construct in which no one can really compel anyone else to do anything. It's not an overnight achievement, but the more we work at it, the better we get—it teaches everyone in the organization to negotiate as peers, *not* like the stereotypical settings in which "superiors" manage "subordinates," or "subordinates" succumb to CEOs. In the process, we build a vibrant, healthy culture at the core of which are free will and free choice.

To restate, this is all about an internal decision to free our minds from the world's machinations. Emma Goldman wrote the following about women's emancipation in the early part of the 20th century, but I think her words apply to everyone regardless of gender: "[T]rue emancipation begins neither at the polls nor in courts. It begins in a woman's soul; . . . every oppressed class gained true liberation from its masters through its own efforts. It is necessary that [every] woman . . . realize that her freedom will reach [only] as far as her power to achieve her freedom reaches." Getting staff members to push politely for what they want, and to stay constructively engaged during the discussions that follow, is not an overnight transition. But as modern-day anarchist professor Mohammed Bamyeh put so beautifully, "freedom is the exercise of freedom." If you don't ask . . .

None of this precludes collaboration or cooperative and professional performance. As anarchist George Barrett wrote in 1921, "To get the full meaning out of life we must co-operate, and to co-operate we must make agreements with our fellow-men. But to suppose that such agreements mean a limitation of freedom is surely an absurdity; on the contrary, they are the exercise of our freedom." If you want a free-thinking organization, you can't have people acting as if they're being forced into doing what they do.

4. A Positive Outlook on, and Belief in, Abundance, a Better Life, People, and the Future

The old model of business and capitalism is all about "winning and losing." It's based on adversarial relationships, "racing to the top," and coming out as "king of the hill." The classic capitalist mindset has been to maximize how much money one makes by keeping employee pay and benefits to a bare minimum. Businesses try to make as much as they can off of their customers; customers, consequently, are supposed to be vigilant to keep businesses from cheating them. Big companies beat down small suppliers by demanding lower prices and longer terms; suppliers respond by either lowering quality or overcharging on other items that no one's watching. It's all a zero-sum game—if I do better, you do worse; if the competition wins, I'm headed for trouble. It is, I suppose, some sort of economic version of Darwin's survival of the fittest. I'm feeling exhausted just from explaining it.

Anarcho-Capitalism, as per hog farmer Emile DeFelice's construct, is the total opposite. We always begin with the belief that things are basically good and that there is ultimately more than enough for everyone to do well. It works well only if you believe that there's plenty for everyone in the long run and that everyone needs to be able to get something good out of almost any activity we engage in. It's about believing that there's plenty to go around if we work together to make sure that happens. We need to believe that whatever it is we're going after is going to work, to believe in the people with whom we're doing it, and to believe in the product that we're making and the service that we're offering.

It's up to each of us to help make more so that everyone can win. As per Servant Leadership, we serve the organization and our community by creating wealth and positive energy for all involved. Proto-anarchist Étienne de La Boétie's views, put down some 600 years ago, still sum up my feelings on the subject: "If in distributing her gifts nature has favored some more than others with respect to body or spirit, she has nevertheless not planned to place us within this world as if it were a field of battle, and has not endowed the stronger or the cleverer in order that they may act like armed brigands in a forest and attack the weaker. One should rather conclude that in distributing larger shares to some and smaller shares to others, nature has intended to give occasion for brotherly love to become manifest, some of us having the strength to give help to others who are in need of it." There's no question in my mind—if we work together, everyone involved can benefit. The bottom line on Anarcho-Capitalism done well is that the business, the employees, the shareholders, the suppliers, and the community can all come out ahead!

5. Creative and Near-Constant Collaboration

I guess it shouldn't come as a surprise that I was reminded to include this essential fifth element only because of a collaborative dialogue with a colleague. If I hadn't been sharing thoughts on Anarcho-Capitalism with Amy Emberling, co-managing partner of the Bakehouse, I'd probably have forgotten to include it. As with most things around here, collaboration came through.

The whole thing happened during a ZingTrain seminar. Amy and I were talking at the side of the room while the attendees were working in small groups on a leadership question we'd put to them. We were talking about something seemingly unrelated, but for whatever reason I found myself coming back to my belief that *the people who are the most successful in our organization are those who are the most self-reflective and also the most consistently collaborative.*

Amy is one of those people. She's been working hard over the years to better understand her own "stuff," and to manage herself in ever more effective ways. Her work has paid off—for her, for the Bakehouse, and for our entire organization. As the seminar proceeded apace, Amy continued to process what we'd been talking about. Coincidentally, a few minutes later, an attendee asked her a question about collaboration. "I realized as Ari and I were talking," she said, "that there are almost *no* decisions that I make here without collaborating with someone else. There are a few that I make talking pretty much just to Frank (Carollo, the other managing partner at the Bakehouse), but those are only about salary rates for our managers. Everything else that I decide is done in collaboration with a pretty extensive group of people." She paused, and then added, "I don't know if I could work anywhere else any more where they expect you to make all the decisions by yourself!"

Like getting good bread, good coffee, or probably good weather, once you've worked collaboratively it's hard to go back to going solo. Collaborating takes time, patience, listening skills, and a willingness to adjust, adapt, and learn from others. It isn't always the easiest change for someone like me who, by nature and upbringing, is very stubborn, single-minded, quick thinking, quick to talk back, impatient, and intuitive. But hey, if I can learn to talk less, listen more effectively, and figure out how to actively engage others in the organization on most every issue, then probably anyone who puts their mind to it can, too.

Collaboration is just better business. When we don't do it we miss out on information that would help us, we lose diversity of views that make for better decision making, and we minimize the contribution of people we're paying to work here. Without collaboration, we move towards isolation, and from there to ineffectiveness. To quote from Servant Leadership savant Robert Greenleaf, "To be a lone chief atop a pyramid is abnormal and corrupting. None of us are perfect by ourselves, and all of us need the help and correcting influence of close colleagues. . . . The pyramidal structure weakens informal links, dries up channels of honest reaction and feedback, and creates limiting chief-subordinate relationships which, at the top, can seriously penalize the whole organization."

As Greenleaf points out, going it alone isn't healthy for the people at the top either: "The typical chief who rests uneasily at the top of the pyramid of any large institution is grossly overburdened. The job destroys many of them—which is reason enough to abandon the idea. But for the institution there is also damage. For in too many cases the demands of the office destroy these persons' creativity long before they leave office." As burnout is setting in and creativity is going down at the top, what do you think is happening in the rest of the organization?

If you've never worked as we do—and most people probably haven't—collaboration is likely to be perceived as all sorts of things other than what it really is. Many people who've come here from outside our organization with upper-level experience have had a hard time assimilating into our collaborative culture. I guess I'll take my cue again from Alexander (Sasha) Berkman, whom I quoted earlier in this essay. In honor of Sasha's sardonic spirit, let me tell you what collaboration at Zingerman's is *not*. It's not chaos. It's not taking forever to get anything done. It's not simple and it's not about being controlled from above. It's not being wimpy or weak-kneed. Collaboration is not about covering our collective butt, avoiding legal problems, or being able to say later that you told so-and-so what you were going to do. It's *definitely* not about compliance, nor does it have a thing to do with compulsion. Misunderstanding this last point is the most common misconception outsiders have. We call for more collaboration, but they hear "command and control." What we have here, friends and colleagues, is a failure to communicate. Everything at Zingerman's, as you already know, is based on free choice, so being "forced to collaborate" is such an absurd concept that I can only smile and shake my head at the thought of it.

So what, then, is collaboration in our context? Collaboration here is about strength, smarts, and success. Freely chosen, with full respect for each individual and the organization overall, collaboration creates the creativity, the better decisions, the positive outcomes, the stuff that has made us what we are. Sure it started out with just me and Paul putting ourselves into partnership together and working this way as peers. But today it's eighteen partners and another 500 folks with us, plus hundreds of purveyors and many more thousands of customers than I can count. But crazy as it sounds, collaboration works.

Leading this way isn't about taking charge and issuing orders. It's rarely glamorous work and it doesn't make sense if you want to be the one in the spotlight all the time. But as Mohammed Bamyeh pointed out quite astutely, anarchism "has no heroes and no need for heroism." Instead, I'm talking about . . . talking. And listening. And learning. All of which happen before a decision gets made, a job candidate is offered a position, a new product is rolled out, a vision is finalized, or a troubled staff member gets fired. Does it take more time? Sure—from the inception of the initial idea to the time the decision is announced. But more time from inception of idea to effective implementation? No. The length of time it takes to get things truly in place actually goes down. More importantly, the quality of the decision goes up.

Collaboration is a better way to work. Max Baginski said, "The individual reaches the highest level of his development through co-operation with other individuals." But in the win-lose way that society has operated for so long, it's highly unlikely to spontaneously start happening. With that in mind, we've built collaboration into most of our systems here at Zingerman's. Partner-level decisions are all made by consensus. Our visioning work is almost always done collaboratively. Open-book finance requires actively talking about our numbers. Our meetings are all open, and anyone who works here can come and participate and get paid for attending. Over time, as Amy pointed out above, we've become so accustomed to the benefits of collaboration that we won't ever go back.

6. Take a Service Orientation

Service—to customers, staff, community, and everyone else we interact with—is an essential element of our approach. If we're not all in a giving mode, caring about and for others around us, none of this will work for very long. Service scores big points with everyone here, and it's just plain better business, a better way to live, and more fun. This spirit of generosity is implicit in anarchism—Emma Goldman advocated that we all would benefit by giving "of one's self boundlessly in order to find one's self richer, deeper, better. That alone can fill the emptiness, and transform . . . tragedy . . . into joy, limitless joy."

Speaking of which, if Emma Goldman is the queen (irony intended) of the anarcho half of this equation, then Robert Greenleaf would be the king of the capitalist part. Greenleaf is amazingly aligned with the anarchists' focus on free will, choice, respect, reverence, and the ineffectiveness of the use of force and coercion. His belief that the leader's primary responsibility is to serve, is, I think, the way that the two seemingly antithetical approaches—anarchism and capitalist leadership—come together in a positive way. If we embrace it, we can in fact put people into leadership roles who aren't exploiting everyone else en route to the single-minded pursuit of profit. And from the capitalist side of things, effective Servant Leadership implies that someone's still steering the ship.

While we as partners may own the business, we still serve with the consent of those we employ, those who supply us, and those who purchase our products. We need the folks who work in the business way more than they need us: customers can obviously eat at about eight million other places; producers can sell to our competitors; and, this being food service, the people who work for us know that they can get new jobs pretty much at will. If the kitchen staff stops showing up and customers start shopping elsewhere, we, the owners, will be left with the leases, a good bit of bank debt, and a large stack of dirty dishes.

In his book *The Ecology of Freedom*, Murray Bookchin refers to old "organic societies" in which it was considered the responsibility of those who had more to freely give back to create a more equanimous setting. Of course, we each also want to get something for ourselves, and there's nothing in this construct to preclude that. To the contrary, the point is that we give a lot and get a lot back in return. It's the responsibility of those of us who have more to freely work to help balance out the inequities that we know exist, as Bookchin believes, "to compensate for differences between individuals. When we're fortunate enough to have more, it's our responsibility to *freely* work to share out and support those who have less."

I can't really prove scientifically that this service stuff is superior, and I can't say that lots of selfish people in the world won't make a lot of money that they manage to keep for themselves. I'm not saying I don't want anything for myself, and I'm not saying that I've got it down, or that I give enough— I'm sure I don't. But the concept is clear and the effort is authentic. When in doubt, my commitment is to give more. As per Servant Leadership, the better the quality of the service we give to staff, the better the service they'll give to customers. The more we give, the more we all get, the better everyone does, the better we all do.

7. Opt for Openness

I know that "transparency" is the big buzzword right now, but to me it's so overused that, in the interest of honesty, I have to admit that the word has started to give me the creeps. I don't personally want to be transparent, and it's not really my desire to see through other people or organizations. I just want to know what's going on, to be up front and on the level. So for the purposes of this piece I think I'll go with "openness" instead. Whatever word you want to use, openness in our organization comes down to two main things:

a. **Let people know what's really going on.** If we want people to use their brains, think creatively, and make good decisions under pressure, they have to know what's really going on around them. Bad or limited information always leads to lousy decisions.

To keep people in the loop, we share information in a host of different ways. Open-book finance means that everyone here is actively involved in running the business, including knowing, understanding, and helping manage the finances. They know the sales numbers, how much cash is on hand, what we pay for each item, and whether or not we're making money. Most all our meetings are open—people are encouraged to attend and participate, regardless of their formal role in the organization. Agendas go out in advance and notes go out afterwards so that anyone who wants in—literally or figuratively—has access. We teach classes on food, finance, service, leadership, and almost everything else you can imagine. Decisions pretty much get made in collaborative open settings and people all around the organization have a chance to influence them. The more they know, the more they buy in, the more they contribute, the better their decisions, the better we do.

b. Speak the same language. The other part of the equation is making the information *real* and *meaningful.* Code words, winks, nods, and "You know what I mean (nudge, nudge)"'s turn corporate culture into a nearly impossible-to-navigate secret society. New employees spend so much time trying to figure out what everyone else actually means by what they say that they have little energy left for serving customers or making creative organizational change. It's so much easier—and more effective—to just say what we mean!

Making it real means cutting the corporate speak in favor of real-life language that everyone can comprehend, language that actually means what it says, instead of something that only insiders can understand because they've been around the dysfunction long enough to intuit when "a" actually means "b." Sure, we have our own Zing-lingo that may sound strange to outsiders—"huddles," "extra miles," "evergreens," "10–4," and "workin'!" to name just a few. But we actively teach the words to everyone who comes to work with us so that they can quickly understand what we're talking about. To wit, in our service work we avoid the oft-overused platitude that "the customer is always right." Almost every company says it, but everyone who works there also knows that the statement is silly—customers *aren't* always right. So why say it? I don't know—so we don't. In our service training we tell the truth—customers are very frequently wrong in what they're saying. But we're going to *act* like they're right even when they're wrong.

The same, I've realized, is also true of how we handle hierarchy. Murray Bookchin got me thinking about this in *The Ecology of Freedom,* when he described a pre-industrial society based on what he calls, "*the equality of unequals.*" It refers, as Bookchin explains, to a culture that "does not yield to the fictive claim . . . that everyone is equal." I know it probably seems absurd for an Anarcho-Capitalist to argue that everyone's *not* equal. But Bookchin's right. While "everyone is equal" sounds superb, we all know that it's actually an impossibility; some people are smarter than others. Some are more skilled. Many have more authority, others have less. Some start life short of support and strapped for cash. Many of us have health issues and have a hard time keeping up. In an organization like ours, some people have more authority, more experience, more ability, and more responsibility.

Rather than pledge allegiance to a fictional equality, I realized after reading Bookchin that we could straighten this one out in the same way we approached that stuff about the customer always being right. My Anarcho-Capitalist take on things is that *everyone's not really equal, but we're going to act like they are anyway.*

When we share information openly, when we say what we mean, when the people who work here are able to act on solid knowledge instead of their best guess about what's really going on, the whole business is bound to work better. And since we're open book, the results to prove the point are all readily available for everyone here to access.

8. The Importance of Acceptance

Acceptance is about making peace with the way things are. And while it doesn't guarantee that everything will go well, it does give us a much better shot at success. It means, quite simply, that we don't waste a lot of energy fighting with, or denying, reality. Rather, we try to see, hear, and experience things the way they are, not the way we want them to be, think they ought to be, or the way our mothers or mentors promised us they would be when we grew up. Much of the world, by contrast, lives in denial. They don't like the way the world works, and rather than accept it they argue with it. The fight isn't necessarily fueled by bad intentions—acceptance isn't easy to attain, especially if you (like most of us) were raised in other, less straightforward emotional circumstances. To quote Gustav Landauer again, "[I]t hurts sometimes to face the truth with open eyes, especially if you are used to dusk and gloom—but it is necessary!"

Basing our efforts on bad information or expending energy fighting with things that aren't ever going to change radically reduces the odds of our succeeding in any significant way. In *Using the Power of Purpose,* author Dean Tucker shares data showing that upper-level executives at big American businesses get only a tiny percentage of the real information available to front-line people. They're steering their ships from the bridge, without knowing what so many others on the front line have long been aware of.

Please note that when I say "acceptance" I am absolutely *not* talking about passivity or fatalism. To the contrary, Natural Law of Business 8 lays out that "You've got to keep getting better all the time." Acceptance makes it easier to make improvements. Once we're working with reality, we can go much farther over the long haul. To tap the insight of poet David Whyte, "Creativity means first accepting creation as it is."

Acceptance is all throughout the Natural Laws—understanding that "success means you get better problems," that "strengths lead to weaknesses," etc., means we don't waste energy fighting with what is. Acceptance also means acknowledging that we're all human. We all make mistakes, and every one of us errs. Acceptance means recognizing that we all have something to learn from everyone else regardless of anything other than the fact that they entered our world. It means that, regardless of resume, experience, age, credentials, or kudos, none of us really fully "know" what we're doing, and that as a result, working collaboratively is likely to get us more positive outcomes.

CEOs Screw Up, Too

Equality, I was recently reminded, applies to errors as well. The ability to make mistakes is not a function of one's place in the hierarchy. I unwittingly proved my own point last year by losing my W-2s. Believe me, I looked everywhere. When I finally gave up the search, I felt silly admitting to a mistake that's most often blamed on irresponsible eighteen-year-olds. As I was apologizing to our payroll staff for the absurdity of the CEO losing his tax forms, it dawned on me that if I was going to honor my belief in everyone's ability to achieve, then that also meant that we all have the ability to make mistakes. As Landauer said, acceptance isn't always easy. Fortunately, our service-oriented payroll crew was quite gracious about replacing them. The good news is that I know they'd have handled it with the same grace and good spirit if it had been a new dishwasher who'd lost his form and not me.

Acceptance also means acknowledging that conflict, while often unpleasant, is normal and, when handled well, is also healthy. It means recognizing that failure and frustration are inevitable. It's being able to admit that we all have biases, bad days, and internal demons to deal with, but that we also all experience (often simultaneously) moments of extreme clarity and achievement well worth celebrating. Acceptance means that we can't dictate the way other people feel. (Telling others not to feel as they do is absurd and an enormous waste of, and drain on, energy. Whether someone *acts* on how they feel is, of course, their choice and a different matter altogether—skip back up to Tenet 3 for more on that.) It means that we all slip and say stupid stuff; that our feelings swing all over the place and that we don't need good reasons for them to swing. It means accepting that change never actually ends unless we close the business, which would be, of course, a change in itself.

Before I close out this section, I want to call out three areas in which acceptance—or the lack thereof—can have a huge impact on our work: *It's all out of control, the world works in paradoxical ways,* and *life is complex.*

For openers, there is the act of accepting that *it's all out of control.* I know this runs counter to standard wisdom. Think about frequently used phrases like "span of control," "cost controls," and "quality control." Management meetings are peppered with people saying things like, "We have to get that situation under control." In bigger companies, they even have a job that's called the controller. You've probably heard the word *control* used a hundred times in the last week alone. But the frequent use of the word only exacerbates the issue. Although it is hard to accept, the truth is it's all out of control. I prove the point every time I teach leadership, simply by asking the class: "Who here has been in a situation where you knew you shouldn't do something, but you went ahead and did it anyway? And then instantaneously regretted the action?" I wait fifteen seconds for almost everyone in the room to raise their hand, and the point is made. If we can't even control ourselves, how much control could we possibly have over other people and outside events? *In truth, all we have are varying degrees of influence over outcomes.*

Second, I'll say that *the world works in paradoxical ways.* To quote Voltairine de Cleyre, "[H]istory is a chain of paradoxes." Paradox, I would posit, makes life more interesting; mastering it makes our work way more productive. When I started working on this section, I was thinking I would say that there is great power in managing paradox. But the more I reflect, the more I've come to believe that it's actually the other way around—*there is no energy to be gained by effectively managing paradox; there's just energy to be lost when you manage it ineffectively.* Fighting with that reality is akin to fighting the full force of history—there is no way to win. By contrast, making peace with paradox frees that energy for other, more positive purposes.

Last, there's the acceptance of the reality that *life is complex.* People want it to be simple but, quite simply, it isn't. Cries of "things are too complicated" seem to be growing by the day, and people try so hard to reduce the world to simple black and white. But oversimplification misses the nuance, denies the density, and dismisses the depth of what's really going on. Railing against the reality that things are complex actually, I think, creates confusion and unproductive, dissonant energy. I'd suggest we'd do better to relax into the natural complexity of the world, to enjoy it for what it is. Writer Wallace Stevens said, "Everything is complicated; if that were not so, life and poetry and everything else would be a bore." Once we make peace with the way the world really is, we have a far better shot at managing it, which, in turn, makes for long-term business success.

Being able to benefit from complexity is a big reason why businesses like ours are more sustainable; they're all about diversity. Real diversity makes for healthier, more resilient, and more successful organizations. Participative management and an inclusive (not highly hierarchical) workplace will always appear chaotic to those from more conventional settings. But Murray Bookchin explained what I'd known for a long time at a gut level: "Ecological stability," he said, "is a function not of simplicity . . . but of complexity and variety. The capacity of an ecosystem to retain its integrity depends . . . on its diversity." Which is why our participative, open, energized way of working—which may seem disorganized to the corporate eye—is actually *far more stable*. We might not have sales booms at the highest of highs, but when all goes wrong in the world, we seem (knock on wood) to do far better than most in hard times. For me, it's about learning to live the way Gustav Landauer did when he wrote of himself a hundred years ago, "I accept my complexity."

9. Commit to Quality—Do Something You Believe In

Quality is the companion of acceptance; the drive to greatness helps to keep acceptance from eroding into passivity and powerlessness. When I say "quality," I'm not talking about meaningless marketing claims or engineering explanations about things being "made to spec." I'm talking about a service or product or pencil sharpener or whatever you produce that you really believe in. What you do doesn't have to be everyone else's passion (though that certainly will help your sales). But it does need to be something that *you* really care passionately about. I always think of the shoe-shine man I met at the tiny airport in Uberlandia in central Brazil (en route to visit our coffee supplier). He kept track of how many shines he'd given and had a sign posted laying claim to being the best in the business. The man mindfully made shoe-shines into something special and brought more positive energy to his little corner of the world than most anyone else I've interacted with.

Quality is also about the drive to do great things, about caring, believing, and conversely, of course, being cared about and believed in. Consider Emma Goldman's great line: "[Anarchism] is the freest possible expression of all the latent powers of the individual, . . . [which is] only possible in a state of society where man is free to choose the mode of work, the conditions of work, and the freedom to work. One to whom the making of a table, the building of a house, or the tilling of the soil, is what the painting is to the artist and the discovery to the scientist—the result of inspiration, of intense longing, and deep interest in work as a creative force." That truly is what I believe we're doing here. Certainly not perfectly, but there's a passion in most every Zingerman's cheese seller, counter person, bartender, and baker that far surpasses what's out there in most of the world. Believing in what you're doing makes a big difference.

When people don't believe, when quality is low, and no one really cares, work becomes the drudgery we all want to avoid. Without caring, without conscious, freely chosen, internally driven commitment to the cause, it becomes pretty clear pretty quickly that there's little point in doing the work other than to pay bills. I can't imagine that any of us who've felt like we were doing mindless and meaningless work ever really felt good about it. Energy drops, insight evaporates, creativity is crushed. It's a sad reality that was well woven into anarchist writing; the industrial scene scape at the turn of the last century was pretty grim. Most every workplace was pretty much working over the people in it, and, although the lights are brighter and the labor laws are more liberal, I don't know that the emotional part of the equation is all that much better now in our own era. Looking back a ways, the anarchists were basically forecasting the energy crisis in the workplace a couple hundred years ago. Early English anarchist William Godwin warned in his 1793 essay, "An Inquiry into Political Justice," "Beware of reducing men to the state of machines." Instead, he advised, "Govern them through no medium but that of inclination and conviction." He continued in "Of Avarice and Profusion," stating that the industrial model "reduces the exertion of a human being to the level of a piece of mechanism, prompted by no personal motives, compensated and alleviated by no genuine passions. It puts an end to independence and individuality, which are the genuine characteristics of an intellectual existence, and without which nothing eminently honourable, generous, or delightful can at any degree subsist." Granted, Godwin's writing is rather 18th century, but you get the point. And he had a point. It happens to be the same one that's being made in most every good business book on the market about leading effectively in today's world: people don't do well when they get treated like removable machine parts.

Lest you think this phenomenon was one only of ancient times, here's an unsolicited sidebar from Pete Sickman-Garner, our longtime marketing manager, who's one of the more spirited, hard-working, creative, and collaborative people I've worked with over the years. "My first job," he mentioned at a meeting one day, "was at a fast-food franchise. I lasted about a month." He laughed and shook his head. "If you want to learn to hate work, get a job like that!" "What did you hate about it?" I asked. "Well," he said, "they don't train you. They don't talk to you. And you get this four-by-four grill you're supposed to work, and that's all you know. You're not supposed to think about anything else." "How long did it take you to get over it?" I asked. He thought about it for a minute. "About ten years," he said.

To go back to Berkman: "Permit [a man] to do the work of his choice, the thing he loves, and his application will know neither weariness nor shirking. You can observe this in the factory worker when he is lucky enough to own a garden or a patch of ground to raise some flowers or vegetables on. Tired from his toil as he is, he enjoys the hardest labor for his own benefit, done from free choice." We know from experience that people treated with respect and expected to do the right thing will probably most naturally want to make something special. They want to be a part of building something bigger than themselves when they go to work. They dearly and deeply love what they do and they really do want to make a difference. They could be nurses, truck drivers, gardeners, or point guards—there are passionate people in every field. I have a friend who gets so excited about archiving (which most people would dismiss derisively as "record keeping"), she can barely contain herself when I ask her what she's working on. As Emma Goldman elucidated, "When we can't dream any longer, we die."

10. Understanding That It's All One Life, and It's an Artful One at That

I'd like to return for a moment to the thoughts of Wendell Berry, whom I quoted in the introduction to this book. As you may recall, it was from a letter he'd written to the editor of *The Progressive*, responding to an article advocating reducing the work week to thirty hours in order to preserve jobs and make sure that people enjoyed a "proper" chance to appreciate "life." Berry is one of the country's great writers, an eloquent advocate for traditional, sustainable agriculture, and an all-around insightful and interesting guy. While he made many good points, one is particularly relevant to this tenet. "Only in the absence of any viable idea of vocation or good work can one make the distinction implied in such phrases as 'less work, more life' or 'work-life balance' as if one commutes daily from life here to work there."

That line still makes me laugh even though I've read it about eighty-eight times now. Where did the idea come from that there was something called "work" and something else called "life," and that the one only started when we clocked out from the other? The way I've long seen it—and Wendell Berry pretty clearly concurs—*we work at all aspects of our life, and we're alive at work.* In the end, it really is all one life. Berry pokes appropriate fun at the writer of the original article, pointing out "the evidently startling possibility that we might work willingly, and that there is no necessary contradiction between work and happiness or satisfaction."

In fact, good work is a significant contributor to a high-quality life. No matter how few or how many hours you spend at work, playing golf, gambling, or getting a college degree, the point is, *it's all one life.* Work doesn't have to be something you do just to get by. Sure, we work in part to pay the bills. But to Berry's beautifully stated point, good work is about far more than that. Good work, I would posit, is something we do to help develop ourselves, and something we do to help the world and those around us. As Gustav Landauer wrote, "What we have to do is but to re-discover what lies hidden in us, what is inalienably ours, that what our true and better selves are called for to represent; namely the binding and unifying tie, the true and full life of the human spirit. To live in a wrong way is to live a life of death." By contrast, choosing (see Tenet 3 above) to enjoy it, to bring positive energy into all areas of existence, is a much more rewarding way to go.

Visioning the Artful Life You Want

Perhaps one of the ways we help bring Tenet 10 to life is by teaching personal visioning classes for our staff. Larry Lippitt, son of Ron Lippitt, the man who developed the approach to visioning we use here every day, wrote in *Preferred Futuring* that "Freedom . . . means being able to actively and consciously participate in the creation of your own future. If your future is decided by others you really are not free. [T]here is a relationship between freedom and our willingness to determine what our future will be." By teaching visioning we're helping everyone here to come clear on their long-term dreams and desires. Once they know where they're going, how their work and family and passions fit together, creating a congruent, rich, and rewarding life is well within their grasp. The message, the belief behind it, and the real-life experience all around it, is that we can all make tomorrow the tomorrow we want. As anarchist and longtime student of the American West, C. E. S. Wood, wrote, "Without Vision life is mere existence." And, Wood went on, "Vision is no empty dream, no floating cobweb. It is man's vital force." Or to quote Gustav Landauer, "Humans have the capacity to freely and independently create a life that is their own." The more we help everyone here understand that, through visioning, they can create the life of their dreams—one that includes family, work, hobbies, sports, art, or anything else that they're drawn to—the more they can bring congruency to all they do. Which in turn improves their energy, makes life more enjoyable and work more effective—in the end, we all win.

I feel very fortunate to have found good work the way I have—I know that many people haven't. I work hard to enjoy what I have and to help others create and live in ways that work for them. That, I think, is a big part of my job. Call it a calling, call it "good work," call it vocation, or, if you want, a "vacation." That's actually what I've started to say. Work, to me, is a vacation. If a vacation is about doing what you want to do, and not "having" to go to work, well, heck, that's what I do every day. Bringing all the elements of our lives into one holistic, sustainable construct is well in synch with anarchist approaches. The anarchists, Murray Bookchin wrote in *Remaking Society*, "saw no contradictions between material well-being and a well-ordered society, between substantive equality and freedom, or between sensuousness, play, and work." I'm in on all counts.

Never Enough Time

One piece of this work for me was the realization that there would probably never be enough time to do as much of all the things that I love to do. When I'm writing, I feel like I could happily do nothing but work on books 100 hours a week and I'd still have more to do. When I'm reading, working through the ever-growing stack of books I've bought, I feel like I could do that for 100 hours a week as well. When I'm on the floor at the Roadhouse, I'm happy doing that all day, too. And when I'm laying on the beach, I usually feel like I could just stay there and never go back. Although most people complain about not having enough time, I realized one day that not having enough time was a given—no matter what it is that I like to do, I will never have enough time for it. But, given Natural Law 9 ("Success means you get better problems"), I'm happy to have this issue. I choose never to be bored, and I love the fact that I have so many things I want to get done. Is there enough time to get in everything I want to do? No. But the alternative is to not have so many things I'm excited to do, and I far prefer the problem I have now!

If there's an issue of balance, I believe it's more about balancing one's energy inputs with outputs. It's much like an organic farmer managing what goes into and later out of his or her soil. The two need to be in synch. The same goes for society at large. Good work, living the Twelve Natural Laws of Business, and mindfully managing your energy (physical, emotional, and vibrational as per pages 78–80) can put a lot of positive power into play. Doing good work and managing ourselves well usually means that there's plenty of energy available to sustain us in whatever we choose to do. Even when we're physically tired, we can still feel nourished. By contrast, bad work, feeling forced, unvalued, and uncared for, and all the other negative stuff that we know dominates society today, leaves people with very little energy to invest in anything. They're depleted, drained, and discouraged. It's no wonder they can't wait for Friday to arrive. Burnout, I believe, comes most to those who aren't feeling gratified by what they do all day, or to those who aren't doing the right work.

The way I see it, whether it's for nine hours a week or ninety, I try to always be fully alive when I'm at work (and anywhere else I go). And in order to make the most of my life outside of work, I actually work at that too. The way I see it, life is art. And work is just as much an art as life. Which then, through the transitive property of prose, leads me to my long-held conclusion that, in a good way, life is also work. A good life includes good work—whether that's volunteering in the community, raising kids, or running a company. And good work is joyful and full of life.

11. Workable Ways for Everyone to Modify and Self-Monitor Systems and Structures

You know by now that Anarcho-Capitalism is all about bringing out the best in everyone in the organization. We know, too, that people do their best work when their motivation and drive come from within. And we know that when people don't know how they're doing, they have a hard time getting to greatness. *For people to do good work, they have to be able to tell for themselves how things are going.*

If you believe in people, then putting self-regulating systems in place and supporting those systems with sound leadership is the way to go. Quite simply, people work better when we give them effective structures to work in. And they work smarter when they know that they can modify those systems to make things run better. The results are significant—more eyes on the prize, appealing to people's self-motivation, and better teamwork, decision making, collaboration, continuity, and succession. Murray Bookchin stated it well: "[E]very normal human being is competent to manage the affairs of society and, more specifically, the community in which he or she is a member."

At Zingerman's we create systems and structures that allow everyone involved (including me) to see how we're doing all the time and correct the course when needed. Having realized how important these systems are, I can see clearly that there are self-regulating regimens all over our organization. They're not very hierarchical, but they are well structured and very clear. All are designed to give individuals here the chance to self-start and to make something special happen.

Open-book finance is the most obvious—everyone knows the financial score, learns how to run a business, and participates in making it better. There are many processes in place. Our Bottom-Line-Change recipe (see page 337) allows anyone here to start a change. Our service steps empower everyone to do whatever it takes to make a customer happy, and our service measurement tells us how it's working. We count quality, too; scoring the food every day lets all of us keep track of how we're doing. And everyone here can participate in our annual planning work.

To quote modern-day business writer Margaret Wheatley, "[A] major act of leadership right now, call it a radical act, is to create the places and processes so people can actually learn together, using our experience." I've learned from ZingTrain's Maggie Bayless and other folks who teach and train for a living that adults need to know how they're doing and why they're doing it, and they do best when they can self-manage for success. Everything I've written about in this essay—being real, accepting the world as it is, respecting every individual and every individual contributing to the group cause—fits with this concept of self-directed scorekeeping. Everyone knows what's going on and how we're doing, and in the process, appropriately, we're undercutting the old parental-corporate model.

12. Make Money Doing It!

Money has never been the main driver at Zingerman's, but it's fairly obvious that it's an essential element of surviving, and hopefully thriving, in the world. The reason this is Anarcho-*Capitalism* is that we don't just want to do the right thing, we want to make money while we're doing it. Per Natural Law of Business 3 ("Without good finance, you fail"), there's really no reasonable or sustainable way around the issue of the dollars and cents of what we do. Unless you make everything you need on your own (we don't) or come from some wildly well-off family (I don't) so that business is basically just a hobby, one has to make money. There are no handouts, no guarantees, no trust funds, no assurance that we're going to get anything other than a shot at doing this tomorrow (and even that can go away when natural disaster or unexpected health issues appear on the scene).

If you look back a hundred years, the anarchists were essentially archenemies of the old-school capitalists. And, not wrongly so. I'm generalizing, but the big business barons were hardly concerned with any of what I've written about above. Quality maybe, but mostly only as a means to make money; the idea of doing it to give people meaningful work in which to believe or to make the world a better place to be was not a high priority. I'd like to bring that animosity to an end and show that anarchism, and its respect for equality and free choice, can be completely compatible with the capitalist idea of the free market and making money. What brings these two seemingly opposite approaches together into one workable, sustainable sort of business is that we don't get to the money-making part until we've worked our way through all the others above. The bottom line really is critical, but I guess it's appropriate that it comes at the end of the list.

Thinking back, I began my business career believing, much as the anarchists did, that business was bad. It was Paul who set me straight. He told me that business was neither good nor bad—it was, he said, "just a tool that you can use for good or for bad things." That idea is what allows us to wed these two historically conflicting ideologies into one harmonious philosophy for working in the world.

When you do it as we do, I really think even Emma Goldman would have been excited about the money-making part of it. She did, we know for sure, like good food, good fun, and nice things (for which, by the way, she often took a lot of flak from her anarchist colleagues). She stood up regularly for her sense of style—one of her best-known lines was: "I did not believe that a Cause which stood for a beautiful ideal, for anarchism, for release and freedom from conventions and prejudice, should demand the denial of life and joy." The reality of the world is that, uplifting spiritual activity and free thinking aside, we still have to pay the bills. But where the old model pitted profit against positive energy, we've put them, so to speak, on the same side—profit here is aligned with, and totally supportive of, our organizational ability to go out and do good things in the world.

Profit 5.1

While I take profitability really seriously and regularly push to make sure ours is at a healthy level, I've never yet gotten up in the morning thinking about making money. I look at profit as I do most every other potentially positive thing in life: something to be created consistently over time and, in moderation, used to contribute to those around me. As with most things, extremes on either end of the spectrum are suboptimal. A diet of binging and purging is unhealthy, and a boom-or-bust approach to business is similarly exhausting: the better we get at delivering a steady profit, the healthier we'll be. Which, of course, is easier said than done. If you aren't familiar with the typical net operating profit for high-end food businesses, it's pretty generally a single-digit percentage of sales. Often it's a rather low single digit. Many food businesses actually finish their year with a minus sign in front of their profit number; fortunately, we haven't had too many of those over the years.

It was Bakehouse managing partner Amy Emberling who reminded me why moderation is an important element in creating sustainable profits.

"Without profit," she explained, "we're out of business, but if we overdo it we're going to end up in trouble, too." Sustainable farming means leaving enough nutrients in the soil to foster future growth; sustainable business takes the same long-term outlook. If you try to drain every last dime out of the business as quickly as you can, you aren't going to be very sustainable. Eventually the energy in your "ecosystem" will be exhausted, and community, owners, staff, and suppliers will all suffer.

To that end, we actually did some work here a few years ago and agreed that a profit level of 5.1 percent would be a rough target for our businesses (I know, we could just as easily have said a flat 5 percent, but 5.1 is more fun). Some years, of course, we aim higher, others lower. But, generally, 5.1 percent is the number that, after *a lot* of long discussions, seemed to provide us with financial health, ensure a fair return to our community and our customers, give a reasonable profit for our investors so they keep investing, set aside savings in case we get hit with unexpected problems, pay for new equipment, and the like. That doesn't mean it's the right number for you or anyone else, but it's one that works for us. What's important here is that the calculation acknowledges all the factors (cash flow, capital reinvestment, savings, benefits, donations, etc.) that are important, rather than fixating on the net profit number in isolation. As Amy said (and I agree wholeheartedly), "Profit, for me, is a byproduct of other goals, never the primary goal."

Wrapping Up

The twelve tenets you've just read have been an integral part of making our organization what it has become over the last thirty years. They've helped us to attain reasonable growth, make enough money to pay the bills, pay people and purveyors, donate a lot to the community, pay ourselves, give out gain-sharing checks with a good bit of regularity, and still set some aside in case the economy should slide. The bottom line is that whether you call it Anarcho-Capitalism or just "that weird way of working they have at Zingerman's," this isn't just some untested exercise in utopian theory—it's functioning fairly well, if imperfectly, to the tune of nearly 500 jobs and $40,000,000 in sales a year.

Although it's not the way most businesses operate, freedom of choice, free thinking, and all that other good anarchist-oriented stuff, dismissed by most of the work world as ridiculous, too radical, or whatever, truly enhances organizational performance. "Diversity" isn't just some silly PC social statement—we can actually use a variety of views, backgrounds, and styles, and seemingly strong and long arguments to get to better results. Living the Natural Laws of Business, showing love and care in all we do, inspiring hope, sharing vision, and all this other good stuff all lead to higher energy, higher engagement, more creativity, and, within the self-managed structures I just mentioned, sustainable finance to go with it.

The funny part to me is that this is not really new news. Gustav Landauer, writing nearly a century ago, said that, "The following has always been true, is true now, and will always be true: people live together in communities; people exchange goods and services over long distances; people are differentiated by language, custom, desire, and need; people believe that everyone looks out for his individual interest; *however, some people stand up, make a change, and point the direction for the spirit and the courage of others.* This is the reality that will always remain."

Landauer was, like me, a peace-loving, nonviolent guy. He argued that, because revolution was all about tearing down and destruction, it was actually *regeneration*—not revolution—that anarchism was all about. I would say the same here: regeneration of spirit is, for us at Zingerman's, the first order. It's helping each of us—those who work here and those we wait on—to feel better about ourselves, and to freely choose to bring our best out into the big wide world in the interest of supporting the greater good.

I offer one last concluding quote from Landauer, who forecasted pretty poetically that "A time will follow in which humans, devoted to both themselves and to their surroundings, will once again climb mountains together to celebrate the renewal of life with fire and light. Inside of us, this time has already arrived. All we need to do now is to keep that spirit alive and spread it." What Landauer described is what I believe we are doing. We can, I think, make money in a respectful, supportive, service-focused, choice-based, sustainable, energy-building, market-oriented, community-minded business. I'm in. You?

Notes from the **back dock**

The Inside Scoop on Working Here at Zingerman's

Nancy Rucker, Facilities Manager, Zingerman's Delicatessen

If I had to narrow down my feelings about working here into one word, that word would be "blessed." I want to thank you for that. If I say more, I sometimes feel self-conscious in a way because it sounds unreal; it seems uncommon to hear people talk about their work with any joy. I could talk endlessly with great enthusiasm and joy about this organization and my work here.

This is so much more than a job for me—if the ZCoB was a meal, the main course would be generosity. I believe this is the ingredient that Ari and Paul brought into this business that made a difference from the start and is one of the reasons I work here. They both have inspired a community with their generosity! Everything we do revolves around giving—whether it's great service, opportunity, a taste, a tale, some time, inspiration, appreciation, a challenge, freedom to act, responsibility, or sharing *our* gains with the community! This energy of generosity opens our hearts and minds and inspires us to collaborate, create, and conquer the work! Generosity spreads. It's like an inoculation of goodness that penetrates everything we do and awakens gratitude, which just makes this all the more potent; creativity thrives in this environment. For me this is meaningful beyond expression—it's a spiritual experience. The connections and expressions of working here are alive with purpose, fertility, and growth. It's fun, action-packed potential that we call work. I love it!

ji hye kim serving really good asian street food from our food cart

A Second Look at Sustainable Business

Buying in the Mainstream May Be Cheaper but Are We Really Paying the Full Price?

Having now shared eleven "secrets," twelve Anarcho-Capitalist tenets, extensive insights on energy, and a host of other assorted stories based on thirty years of learning, I hope it's been of help and that you've learned at least a few things from the book that you can effectively put to work in your life. But I want to end the book with this epilogue, by turning the tables on myself and share something I learned from writing it. What follows has been a huge help to me in framing our work and the way we fit into the world—I hope it's of equal value to you.

It was only when we were getting close to sending the *Guide to Good Leading, Part 1* to our local printer that the metaphor of our organization as a sustainable small farm, or maybe an organic garden, came to my mind. We'd long been believers in sustainable produce, so it only made sense that we view business in much the same way. In fact, I liked the idea so much that a few weeks before we put the book to bed, I snuck in a last-minute postscript to the essay on sustainable business. (It's at the end of Secret 15, on page 240 of *Part 1* if you want to look it up.) What it says, in a nutshell, is that the old model of business is mostly about maximizing the bottom line and extracting as much as possible from everyone and everything it comes in contact with. In a *sustainable* business, by contrast, although things may not look as superficially neat and hierarchically ordered, everyone and everything involved should come out *ahead*—staff, customers, suppliers, community, and the environment. The metaphor made an impact. I've been thinking about it, teaching it, and learning from it ever since.

But as I worked on *Part 2*, it became increasingly clear to me that in my first go-round with the model, I hadn't grasped the full impact of the image. Knowing what I know now, I see that I'd totally missed the element of energy—it just wasn't something we were working on at that point. Today, the connection couldn't be clearer. As per Secret 19, we know that when organizations operate in violation of the Natural Laws of Business, an energy crisis in the workplace will ensue. Building on that insight, what came to me during the writing of *Part 2* is just how much impact the energy in the business—for better and, unfortunately, for worse—carries over into the family lives and communities of the people we work with. It is, I suppose, the business equivalent of agricultural runoff; what starts on the farm doesn't stop flowing when it gets to the property line. Doing *bad work* poisons people's spirit. When the energy in a business is bad, it's inevitable that the people who work in, buy from, and sell to that business are going to pass all their work-related negativity and frustration on to the rest of their community. A business that's based on bad work will slowly but surely poison the environment around it.

On the upside, a sustainable business has a hugely positive influence on the lives of the people who are part of it. Doing *good work* every day alters the way those people relate to the world. They feel better, and they feel better to be around. They learn skills and take home tools that are of equal value in every other aspect of their lives as well. They start to do visioning work at home, they give good service to their families and friends, and they bring positive energy everywhere they go. They begin to believe in themselves more strongly. Everyone around them benefits from the way they're working. And just as no one who's gotten used to eating good bread, good cheese, or good chocolate will ever willingly go back to bad, people who work in sustainable settings will never willingly accept bad work—once you're in a more positive setting, it's hard to put up with passé. The energy gap between those who work in sustainable businesses and those who work in old-school, unsustainable settings is vast.

Positive Energy, Packed to Go

The more I worked on the essays in the book, the more I realized just how much impact what we were doing in the workplace was having on the lives of the people who worked here. To wit, check out what happened the morning I sat down to start writing this essay. Somewhere on the sunnier side of 7:00 a.m. one midsummer day, I was at work at the back corner table of the Deli where I frequently set up to sip coffee and get organized. Out of the corner of my eye, I got a sense of someone approaching at a rather rapid pace. I looked up and saw Grace Fisher coming my way. For context, Grace is in high school, so I'll guess she's somewhere around seventeen, and, at that point, she'd probably been working at the Deli for about six months. She walked up and politely asked if she could talk to me for a few minutes. This accessibility is one of the benefits of what I could call "management by sitting around"—by working out in the open as I do (instead of being in an office all day), people spontaneously tell me things they'd probably never make time to do if they had to compose a long letter, make an appointment, or request some special audience with the boss.

Grace's energy as she approached me was pretty high. She sat down, smiled, and sort of nervously said, "You might get sick of hearing this, but . . . can I just tell you?" She paused and I got a bit nervous myself—I couldn't quite tell if she was upset or upbeat. I reassured her that I was very happy to hear her thoughts. She took a deep breath and announced: "I just have to tell you. I *love* this job!" I was excited. Professions of passion for a job are not something you typically hear from a seventeen-year-old. But Grace was just getting going. "I *really* love it!" she repeated. "I feel so good about it. It carries over into my whole life. I feel like I can make suggestions here. And that when I do, people will listen to me. And that I can be creative. I really love it and I wanted to tell you that. Last night I went home and tasted three different chocolate bars and it was great. I decided that I'm gonna get really good at it. And there's so much to learn!"

Segue back, for a second, to Pete Sickman-Garner's story (see page 284) about learning to hate work when he was roughly the same age as Grace. It took him ten years to recover, to finally start to see work as a positive thing, not as something he should stay as far away from as possible. Which means that for a solid decade a smart, creative, caring guy was working way below capacity, feeling bad about what he did and about himself, for at least 40 hours a week. You think that didn't impact his relationships when he went home every day? How can you hate what you do eight hours a day and not have that cause hardship to all you interact with? No way that I know of.

A bit further afield is the impact that our approaches have made through ZingTrain. Teaching them to people who are working to build sustainable businesses of their own is an amazing and rewarding thing to be a part of. Barely a week goes by that we don't hear back from someone who's been to a ZingTrain session about how much positive impact our ideas have had in their businesses. Recent seminar attendee Beth Fahey, who co-owns Creative Cakes with her sister on Chicago's southwest side, saw me pouring water at the Roadhouse the evening after we'd finished a two-day ZingTrain session on visioning. She took my hand, looked me straight in the eye, and said, very seriously, "I want you to understand. The last few days were transformative. I will never look at life the same way again."

It's probably not a coincidence either that, as I was working on this epilogue, I happened to have tea with J. D. Loeks. J. D. is the president of Celebration! Cinemas in Grand Rapids, Michigan, a family-owned chain of ten upscale theaters spread across the western side of the state. He'd driven the two hours down to Ann Arbor to share a few thoughts. "You guys teach so many people through ZingTrain. But I don't know how much you hear back from people about how what you teach has impacted their organizations. I wanted you to know that the impact on our organization has been profound. We came to the ZingTrain service seminar in 2008, and I mark that date as a significant turning point in our business. Three years later, we have our own service training, based on yours, but adapted to what we do. And all 600 of our employees have been through that training." Since that time Celebration! has also adapted our approach to open-book finance and our process for organizational change. "It happens gradually," J. D. said. "But we've changed a lot. It's profound. I hear from people that this is an exciting time to work for this company. I've got a team of VPs, two of whom are hitting thirty-five years working for the company, really good guys who do good work. And they're saying that of all their years here, this is the most exciting time that they've worked for this company. The things we learned from you have changed the way people here feel about work."

Coming back closer to home, check out the story that follows from Carole Woods. She's worked here for many years now so I know she has plenty of good Zingerman's tales to tell. But this one, about the value of visioning and its impact on her life outside of work, is particularly poignant. It still makes me cry every time I tell it. In fact, Carole and I have that in common. "I think I stopped telling this story every time I teach our M.O.R. Money class," she shared, "because I almost always get teared up and it gets sort of embarrassing! When we began the first Money Club here at work, we decided to start the year off with writing a vision of where we each wanted to be by the end of our year together. At the beginning, I had terrible credit and huge credit card debt and really no idea of how I could get out of it. I wanted to buy a house, but knew I was in no position to even begin that process. My vision stated that by the end of the year, I'd have reduced my debt and increased my credit score so that I'd be able to start talking to someone about getting a mortgage. It felt weird to just write that down because I didn't really believe at that time that I could do it. But month after month, I plugged away at my goals and with the help of the group—the people whom I communicated my vision to— I did in fact get into a position to apply for a mortgage. And right now, as I write this, I'm sitting at the computer in my house that I've lived in for the past three years. I've paid the mortgage on time or early every month and now have more savings than I've ever had. Writing a vision, putting it down on paper, and sharing it with others—what can I say? Life changing."

There are about two dozen similar stories that demonstrate the positive impact that sustainable businesses can have on the community a few pages from here in "Notes from the Front Porch" (insights and comments from people who've put ZingTrain teaching into play in their own organizations, on page 307) and in the "More Notes from the Back Dock" (more thoughts about working in a sustainable business from other Zingerman's staff members, on page 317). I know that their words had an enormous impact on me. What really became clear as I was writing this book, processing the views of so many good people who are touched by what we do, is that the real cost of a business's products isn't fully covered by the price tags on its products or in its profit and loss statements. *To calculate the true cost, one needs to add in the impact the business has on its staff and, further still, the impact they have on others in their lives and on the place they live.*

Paying the Full Price

To frame this insight about the real cost of doing business, let me take you back to a story from an American Institute of Wine and Food conference on organic agriculture I went to in the mid-'90s in Washington, D.C. At that time, the idea of sustainable farming was far less mainstream than it is today—there were no mass-produced organics back then. A panel of half a dozen experts presented their views on the subject. At the end, the audience—filled with chefs, academics, and writers—got time to ask questions. One attendee sort of called out the people on the panel. "I don't mind paying ten percent more for organic," he offered (with that rather belligerent, "let's see how you're gonna handle this one" tone of voice that we've all heard way too many times), "but how exactly do you justify charging double?" His implication was obvious—organics are mostly just a marketing sham used to justify charging consumers more money.

The audience, as I recall, got rather quiet, waiting for the panel's response. One of the presenters, whose name I unfortunately can't recall, decided to field the question. "Look," he said, quite calmly, reclaiming the tone and energy of the exchange, "When you pay for conventional produce at the cash register, you aren't really paying the full price. Sure, you give them what they tell you that you owe. But the price they quote you doesn't actually cover the whole cost of what you're buying. Later, you're going to pay for the rest of its cost in the form of environmental clean-up, health care for the people who worked in the fields, soil restoration, etc. You won't see that stuff in the price they're charging you in the store, but the money's going to get paid out down the road in the form of taxes, insurance rates, and environmental surcharges. But when you buy organic produce," he pointed out, "what you pay at the cash register really is the full price. Because the organic farmer always leaves the soil in at least as good, and usually better, shape than when they started."

That story has stuck in my mind ever since. Although I was already inclined towards organic agriculture, his simple, nonscientific explanation made total sense to me. So much so that I started to use it a decade later to explain our 2020 vision of leaving our world better than we found it. As with organic (or what we'd now call sustainable) growing, I explain, our vision states that everyone and everything we interact with—staff, customers, community, environment, each other—will be better off for having interacted with us than they were before we started. I'd been sharing the story for many years when, one day, smack in the middle of teaching a ZingTrain seminar, it dawned on me that I'd been missing half of the point each time I told it. I'd quickly adapted the part of his explanation about the sort of positive impact we wanted to have by leaving everyone who interacted with us better for the experience. But I'd somehow completely missed the parallel in the start of his story about the price the customer was paying.

What I realized was that the same thing he was saying about the incomplete price of commercial produce at the cash register—in contrast to the fully-paid-on-the-spot price for organic produce—was equally relevant in the context of customers buying from any business. Take out the word "produce" and plug in "business" and the conclusion is identical. *When we buy from a business that doesn't subscribe to a sustainable approach, we aren't really paying the full price when they give us a receipt at the cash register.* Later, there will come costs for the stress carried back to families, the cost of staff who get their medical care by going to the emergency room, and the seemingly intangible but still significant cost of the tension and bad energy they emit to the rest of the community. The tension that comes from going to work day after day when you really don't want to go adds up, and adds up to poor health, weight gain, substance abuse, and a hundred and a half other problems. Whether those costs show up on your invoice or not, they're most certainly still there—they amount to a secret, after-the-fact, surcharge on society.

By contrast, when you buy from a sustainable business—and, flawed though it is, I believe ours is one—I think you are paying the full price. Because our impact on the world around us is positive, when we present our customers with a bill at the counter, those people really *are* paying the full social price. The difference between the two situations and their opposing impacts on society are, I suppose, the energy equivalent of a differential equation. It's a long, long way from barely getting by doing bad work every day to getting to do good work.

Thinking of Grace Fisher, but quoting from Emma Goldman, "[T]he true function of organization is to aid the development and growth of [the individual's] personality." Our responsibility, remember, is to help everyone who works here grow, develop, and learn to constructively be themselves. The better we do that work, the better people feel, the better they feel, the better the business does, too. From all of that emerges the kind of innovation, creativity, and energy that's naturally present in everyone when they're born, but has since been lost to so many from destructive work and social settings. Most organizations are still struggling hard to rediscover it, pushing their people to be more creative and to innovate more often. Sustainable settings, by contrast, working with (and not against) the Natural Laws of Business, gently and effectively bring it out organically as people learn to be themselves. Quoting again from Emma, "It is the harmony of organic growth which produces variety of color and form, the complete whole we admire in the flower."

There's Still a Farmer

The other key learning point for me in this sustainable business metaphor is brief. Although what we do here may appear to just happen organically, it's most definitely not unmanaged. *There is still a farmer!* And that farmer is you or me, the leaders who are at work trying to help make good things happen for everyone around us, the people who have chosen as their calling to serve their organizations, to work in the best interests of everyone around them. The farmer, in this metaphor, makes hay by respectfully, gently but firmly, working to do all the things that I've written about in the first two parts of this series (as well, I'm sure, as many good things I've not yet thought of or written about).

Sustainable farms and organic gardens are great, but in case you had any illusions to the contrary, farming is a lot of work. Most of that work is anything but glamorous. But in the end it makes for some great-tasting produce grown in respectful and environmentally sound ways. Being the leader in a sustainable business setting is also a lot of work. While it may look softer from the outside looking in, working this way requires very strong and effective leadership. It's not leadership in the old context, the one that calls for closed-door meetings, careful assignment of titles, extensive commanding, and a lot of controlling. It is, as you now know, a style of leadership that embraces vision, values, service, stewardship, staff involvement, sharing information, sensitivity to individual dreams and desires, free choice, complexity, paradox, and the import of asking for help.

In agriculture, the farmer figures out what and where to plant; it may all be organic, but he or she is ultimately in charge. They make those decisions with nature's and everyone else's interests at heart as well as their own—decisions that are all about abundance, appreciation, and looking at things from the big picture with a long-term perspective. The same goes for business. Leaders in a sustainable setting still make decisions about people, products, prices, new programs, promotions, etc. It's about guiding without dominating, making diversity into an advantage instead of driving it out, helping bring out the best in everyone instead of trying to get everyone to just give their best. But they do it in a way that's respectful and inclusive of all those around them, not just for a higher return on shareholder value. Whether it's a skilled farmer working an organic garden or a skilled business leader working a sustainable business, they're leaving their part of the world a better place than when they found it.

The End of the Epilogue

Despite my passion for all this work about sustainable business, Anarcho-Capitalism, Servant Leadership and the like, I'm not on a mission to convert the world overnight or anything of the sort. Lecturing those who don't want to hear how they should live a better life never, ever works. I'm more for setting a good example, sharing what we've learned here, and showing that the way we work is a viable, shall we say, sustainable, alternative to what most everyone else is doing. As per Gustav Landauer—"Revolution of spirit is, for us, the first order"—my commitment as a leader, going forward, is to be a better sustainable "farmer"; to do an ever better job of living our mission by enhancing the experiences we bring to customers, the community and our co-workers; to live the Natural Laws of Business, to provide Servant Leadership, to manage my own energy and help them manage theirs, to make sure we have inspiring, strategically sound visions, and to find ways to keep pouring water as we go forward; to remember that it's important to be the beekeeper a lot of the time. And through that effort, to continue to effectively share with others the tools and techniques that have helped to make our work more effective and our own organization here more sustainable.

All of which leads me to think about how many people who came to work here (or at other sustainable businesses) left and went on to start or lead a healthy organization of their own. The approaches we teach here are spreading slowly but steadily across the country. Ask anyone in Santa Barbara about Michael Graham's C'est Cheese; in Chattanooga about John and Angela Sweet's Niedlov's Bakery; or up in Northport, Michigan, about Jess Piskor and Abra Berens's Bare Knuckle Farm. All of these former Zingerman's staff members have established sustainable businesses of their own. All have put their own stamp on what they do, but each in some way uses elements of what they learned while they were here. Or ask any of the many organizations from around the country that have come to ZingTrain seminars and taken back and adapted many of these approaches to leadership and business building. I'm thinking about the folks at the Old Lahaina Luau on Maui; Celebration! Cinemas in Grand Rapids, Michigan; Harvey Sackett and the others at his law firm in Los Gatos, California; Wheatsville Co-op in Austin, Texas; or the Merc Co-op in Lawrence, Kansas. In their own ways, they're all building sustainable businesses in their settings as well.

Which is, really, what I hope you will do with the "secrets" in the book. Take them, adapt them, and put them to good use where you work and where you live. In the process, slowly, productively, and positively let's spread the word by letting others choose freely to adapt them to their world as well. As Gustav Landauer wrote, "Inside of us, this time has already arrived. All we need to do now is to keep it alive and spread it."

Here's to better leadership and to building sustainable businesses. All the best in all you do!

working the bar at the roadhouse

Extra Bonus Stuff

the black bench out front of the delicatessen

Notes from the Front Porch

As I'm sure you've noticed in going through the last three hundred pages, I'm adamant that all of these "secrets" work well in businesses other than our own. They can, as you'll see below, be organization-altering experiences. What follows are stories from folks who've adapted our ideas and approaches to their businesses. They offer, I hope, a different but productive perspective on what it means to put all this to work in places that are far afield—geographically or professionally—from our Zingerman's Community of Businesses in Ann Arbor.

Whether it's been the ZingTrain Art of Giving Great Service seminar, Fun Flavorful Finance, or reading Ari's last book, individually and collectively, each of these experiences has resonated both professionally and personally for my staff and me. During a custom ZingTrain program attended by our entire staff in Ann Arbor, Ari said, "It doesn't cost anything to be nice to people." Today a sign with this quote adorns our office. Why is this important? The ZingTrain experience has taught us to actually take the time to be kinder to our clients and each other. As a result, the sense of team we have is not simply a phrase, but a bona fide part of our culture. Clients pick up on this energy; those of us who work together day in and day out feel it and are more productive because of it. Clients walk away having felt like their experience with our firm was a good one. One tangential result of this: the number of client referrals has increased exponentially. And, to take it one step further, this means we can spend less on marketing our services because we're doing it ourselves by virtue of how we treat our clients.

This sense of teamwork has also been felt by practicing open-book finance. Staff members are not cogs on a wheel but, rather, critically important frontline participants in the decision making of the firm. After all, who knows best as to what is really going on than those who are in the proverbial trenches? Because of their active and ongoing engagement, staff members feel a greater sense of belonging and contribution. How does this shape up? Well, we make smarter, more insightful decisions earlier on. This allows us to deal with the "good" and the "bad" with enhanced foresight and skill. My partner and I don't run the firm; truth be told, because of their heightened participation, the employees are the ones who really do.

And, because ZingTrain has given us greater perspective to see things, we think about the future much differently. Visioning has freed us up to think big and boldly about the future. We do so with reasoned reflection, but with an unshackled and more knowledgeable understanding of where we want to go. Before we learned about visioning, if asked to describe what the future would look like, I would become anxious to the point where I'd seemingly want to crawl into the fetal position. Thanks to our work with ZingTrain and Ari's book, I no longer fear the unknown but covet the opportunity to create it.

What's the upshot of all of this? I'd like to think that my relationship with ZingTrain has made me a more effective and caring leader, and perhaps just a little bit nicer of a person.

Harvey Sackett, Attorney at Law, Los Gatos, California

We randomly came across ZingTrain while shopping for mail-order gifts on the Zingerman's website. At first we were excited by the Zingerman's food tours of Italy, but then a few clicks away we found ZingTrain—a food service business doing management training. This was intriguing, and since we were already huge fans of their products, it seemed worth pursuing. It wasn't exactly a stone's throw from Maui, but less than two weeks later we found ourselves sitting in the Zingerman's Experience seminar in Ann Arbor. Wow! We were beyond impressed, not only with the quality of the information that was shared, but by the enthusiasm that we felt in every aspect of the Zingerman's organization. Ari and Maggie were delightful and insightful teachers. And their work and vision is evident everywhere in the ZCoB. Since that seminar we have brought ZingTrain to Maui three times to teach Zingerman's approaches to our management team. Because of that work we are a very different company than before our relationship with Zingerman's began. In so many ways what we have learned is making us better and better at what we do.

During that time, Ari's book, *Zingerman's Guide to Good Leading, Part 1: A Lapsed Anarchist's Approach to Building a Great Business* has become a constant resource for our company. Our key leaders are reading the book as a group and are using it as an outline to develop in-house training around the contents. While we certainly believe we have created a successful and well-regarded *ohana* (family) of businesses, the guidance, knowledge, and experience that Ari shares in his book has proven to be of enormous value and will most certainly continue to contribute to our future success. As Ari has told us, it's hard work, and, honestly, sometimes it feels really hard, but we are reminded daily of its value and how much we are growing through our partnership with Zingerman's and ZingTrain. They have become an integral part of our vision for success. The Zingerman's "recipes" for Servant Leadership, visioning, etc.— the list of concepts and practices that we are embracing from Ari's writing and ZingTrain's teaching—are dramatically improving our organizational culture. We are daily witnesses to the new level of enthusiasm and confidence from our leadership team. Many who never conceived of the concept of visioning are using it effectively at work as well as in their personal lives. To hear of someone on our team creating a vision with their family at home is an amazing thing. Helping people to improve their lives that way is one of the reasons we want to be in business.

Everyone learns best by honest example and Ari, Maggie, Stas', Paul, and *everyone* we have worked with at Zingerman's comes to their role with amazing compassion, kindness, and understanding. When we have seminars here on Maui, they bring a true respect for the culture and for our diverse ohana. I love the moments at a workshop when I see one of our team members who, normally shy and quiet, is completely engaged in an animated conversation with Ari. Their honesty and ability to communicate to our team has brought out the very best in all of us. We have a lot to learn and we are so very fortunate to have found a partner in learning with so many common values and principals to help guide us. We look forward to working with Zingerman's for a very long time, and are forever grateful for their guidance in helping us realize our vision.

Tim Moore, Partner, Hoaloha Na Eha, Lahaina, Maui, Hawaii

I've read several of Zingerman's books, and there are always nuggets of info to take away, but I had an entirely different experience when I read *A Lapsed Anarchist's Approach to Building a Great Business*. While I was reading, I kept thinking about how I might apply different ideas to my business, but there are so many spectacular ideas in this book that I went another way. I bought copies of the book for my whole staff! We read it like a book club and met monthly to discuss two or three chapters at a time and look at how we might apply different ideas. Our biggest takeaway was that we were able to construct a draft of our five-year vision written by all staff members. It has solidified our group and brought a cohesiveness that I was previously struggling to attain in the business.

Not only have we implemented the vision, but we have begun tracking many ideas, successes, failures, and more. I am so grateful 1) that this book was written, 2) that I read it, and 3) that my staff saw what I saw in its ideas. Thanks, thanks, thanks!!!

Sharon McRill, President, Betty Brigade, Ann Arbor, Michigan

I've had several significant experiences using Zingerman's style of positive visioning and have been delighted by each process and outcome. The first experience was with the National Co-op Grocers Association during a very important and difficult transition. Ari and Stas' spent time working through a variety of exercises, including a very cool headline exercise that helped a rangy bunch of co-op managers find our agreement and develop a powerful united vision for the future. Honestly, I was amazed at the outcome of the process that I was, also to be honest, really skeptical about at first!

That led me to hiring Maggie and Zingerman's to help my co-op as we planned a major renovation that we knew would include some challenging cultural change along with a nice new building. She helped lead a wide range of my staff through a process that developed a shared vision of what success at the newly redecorated Wheatsville would look like. We also created a shared list of the things that would be retained and preserved in the new store and the things that would "stay behind." This wasn't just a list of physical attributes; it also included how we were going to treat our customers, and each other and to deal with problems constructively going forward.

This vision also included all the many positive impacts we would have with a successful project. Three staff members ended up writing a narrative of the future that was simply amazing. We still bring it out occasionally to relish in this awesome (and largely accurate) world that we agreed to create!

We've also used positive visioning for project implementation, most notably our implementation of open-book management. These visions typically look out a year or so and imagine what success would look like. They're pretty simple, really, but using them and writing them in a narrative, descriptive way really helps to bring people along with enthusiasm. *And* reading the narrative at the end of the vision's period has been very gratifying for us. It makes us even bigger believers in our ability to plan and achieve the future we want at Wheatsville.

Dan Gillotte, General Manager, Wheatsville Co-op, Austin, Texas

We are an organization that traffics in words and images. At times it's really difficult to communicate our ethics to members, donors, even employees. The best tool we have—bar none—is the values statement we honed with the help of ZingTrain. It's a distillation of our better organizational self, a living embodiment of who we are and what we hold dear. I'm not being nice in that Southern sort of way. I'm serious.

John T. Edge, Director, Southern Foodways Alliance, Oxford, Mississippi

When I went to college in Ann Arbor, I remember thinking that I hoped to see many more companies in my lifetime as energetic and soulful as Zingerman's. Twenty-three years later, after learning about thousands of companies, reading hundreds of business books, and following just as many business best practices, I still return to Zingerman's as the best example out there. What Zingerman's has figured out and documented is the most comprehensive system of how to organically grow a soulful, inspiring company.

The culture and energy of one of my companies, www.PosterBrain. com, has Zinged to an entirely new level because of what Ari recently shared about Zingerman's philosophies and "recipes." We started giving our staff the kind of service I was wanting them to give our customers. We started setting expectations weekly by having team huddles around a Zingerman's-inspired dashboard and sharing appreciations for each other. The whole company did visioning and energy-check exercises. We designed a new employee training that gave a *much* deeper sense of our history and purpose.

Within weeks, the excitement and energy of everyone in the company went through the roof. We all felt more connected, happier, more creative, and more productive as a result. Our sales and customer feedback increased along with our profitability. As a result a couple new ideas cut our waste in half, nearly eliminated our late shipments, and increased our early shipments. Our newest hire comments regularly on what an amazing place it is to work.

Thanks, Zingerman's, for sharing your wisdom and inspiration with us!

Bill Flagg, The Felix Fun, Boulder, Colorado
P.S. I decided today to drop the *d* on "Fund."

I may be one of the luckiest entrepreneurs in the world. We started Menlo Innovations in 2001, and we've been in the same Kerrytown neighborhood with Zingerman's almost our entire lifespan. What this has meant for me is that I have gotten to know Ari, Paul, and many on the Zingerman's team as personal friends. Their impact on me and my business has been profound.

Ari often speaks of the *terroir*, the effect that something has been planted in has on the fruit it bears. The Kerrytown neighborhood is an amazing place, and Zingerman's is a huge part of it. When I coach entrepreneurs, I often speak of passion as a key ingredient. You can see that passion in everyone at Zingerman's, and it starts with Ari and Paul. They love everything about what they do, who they do it for, how they do it. And they sweat every detail. And if it's not working, there are code reds, an impartial device Zingerman's uses to report problems, actionable problems. Then they fix them.

I was first exposed to open-book management at Zingerman's—all the financials and key performance indicators on the walls where *everyone* can see them. Whenever I'm discussing open book with a Menlo visitor, if they are really intrigued, I walk them across the street to see Zingerman's numbers. I don't call ahead, I don't ask permission, and I'm welcomed every time. Amazing.

One of my favorite books is *Zingerman's Guide to Giving Great Service.* Every entrepreneur should read this book. My particular favorite is the 10-4 rule. Smile and make eye contact with a customer when you are within ten feet, and say hello when within four. Ari says if you don't smile during the interview, you'll never smile when you are working, so you won't get the job! I also love their basic approach to service: if you see a problem, ask if you can help and then *listen!* (Most of us overlook this point.)

Perhaps the most impactful lessons come from their approach to mission, vision, and values that are covered in *Zingerman's Guide to Good Leading, Part 1.* Ari writes about the mission being the North Star, guiding you along a journey, but you'll never get there—it simply reminds you of the direction you've chosen. Our mission is "to end human suffering as it relates to technology." The vision process is fun and compelling—pick a day in the future and describe it in terms everyone can understand. It should be inspiring, achievable, written down(!), and communicated. One day you will achieve your vision, and thus it is something you need to revisit every few years or you may end up having achieved something great and then begin drifting (formula for disaster).

Passion, service, mission, vision, and values—and measuring your results every moment along the way to avoid drifting into complacency. These are the basics to ensure you are building a great business. Oh, and then hard work, a ton of hard work!

Thank you Ari, Paul, and Zingerman's for being an inspiring example for the rest of us!

Rich Sheridan, CEO, Menlo Innovations, Ann Arbor, Michigan

Why does Zingerman's make me feel so good? Not just about food, but about *life?*

I've often pondered this question while noshing a Montreal Reuben, slathering butter on warm Roadhouse bread, sipping a toasty cup of Brazilian Peaberry coffee, tucking into a pile of pork and collards, swooning over chocolate gelato, or watching my wife jump (literally!) for joy when she discovers a Zingerman's Mail Order box on the front porch. What the heck is going on here?

Reading and taking time to re-read Ari's writing—whether it concerns food or business—does a lot to explain it. Ari is an authentic, big-hearted, tree-of-knowledge guy who can guide you, if you take the time and effort to follow him, into what he would describe as an "artful life." A life that is necessarily all your own, in line with your heart and fully engaging your master passions, where your work is not just a job, but your vocation.

In his book Ari describes it as "a new way to work" and the employees in the ZCoB are necessarily immersed in the culture it creates. So when my life intersects with the lives of ZCoB employees, I think I'm tapping into all the individual visions of greatness, passionate pursuits, ideals, and convictions for which they've been given the tools and opportunities, through successful leadership, to discover and materialize for themselves. It's anarchism of the best sort, and it makes me feel good.

It's equally good to learn how to put these tools to work in my *own* life. Like many folks, I've had many jobs, in many places, doing many different things, none of which sustained me. From offices to auto plants, from record stores to refineries, I've often toiled at work and life (sometimes miserably) instead of thriving, and I've been lost in the proverbial woods. Ari and his writing have helped me find my way. I've discovered my vocation, I've started my own business, and I passionately agree with him (and his *own* guides whom he quotes so well) that being in business is "a way to become who you are." And that's the most important work any of us can be doing.

Keith Ewing, Proprietor, Humble Hogs (Envisioned 2010),
Ann Arbor, Michigan

When I returned from the very first ZingTrain visioning (Small Giants) seminar, I was charged up and ready to take our little olive oil business, Pasolivo, into the next phase of its life. We had used the Zingerman's approach to visioning, and—like good students—both Jillian and I had memorized our vision (we attended the workshop together and share an office the size of two phone booths). Doing that work, you imagine using it to navigate new adventures, exciting opportunities. Good, big things!

What surprised me and proved the value of vision work for a business like ours is how we came to depend on it when things got very, very tough. There was a chance we'd lose the business, and rumors ran wild in the wine-industry town we live in. We had to deal delicately with vendors, employees and customers who had known us as one thing and were alarmed that we may become something other than that. Time and again we went back to the vision. Everyone else may think we're A or B, but by keeping true to what mattered to us, our behavior overrode the craziness. We just kept doing what we do, in the way that felt right to us.

Three years later, our vision is pinned above my desk. I remember the exercise where you imagine five years forward: what you'll be wearing, who will be there, what your work place will be like. It may not be at the grand butcher-block table I'd imagined, but sure enough, my daughters will come home to do their homework with me at my Ikea desk here at Pasolivo this afternoon. Our team is wearing striped aprons just like I imagined, and—just like in my dream—there are tomatoes in the kitchen that we grab and drizzle with oil for customers. It works, even when you don't realize it, and I'm grateful professionally and personally for the Zingerman's experience that launched it for us.

Joeli Yaguda, Pasolivo Olive Oil, Paso Robles, California

After my long and harrowing day yesterday, I stopped at the Roadhouse around 7:30 for a bowl of soup to revitalize, get babied, and also come down off my adrenaline high. I ended up at the chef's counter facing the kitchen and had one of my top three most delightful times ever at a restaurant. My experience was illuminated by having sat through several of Zingerman's training sessions.

In brief, the waiter was the quintessential Zing employee—helpful, sweet, charming, funny, genuine, and attentive (*without* making me feel like a diabetic drowning in syrup, as the earnest new employees sometimes do). He offered samples when I vacillated, had only positive responses when I changed my mind, teased me like a kid brother, and responded to my customer cues by generally giving me a *relationship* experience with my dinner. It was fantastic. If I had been able, I would have left a $100 tip with my $17 check.

In chatting up my bar mates, I discovered a Zingerman's fan next to me who was a little displeased with her meatloaf . . . making interesting and detailed comments. Not sure if I did anyone any favors, but Kieron, the head chef, was walking by (he handed me a donut in a bag with a wink because he had seen me eyeing plate after plate of them going to the back-room party), and I told him she had some interesting feedback. This turned into the sweetest exchange I have *ever* witnessed, and he must know that the care he heaped on this lady is probably some of the most unconditional love she has ever experienced. She teared up when he brought her a playful sampler plate of food (she was too embarrassed to respond when he asked what she liked or what he could bring her).

Although this woman told me she saves a long time to be able to come to Zingerman's once a year for her birthday meal (apparently she's been coming for your meatloaf since you opened and she worked across the way at the then-Blockbuster store), and may not be the frequent big-bucks tab, she has a mouth. She told me that she works at Blockbuster and has thousands of customers. She was offering to tell them about my store, so you know she'll be telling them all about yours. At one point she was on the phone with a friend who called her: "No, I'm at Zingerman's. I've got to go, the *chef* is coming!!" Kieron hung around (he said it was his night off, what a trouper) for quite some time, bringing her purslane from the back and more and more and more. She loves food, and reads up and studies all kinds of prep, and her private disappointment turned into what must have been one of her best nights ever. Not to mention that he asked her to come to a meatloaf tasting that upcoming Wednesday night!

There was positive eye-to-eye contact with probably more than a dozen of your employees last night. The whole staff shined in many small and large ways, and their affection for each other (even as personality discord was acknowledged) radiated as a moving, living ribbon through the business. As a student of life and a business owner, I saw it as a $10,000 practicum of best intent plus great training and highest model of vision in action. I treasure my experience, and they all deserve a gigantic standing ovation for putting it together in a brilliant evening of pulling in the same direction and doing their jobs very well.

And a big round of thanks to all of you who have crafted and sweated this training program and management style that made it possible for them to have such a lovely experience *at work* as well! I appreciated the chance to have an uplifting experience, food for my soul, as well as a delicious plate (I got the fried chicken, which was perfect).

Beth Barbeau, Traditional Midwife, Childbirth Educator and Owner, Indigo Forest, Ann Arbor, Michigan

Hi, Ari. As you may remember, I recently accepted a job working with a new company on the housewares section of their website. Today is my fourth day, and as has been pretty typical in many of my post-Zing jobs, there's no real training, only a little guidance, and virtually no plan in place for me as I come into a new position, and as a result I have been kind of flailing around a little bit. Happily, I have the concept of *vision* to fall back on, and it is serving me well to help me find my way!

I have already introduced the concept of visioning, as you taught it to me, to my supervisor and got his approval for my working within this structure. My manager was interested and impressed, I think, and said that nobody else in this company is ever that specific with their goals, and that typically there's not anywhere near as much follow through and measurement as would be ideal. I have just today written the first draft of my vision for the housewares website through to the end of 2011. I think I'll have something to show him on Monday, and it is my goal (vision?) to have the four or five other people who are closely involved in my area in agreement and willing to support me in my pursuit of my vision.

Visioning has, without a doubt, really made a difference in my life! Thanks for this valuable tool. I will treasure it always!

Allison Schraff, Former Zingerman's Delicatessen Staffer, New York, New York

more notes from the back dock

The Inside Scoop on Working at Zingerman's

What follows are some additional comments from real live folks about what it's like to work here.

I applied to be a server at the Roadhouse with lots of great things on my resume, including international tour guide, school fundraising consultant, professional memory training speaker, and recruiter/sales manager. I had some perspective. These things sound good, and there were really great things about each experience. But as a server at the Roadhouse, I laugh *a lot,* and make others laugh. I sing while I'm serving, and often someone joins in and sings with me. I love feeling encouraged to be myself. There is good energy in the building. Guests are smiling and loving the food and having fun. Zingerman's attracts sharp workers with strong personalities, so there are usually some great conversations happening as you walk through the building. I eat great food throughout the day as part of my job. I get plenty of exercise. I feel part of a community, part of something special. I am genuinely impressed on a daily basis by the level of hard work and enthusiasm that surrounds me. I think our meetings are useful and worthwhile. I am grateful for open-book finance and love talking with guests about it. I am proud of all the food coming off Zingerman's Cornman Farms and love telling guests about that also. I love having an open kitchen where the front of house and guests can see all the stations. When I find myself talking with friends who work other places about their jobs, I find that I am usually the most satisfied. The best part is that I am able to say this in Michigan in 2011, when lots of people do not have a job and lots of others don't love their job. I am pretty sure this is the first job that I've had that I enjoy and respect pretty much all the time.

Shelly Smith, Server, Zingerman's Roadhouse

My favorite thing about working at Zingerman's is when someone sits down for a meal, looks around, and asks me, "Are all you people *seriously* this happy?" I generally chuckle, then reply, "In fact, yes, we all are really this happy. Working for a company that provides fantastic benefits (better than when I was a full-time manager at a previous employer), with 401K and gain share, and that pays us for taking classes such as personal finance and how to buy a house, all for an hourly employee, how couldn't we be happy?! Employees here are actually appreciated for the work they do, encouraged to challenge themselves and try out new opportunities, and are allowed to have fun while providing an incredible experience to the guests. Yeah, I'd say I have a pretty stellar job!!" The short answer of course is, "Yes, I actually am this happy, so are the rest of us, and no, we don't take happy pills!"

Jami Kowalski, Bartender, Zingerman's Roadhouse

Years ago I worked with thousands of professionals within a multinational company. Yet, Mr. Watson, the chairman, maintained an open-door policy—meaning any employee was invited to walk through his door (literally, or by phone) for a one-to-one interaction. I never dreamed in my lifetime I'd have another opportunity to work with such an open company. Can you imagine that Zingerman's implementation of open is exponentially greater? I know what I need to know—goals, plans, and forecasts. It gets me on board to contribute to a successful business day, week, month, and fiscal year. Plus I'm free to approach management, even Ari and Paul—especially Ari and Paul—anytime.

Nancy McClintic, Sales and Consulting, Zingerman's Catering

It is a true gift to be a leader within Zingerman's Community of Businesses; to have the freedom to be a true leader and be true to yourself. Not that there isn't pressure, but the pressure is largely self-imposed to live up to the expectations we have set for ourselves and our organization. In my 25-plus-year career, I have never felt more appreciated, engaged, challenged, and rewarded.

Elaine Steig, Zingerman's Service Steward

The Zingerman's Experience is definitely worth experiencing. There never seems to be a dull moment. We're always brainstorming to come up with new ideas. Not just to make a profit, but to make the business grow, to be a better place to work and to become increasingly more environmentally friendly. Working with the Zingerman's Community of Businesses is quite rewarding. Not only do we get discounts at every Zingerman's establishment, but we're usually on a first-name basis with the staff! Working at Zingerman's is like being a spoke that's connected to a huge, forever-turning wheel.

Bert Bisset, Shipping Supervisor, Zingerman's Creamery

I have worked for years in food and in customer service, which includes serving tables, cooking, and bartending, and now I work in catering at Zingerman's Deli. Growing up in food service, you get people asking you about where you are going to school and what for, since this couldn't possibly be your "real" job. I actually had a woman at an event tell me that I "could do better." The best thing about Zingerman's is you never feel that this isn't a *real* job. I have had, and jumped at, the opportunity to grow and learn many things across the board (like finance) that I didn't learn in my college years getting my BA in psychology. Zingerman's has helped me in so many ways that to list them all could make a small book in itself. But knowing that I am a part of a great company and that it is a *real* job makes me very proud.

CeCe McClintic, Server, Zingerman's Catering

Perhaps the most magical part of working for Zingerman's is the chance to be a part of a vision-oriented community. Something wonderfully mysterious happens when a group of people get together, define what success will look like at a particular moment in the future, and then set out to make that vision a reality. There's just no denying its effectiveness; it's dependable, measurable, and tangible. It happens every day at Zingerman's, and on all scales—from one department's vision for a single eight-hour shift to the ZCoB-wide vision for 2020. Simply put, visioning is a way of life at Zingerman's. And it makes life at Zingerman's really, really good.

Rebecca Sunde, Co-Chocolate Specialist, Zingerman's Delicatessen

two of our local suppliers

Thoughts on Books

You don't need to be much of a futurist to forecast that in the coming years old-style books are likely to fall ever further behind electronic media in terms of everyday importance. I should know—I never go anywhere other than jogging, to the beach, or to bed without bringing my computer. I know a lot of people have already written books off as old-fashioned and unnecessary baggage, justly jettisoned in the interest of easier access to information. When you add in iPads, smart phones, video games, DVDs, YouTube, Facebook, ebooks, and whatever else someone out in Silicon Valley invents in the coming decades, it might well be that paper is practically a thing of the past. I hope not, though. Business and leadership aside, I do have a case to make for bound books.

Interestingly, although books had nothing in particular to do with their politics, the anarchists were all about putting things into print in artful and aesthetically pleasing ways. Many had a serious love of learning, literature, poetry, and prose. Emma Goldman regularly spoke and wrote about theater, and the list of writers and artists who associated with anarchists is long and prestigious. Anarchist books were often as interesting for their art as for the intellectual activity inside: drawings, woodcuts, and etchings abound.

Some of the most amazing of the anarchist work was put out by Joseph Ishill and his Oriole Press. A Romanian Jewish immigrant to the United States, he published over 200 pamphlets and books on his hand-cranked press in Berkeley Heights, New Jersey. Many were small chapbooks of poetry and the like, but some were more substantial collections—300- or 400-page tributes to the anarchists, anarchist ideas, artists, and free thinkers he knew and held in high esteem. The two volumes of *Free Vistas* he produced—the first in 1933 and the next in 1937—are truly some of the most beautiful books I've ever seen. They're definitely about anarchism, but they're also incredible works of art. Each was printed, by hand, in very limited editions—less than 300 copies. Each volume includes a dozen types of paper, each of different textures, colors, and sizes, all bound together into very beautiful books. Each edition has a goodly number of remarkable woodcuts and sketches, woven in with articles, essays, politics, and poetry. To say they are amazing is an understatement—if you're into books, I'd make the trip to Ann Arbor just to go see them in the Labadie Collection on the seventh floor of the Graduate Library.

While I've certainly read old anarchist work online—working on the web is great when I'm in a hurry, and it's a lot faster to copy and paste than it is to retype the parts that I want to transcribe—I still would far rather read it all in the original. When I look at the copy on the computer I feel a little like I'm reading a half step or so removed. There's just something to be said for holding the paper, the same, slightly weathered and worn pages that someone, maybe not unlike me, might well have held in their hands a hundred years ago. Emma Goldman's essays certainly read fine and for free online, but, for me at least, the spirit is far more sensually present when I actually hold my well-worn copy of her pamphlet, "The Place of the Individual in Society," in my hand.

It's with that sort of stuff in mind that, three years ago, we made the move at Zingerman's to go back to putting out our own books—to, as author Hugh MacLeod admonished, "ignore everybody" and move away from the big, not-so-much-fun (for me at least) world of mass-market publishing and go our own way. It wasn't a snap decision. When I'd opted to do a couple of books with mainstream publishers earlier on, I made that move mindfully as well. I'd heard enough stories to know it might not be ideal for me, but I figured I should try it firsthand before I ruled it out altogether. So I did. It's hardly evil, or horrific, and there are far worse fates in life than having to put out a book with a big publisher. But I'm about a hundred times happier doing it on our own; for me, our way definitely beats the highway, even when the "highway" means a far higher rate of short-term sales.

The book you're holding right now has its issues (what doesn't?), but the decision to go to print with them was no one's but ours; while we don't have control (see page 279), we do have a very high degree of influence. When I hold one of our books in my hands, I feel the same way about it as I do a loaf of handcrafted bread from the Bakehouse, hand-ladled, paper-wrapped goat cheese from the Creamery, a made-to-order sandwich from the Deli, a carefully constructed fresh candy bar, or a rack of ribs (nine hours of smoking, braising, and steaming before they're ready) from the Roadhouse. I appreciate the paper quality, the design done by our staff, the scratchboard drawings, and the feel of it every time I pick up a volume to show it to a customer. While the words inside are the same in a book that's printed on poor quality paper with a suboptimal sense of design, well-made old-fashioned books do feel better! At the small scale at which we're working, there's a connection between the writer, the editor, the designers, the people who produce them, and the folks from whom you're buying them. It's the same sort of shorter, mindful supply chain we've worked so hard to establish with what we eat. Only in this case it's about products that are in print, not on your plate.

Going back to the small-scale publishing of the anarchist world of the early 20th century, not far behind *Free Vistas* on the beauty scale was a book Joseph Ishill issued as a tribute to Élie and Élisée Reclus. While you've likely never heard of them, the brothers were apparently special people and very highly respected back in their day. Élisée was a world-famous geographer, and his older brother, Élie, was a world-renowned anthropologist; both were also avowed anarchists. The Oriole Press book, published in 1927 (two decades after the two had passed away), is a collection of essays, letters, and articles by and about the brothers. In the introduction, Ishill himself wrote about its production: "One by one," he said, "the pages [of this book] were set up and printed by a single pair of hands, and the first crow of the neighbor's cock, indicating the passing of midnight, was the signal for me to 'lay off' for the night. In spite of handicaps, however, I never felt really fatigued with my work. There was always nervous energy to eke out the physical, and I felt a certain exaltation in the thought that I *was* burning the candle at both ends, [and] it was for a social cause. I felt what almost every other individual would feel in a society differently constituted from the present one. I was doing the work I loved—doing it with enthusiasm, if not physical strength, unimpaired."

To use Wendell Berry's worldview (see pages 28–29), that is as about as good as good work can get. Joseph Ishill's art, his books, and his insights are all pretty inspiring. He closes out the introduction with something that struck me, book lover that I am, as very timely. "Until the dawn of a more luminous day," he wrote, "let at least the few in quest of truth and beauty find their meed of content in the written word. Nothing, alas, in this era of harsh reality can quite take the place of books." I'll stand by what he said—times are still tough, so, for me at least, nothing really takes the place of a well-made book. To Mr. Ishill's point, great books are beautiful; if you couldn't already tell, I love them. Which is why, then, I really wanted to make books that I love, books that are in synch with all the other traditional, carefully crafted foods we're selling here at Zingerman's. I hope that we've at least come close to succeeding with what you have in your hands.

One last note and a bit of book-oriented laugh, so to speak, for the road. In her biography of Emma Goldman, *Red Emma Speaks,* author Alix Kates Shulman shared that the queen of the anarchists "was arrested so often that she never spoke in public without taking along a book to read in jail." I hope none of us will be getting arrested any time soon, but it's not unlikely we will get stuck in an airport, arrive early for a dinner date, or find ourselves waiting for our doctor to finish with the previous patient. I guess you can probably just do email on your phone while you wait, but, hey, why not bring a book? And, better yet, one that's on nice paper, that feels good when you hold it in your hands, and, even better still, in your mind when you work your way through its contents.

A List of Suggested Reading on Business, Writing, and Anarchism

What the Anarchists Knew a Hundred Years Ago

In his book *Crossing the Unknown Sea*, author David Whyte wrote that "A good artist, it is often said, is fifty to a hundred years ahead of their time; they describe what lies over the horizon in our future world. . . . The artist, of whatever epoch, must also depict this new world before all the evidence is in. They must rely on the embracing abilities of their imagination to intuit and describe what is yet a germinating seed in their present time, something that will only flower after they have written the line or painted the canvas. . . . The artist's sensibility is one that grants life to things outside of our normal human ken." I'm sure David's point applies to any number of artists of all sorts who find themselves moving against the current, fighting the mass market to put their own individual creative stamp on their work. But in particular, it's precisely what I stumbled on in going back to study the anarchists. While they certainly didn't have it all figured out, they were very definitely talking and writing, decades before we opened the Deli, about a whole lot of the ways of working that we've put in place here at Zingerman's.

Other modern writers have said much the same thing about the anarchists of that era. The great writer Irving Howe, in the introduction to his book *The Anarchists*, said that, "The anarchist tradition is a particularly fruitful, and frightfully neglected, source in the common human effort to overcome manipulation with the only genuinely effective instrument we have—clarification." Modern-day anarchist Murray Bookchin goes even further, writing in his book, *Remaking Society*, that "it is very important that we examine the libertarian movements that emerged at each of history's turning points and the ideas of freedom they advanced. Here, we shall find a remarkable development of ideas that sought to countervail civilizations' immersion into evil." And, he explains, "So the thinkers of the liberatory, indeed revolutionary, tradition must be appreciated as much for what they add to our time as they did to their own if the abiding character of their work is to be grasped."

Similarly, early 20th-century German anarchist Gustav Landauer expressed that same view a century ago. "In the era of individualism," he posited, "geniuses precede events. Their work often remains ineffective for an extended period, appearing to be dead. It remains alive, however, waiting for others to apply it practically." Landauer was writing about Étienne de La Boétie, over 400 years after the twenty-something-year-old Frenchman authored the amazing, essentially proto-anarchist essay, "A Discourse on Voluntary Servitude." La Boétie's work was practically lost in the vaults of history and assigned little value, until people like Landauer picked up on it late in the 19th century. Ironically, or maybe appropriately, what Gustav Landauer wrote about La Boétie has also turned out to be true about his own work. I'm not fixated on identifying huge international turning points, nor on telling everyone what all the upcoming trends are going to be. But maybe that moment of applying Landauer's insights "practically" has actually arrived here in Ann Arbor.

I don't have any way to know it for sure, but I'm pretty confident that I could have had some very interesting conversations with Gustav Landauer, Emma Goldman, and others of their peer group. Now if we want to dialogue with them the only real way to do it is to read what they wrote and imagine the conversation that might follow. Below is a list of some of my favorites from amongst the anarchist writings. Remember when you read them that most of the authors were living in a different time than we are, one in which the idea of creative or constructive capitalism seemed silly, almost unthinkable. But, still, the seeds of what we're doing here at Zingerman's, and at many other progressive organizations as well, are certainly well present in what they wrote.

ANARCHIST READING LIST

Carlotta R. Anderson, *All-American Anarchist: Joseph A. Labadie and the Labor Movement*

Paul Avrich, *An American Anarchist: The Life of Voltairine de Cleyre*

Paul Avrich, *Anarchist Voices: An Oral History of Anarchism in America*

Mohammed A. Bamyeh, *Anarchy as Order: The History and Future of Civic Humanity (World Social Change)*

Alexander Berkman, *Now and After: The ABC of Anarchism*

Étienne de La Boétie, "Discourse on Voluntary Servitude"

Murray Bookchin, *The Ecology of Freedom: The Emergence and Dissolution of Hierarchy*

Murray Bookchin, *Remaking Society: Pathways to a Green Future*

Murray Bookchin, *Toward an Ecological Society*

Voltairine de Cleyre, *Exquisite Rebel: The Essays of Voltairine de Cleyre—Feminist, Anarchist, Genius.* Ed. Sharon Presley and Crispin Sartwell

Candace Falk, *Love, Anarchy, and Emma Goldman*

Emma Goldman, *Anarchism and Other Essays*

Emma Goldman, "Anarchism: What It Really Stands For"

Emma Goldman, *Living My Life*

Emma Goldman, *What I Believe*

Tom Goyens, *Beer and Revolution: The German Anarchist Movement in New York City, 1880–1914*

Peter Kropotkin, *The Conquest of Bread*

Peter Kropotkin, *Fields, Factories, and Workshops*

Peter Kropotkin, *Mutual Aid*

Gustav Landauer, *Revolution and Other Writings: A Political Reader.* Ed. Gabriel Kuhn

Peter Marshall, *Demanding the Impossible*

Benjamin Tucker, *Why I Am an Anarchist*

If you're looking to buy anything of an anarchist nature, check out Bolerium Books in San Francisco; they have a great collection. AK Press in Oakland and Black Rose Books in Montreal do as well.

Business Reading List

The books that follow aren't likely to be found in any of the anarchist bookstores. All have helped me to arrive at where I am.

Ichak Adizes, *Corporate Lifecycle: How and Why Corporations Grow and Die and What to Do about It*

James Autry, *Life and Work: A Manager's Search for Meaning*

James Autry, *Love and Profit: The Art of Caring Leadership*

Warren Bennis, *On Becoming a Leader*

Peter Block, *The Empowered Manager: Positive Political Skills at Work*

Peter Block, *Stewardship: Choosing Service over Self-Interest*

Bo Burlingham, *Small Giants: Companies That Choose to Be Great instead of Big*

Bo Burlingham and Norm Brodsky, *The Knack: How Street-Smart Entrepreneurs Learn to Handle Whatever Comes Up*

Anese Cavanaugh, *The Little Book of Bootism*

Chip Conley, *Peak: How Great Companies Get Their Mojo from Maslow*

Stephen Covey, *Principle-Centered Leadership*

Max DePree, *Leadership Is an Art*

Max DePree, *Leadership Jazz*

Peter Drucker, *The Effective Executive*

Peter Drucker, *The Practice of Management*

Robert K. Greenleaf, *On Becoming a Servant Leader: The Private Writings of Robert K. Greenleaf*

Robert K. Greenleaf, *Servant Leadership: A Journey into the Nature of Legitimate Power and Greatness*

Paul Hawken, *Growing a Business*

Rosabeth Moss Kanter, *Confidence: How Winning Streaks and Losing Streaks Begin and End*

Lawrence L. Lippitt, *Preferred Futuring: Envision the Future You Want and Unleash the Energy to Get There*

Hugh MacLeod, *Ignore Everybody: And 39 Other Keys to Creativity*

Dawna Markova, *I Will Not Die an Unlived Life: Reclaiming Purpose and Passion*

Gifford and Elizabeth Pinchot, *The End of Bureaucracy and the Rise of the Intelligent Organization*

Daniel H. Pink, *Drive: The Surprising Truth about What Motivates Us*

Tom Peters, *In Search of Excellence: Lessons from America's Best-Run Companies*

Tom Peters, *Re-Imagine! Business Excellence in a Disruptive Age*

Ricardo Semler, *Maverick: The Success Story behind America's Best-Run Companies*

Peter M. Senge, *The Fifth Discipline: The Art and Practice of the Learning Organization*

Jean-Louis Servan-Schreiber, *The Art of Time*

Simon Sinek, *Start with Why: How Great Leaders Inspire Everyone to Take Action*

Jack Stack and Bo Burlingham, *The Great Game of Business: Unlocking the Power and Profitability of Open-Book Management*

Jack Stack and Bo Burlingham, *A Stake in the Outcome: Building a Culture of Ownership for the Long-Term Success of Your Business*

Dean E. Tucker, *Using the Power of Purpose: How to Overcome Bureaucracy and Achieve Extraordinary Business Success!*

Brenda Ueland, *If You Want to Write: A Book about Art, Independence, and Spirit*

Brenda Ueland, *Strength to Your Sword Arm: Selected Writings by Brenda Ueland*

Robert Wall, Robert Solum, Mark R. Sobel, *The Visionary Leader: From Mission Statement to a Thriving Organization, Here's Your Blueprint for Building an Inspired, Cohesive, Customer-Oriented Team*

the deli renovation, 2011

A Handful of Organizational Recipes

Here are a dozen or so of our organizational recipes. Adapt at will!

twelve tenets of anarcho-capitalism

1. All for One—Bringing Out the Best in Each and Every Individual in the Organization

2. One for All—Individual Responsibility for the Organization's Success

3. Frame Everything in Free Choice

4. A Positive Outlook on, and Belief in, Abundance, a Better Life, People, and the Future

5. Creative and Near-Constant Collaboration

6. Take a Service Orientation

7. Opt for Openness

8. The Importance of Acceptance

9. Commit to Quality—Do Something You Believe In

10. Understanding That It's All One Life, and It's an Artful One at That

11. Workable Ways for Everyone to Modify and Self-Monitor Systems and Structures

12. Make Money Doing It!

twelve natural Laws of business
from zingerman's guide to good leading, part I: a lapsed anarchist's approach to building a great business

1. An inspiring, strategically sound vision leads the way to greatness (especially if you write it down!)

2. You need to give customers really compelling reasons to buy from you

3. Without good finance, you fail

4. People do their best work when they're part of a really great organization

5. If you want the staff to give great service to customers, the leaders have to give great service to the staff

6. If you want great performance from your staff, you have to give them clear expectations and training tools

7. Successful businesses do the things that others know they should do . . . but generally don't

8. To get to greatness you've got to keep getting better, all the time!

9. Success means you get better problems

10. Whatever your strengths are, they will likely lead straight to your weaknesses

11. It generally takes a lot longer to make something great happen than people think

12. Great organizations are appreciative, and the people in them have more fun

Secrets 1-18

from Zingerman's Guide to Good Leading, Part 1: a Lapsed anarchist's approach to building a great business

1. Twelve Natural Laws of Building a Great Business

2. Contrast, Composition, Content

3. Creating Recipes for Organizational Success

4. The Zingerman's Business Perspective Chart

5. Building a Better Mission Statement

6. Revisiting the Power of Visioning

7. Writing a Vision of Greatness

8. Vision Back

9. An 8-Step Recipe for Writing a Vision of Greatness

10. A Question of Systems

11. Writing and Using Guiding Principles

12. 5 Steps to Building an Organizational Culture

13. Creating a Culture of Positive Appreciation

14. Why I Want to Finish Third

15. Building a Sustainable Business

16. 28 Years of Buying Local

17. A Recipe for Making Something Special

18. Finally, Some Food!

3 elements of energy

Physical

Mental/Emotional

Vibrational

4 steps to effective energy management

1. Read it

2. Vision it

3. Manage it

4. Repeat it

6 elements of the entrepreneurial approach in action

1. Sell our ideas and beliefs to our staff

2. Use free-market concepts to reward what you really want

3. Rotate rewards to maintain high yields

4. Use creative consequences

5. Try group rewards and consequences

6. Use the Entrepreneurial Approach in all directions

6 elements of effective Servant Leadership

1. Provide an inspiring and strategically sound vision

2. Give great day-to-day service to the staff

3. Manage in an ethical manner

4. Be an active learner and teacher

5. Help the staff succeed by living the training compact

6. Say thanks

3 Steps to Great Service

1. Find out what the customer wants

2. Get it for them
   - Accurately
   - Politely
   - Enthusiastically

3. Go the extra mile

5 Steps to handling a Complaint

1. Acknowledge the complaint

2. Sincerely apologize

3. Take action to make things right

4. Thank them for letting us know

5. Document the complaint

Stewardship Compact

Leader agrees to:

1. Document clear performance expectations

2. Provide the resources to do the work

3. Recognize performance

4. Reward performance

5. Provide the freedom to manage the day-to-day work within the guidelines established in the expectations

Staff agree to:

a. Deliver on the expectations that the leader laid out

or

b. Negotiate through to agreement and then deliver on an alternate set of expectations

6 key components of effective stewardship work

1. An effective exchange of purpose

2. Emphasis on performance results

3. Negotiating to agreement (including the opportunity to say no)

4. No abdication

5. Freedom: you really can make a difference

6. Conscious commitment

5 Steps to bottom-Line change

1. Create a clear and compelling purpose for change.
2. Create a positive vision of the future and develop leadership alignment around that vision.
3. Engage a microcosm to determine who needs to know and how to get the information out.
4. "Officially" present the vision and create an action plan.
5. Implement the change.

training compact

Trainer agrees to:

1. Document clear performance expectations
2. Provide the resources to do the work
3. Recognize performance
4. Reward performance

Trainees agree to:

Take responsibility for the effectiveness of their training at Zingerman's

management's role in zingerman's training compact

1. Provide context for the training

   • Agree on a shared vision of why this training is important to the trainee's—and the business's—success.

   • Agree on what the trainee will know and/or be able to do after the training.

   • Decide how that will be measured as part of the employee's day-to-day work.

2. Reinforce how the training supports the trainee's (and the organization's) success.

   • Before: Give suggestions for how the trainee can get the most out of the training.

   • After: Touch base with the trainee to discuss what's working or not working.

3. Help the trainee put the new learnings to good use.

   • Make sure the trainee has an opportunity to use what was learned within 2 days back on the job.

   • Decide if and what additional training is needed to meet the vision of success for the trainee (and the organization).

4 steps to productive resolution of your differences

1. Go direct.

   Speak directly to the individual involved and express your concerns and work towards resolution.

Keep in mind that

   a. Everyone who has made a decision to work within the ZCoB has made a commitment to upholding Zingerman's guiding principles. We are committed to holding ourselves and everyone else accountable to that commitment.

b. Interpersonal problems, conflict, and frustration are normal obstacles. While we all wish it wasn't so, we recognize that people will sometimes fall short of expectations.

c. In the spirit of effective partnerships, we are committed to addressing these problems quickly, constructively, and, most importantly, directly.

d. We acknowledge that it takes courage and determination to act directly to work difficult issues through to resolution. But we are committed to doing so, and we ask that you do, too.

e. If one of us is falling short in our work, please let us know how we can improve.

f. We understand that if each of us does not follow through with the process, we are choosing to accept and support the very behavior or work problems with which we are frustrated. If you aren't satisfied with the outcome, then . . .

2. Put it in writing.

Address your concerns in writing to the individual involved (with a copy to their supervisor or manager and owner-operator), then meet with them again. If you still aren't satisfied with the outcome, then . . .

3. Put it in writing and meet with a manager present.

Follow up in writing (copy to supervisor or manager and owner-operator) and ask for a meeting with you, the other individual, your supervisor, their supervisor, and/or the owner-operator. If that meeting still doesn't meet your needs, then . . .

4. Present your issues at the Partners' Group.

Follow up in writing again (copies to everyone) and ask for time at the Partners' Group where you can both present your case and ask for help. The Partners' Group is the final spot to reach resolution.

mike broman scooping gelato at the creamery

An Interview with Our Illustrators, Ian Nagy and Ryan Stiner

The Story of Scratchboard in Zingerman's Guide to Good Leading

Ari: I love the illustrations in the books, and I really appreciate the amazing artwork you've contributed to them, so I thought it might be nice for folks to get a better sense of who you are and the story behind the drawings. How did you get to Zingerman's?

Ian: Thanks, Ari. I started in 1991 as a sign maker when the only business was the Deli and became the first full-time Zingerman's illustrator in 1997. A friend of mine who worked at "the Zing" taking sandwich orders (thanks, Vicky!) told me there was a job opening in the art department and I practically begged to work here. Before that I made art soon after birth, encouraged by my fantastic family and inspirational, art-degree-having mother. See iannagy .com for more details and stuff I've made.

a scratchboard illustration's progression

Ryan: Thanks! I've been here about seven years now. I started out as a part-time illustrator, but quickly started building signs and other random constructs. Now I'm a full-time illustrator and thing-maker. Otherwise, I've been creating stuff since I was a kid. I went for a year to the School of the Art Institute of Chicago, lived there for a few years, and then I moved to Ann Arbor. Soon after, my future wife (thanks, Lauren!) saw a flyer that Zingerman's was hiring a part-time illustrator and the rest is history. Also, feel free to take a peek at ryanstiner.com if you are interested in more.

How do you feel about getting to draw and do design for a living?

Ryan: It's pretty amazing. It can be easy to take it for granted, but when I see other artists who are in the same spot I was seven years ago, talented people who can't do art for a living, it reminds me how amazing it is.

2

Ian: Ryan pretty much summed it up right there, I agree with everything he said. It is the best job I have ever had and there is nothing else I would rather do.

How did you decide on scratchboard drawings for the Guide to Good Leading series?

Ryan: Well, you'd asked us for something in the style of woodblock printing, of the art from the '30s and '40s. Ian and I talked about it, and he really pushed for scratchboard. It was a way we could give you what you were looking for, and also do something special that we liked.

3

Ian: We kicked around several different techniques but I thought scratch-board would look the best for the entire book. It's one of my favorite ways to make pictures and I feel it is the best black-and-white medium.

What's the history of scratchboard? Where and when did it originate?

Ian: This is what our friends at Wikipedia say:

"Modern scratchboard originated in the 19th century in Britain and France. As printing methods developed, scratch-board became a popular medium for reproduction because it replaced wood, metal and linoleum engraving. It allowed for a fine line appearance that could be photographically reduced for reproduction without losing quality. It was most effective and expeditious for use in single-color book and newspaper printing. From the 1930's to 1950's, it was one of the preferred techniques for medical, scientific and product illustra-tion. During that time period, Virgil Finlay made very detailed illustrations, often combining scratchboard methods with traditional pen & ink techniques, and producing highly detailed artworks. In more recent years, it has made a comeback as an appealing medium for editorial illustrators of magazines, ads and graphic novels."

4

5

Ryan: Uhmmmm, that sounds about right.

The drawings look fantastic. How does the process work?

Ian: After Ryan so kindly takes reference photos for us based on ideas we brainstorm beforehand, I crop the photo, sketch it on paper, transfer the sketch to the scratchboard, then scratch like a maniac while touching up a few things with marker. The scratchboard we buy from an art supplies store comes pre-inked on hardboard, and we scratch it off with a small tool that looks like a tiny metal spear and fits into a basic pen-tip holder. The white part of the board that the black ink sits on is a thin layer of clay, so you have to be careful not to scratch off too much or go too deep because you will hit brown board!

done!

Ryan: I almost always hit the brown board.

How long does it take to do one of these pieces?

Ryan: The one I just finished today, the one with Robert Greenleaf and Emma Goldman in front of the Deli (page 258), took me about eight solid hours of artwork. Some take more than that, some are less, but that's a good ballpark number.

Ian: About a day's work minus the photos.

What do you like about it?

Ryan: There's a certain finality to it. I mean, you can adjust a little bit after the fact. But, really, once you cut away the ink, that's it. That isn't necessarily there with other styles of drawing. And I like that. Plus it's out of the ordinary. You don't often get a request for two dozen pieces of scratch-board art!

Ian: One of the things I love about it is the "noise" that you can leave in any area. For example, if you're depicting a loaf of bread that had a black outline, you can roughly scratch the inside of the loaf. This leaves small jagged pieces of visual shrapnel, or tiny organic black and white shapes. The more you scratch, the less noise you end up with. The noise is my favorite part! I leave as much of it as I can.

Zingerman's Timeline

1902—The building now known as Zingerman's Delicatessen is built on the corner of Kingsley and Detroit Streets in Ann Arbor, Michigan. It opens as Disderide's Grocery.

1975—Paul Saginaw leaves graduate school at the University of Michigan to work at a local seafood restaurant.

1978—Ari Weinzweig graduates from the University of Michigan and goes to work washing dishes at a local restaurant, Maude's, where he meets Paul Saginaw, Frank Carollo, and Maggie Bayless, his partners-to-be.

1979—Paul opens Monahan's Seafood Market in Kerrytown with Mike Monahan (which is still there and still one of the best in the country!)

1980—Ari and Paul begin a conversation about how Ann Arbor could use a traditional Jewish deli like the ones they grew up with in Detroit (Paul) and Chicago (Ari).

November 1981—Paul notices that the building on the corner of Kingsley and Detroit is available. He calls Ari to see if he's ready to open the deli that they had talked about.

March 7, 1982—Ari and Paul are making final plans to open "Greenberg's Delicatessen" named in honor of Hannah Greenberg, one of Paul's regular customers at the fish market. Ari takes a call from a man in Michigan who has already filed papers with the state to own the name "Greenberg's Deli." After being told they can't use the name, they have a quick brainstorming session to find a new name (since Weinzweig is unpronounceable and Saginaw, though derived from the Jewish name *Sagin' Or*—which means "seer of light"—has decidedly non-Jewish connotations in Michigan). They settle on Zingerman's (in part because it starts with Z and will be easy to spot at the end of a list).

March 15, 1982—Zingerman's opens its doors for the first time. Ari and Paul are behind the counter making sandwiches and cutting bread and cheeses, working with one full-time and one part-time staff member. There are five tables and four stools along the counter in the front window. We feature a small but meaningful selection of sandwiches, traditional Jewish foods like chopped liver and chicken soup, cheeses, smoked fish, cured and smoked meats, and breads and pastries from local bakeries. (Before the Bakehouse, the Deli made daily trips to Detroit to get quality bread!)

1985—Steve Muno begins work on the retail line. His inventive sign making would come to exemplify the Deli's signature artistic style and his unique handwriting, eventually dubbed "*muno bold*" (pronounced "mew-no") would become the standard font for all Zingerman's signs and posters. Steve is still a regular Zingerman's customer.

1986—The 700-square-foot addition to the original Zingerman's building is completed. The pie-shaped wedge houses the sandwich line and provides expanded room for dry goods.

1988—Zingerman's Magic Brownies are baked for the first time. The recipe was developed courtesy of Ms. Connie Prigg, a Zingerman's staff member at the time who now lives in Baltimore.

1988—Zingerman's begins a food rescue program to feed the hungry in our community. **Food Gatherers** collects nutritious food from shops, restaurants, and hotels and quickly delivers it to the people in need in our community.

1991—Ian Nagy begins work as Zingerman's first full-time illustrator (he's still here, too!) and goes on to define the Zingerman's style that has become famous nationwide, thanks to our mail-order catalogs and websites.

Zingerman's Next Door opens up in a converted residence one door south of the Deli on Halloween.

April 1992—Frank Carollo, an old friend from Maude's, gets together with Ari and Paul, and the three of them meet up with Michael London, bread baker extraordinaire, at his bakery in upstate New York. Michael teaches his techniques to Frank and the seeds of **Zingerman's Bakehouse** are planted.

October 1992— The first official loaves of bread emerge from the Zingerman's Bakehouse ovens and head to the Deli breadbox and sandwich line. Among the original Bakehouse staff of eight is Amy Emberling who, after a hiatus to complete her MBA from Columbia, returns to Ann Arbor to join Frank as Bakehouse co-managing partner.

1993—We write our mission statement and guiding principles.

Zingerman's first mail-order catalog is released. Deli staff members Mo Frechette and Jude Walton take the lead in shipping food to hungry guests looking to get their Zingerman's fix from afar. Four years later food writer Ed Behr describes Zingerman's mail-order catalog as "the most discriminating selection of foods that I am aware of."

1994—After years of pondering how to grow their business and still stay rooted in the local community (and after rejecting numerous offers to franchise), Ari and Paul release Zingerman's 2009, a unique vision for organizational growth that plants the seed of the **Zingerman's Community of Businesses**.

Ann Arbor becomes a sweeter place to live when Zingerman's Bakehouse begins baking sweet stuff to go with bread. Big O's (oatmeal raisin cookies baked with real maple syrup), Funky Chunky Chocolate Cookies, and AmaZing Cheesecake start emerging from the Bakehouse's new ovens in addition to the already successful Magic Brownies.

In response to numerous requests from others in the business world to learn the secrets to Zingerman's success,

ZingTrain—Zingerman's consulting and training business—is born under the aegis of Maggie Bayless (a friend from the old days at Maude's). ZingTrain offers all sorts of interesting information on service, training systems, and other tools and techniques used throughout the ZCoB.

1996—Zingerman's Catering, famous for extraordinary deli trays and for bringing the Zingerman's Experience beyond the Deli's doors and into southeast Michigan, is launched. The Deli's catering department grows to provide everything from casual meals to planning and catering for 2,000-person events.

1997—The new bread bag from Zingerman's Bakehouse earns national design recognition from *Print* magazine. Zing artists become *Print* favorites, receiving similar recognition the next three years in a row for four other Zingerman's design projects.

1998—Food Gatherers delivers over 2,000,000 pounds of food to help feed those in need in Washtenaw County. After three years of outstanding effort, Jude Walton and Maurice (Mo) Frechette make the jump to full-fledged managing partners of **Zingerman's Mail Order**. The push towards Zingerman's 2009 continues.

1999—Led by managing partners Tom Root and Toni Morell, **Zingermans.com** goes online.

2000—*USA Today* names Zingerman's one of the country's top ten places to buy "a genuine Jewish nosh."

As demand for ZingTrain seminars and workshops continues to grow, Stas' Kazmierski joins ZingTrain as Maggie's co-managing partner.

2001—Zingerman's Creamery opens up in Manchester, Michigan, and cheesemaker and managing partner John Loomis begins making fresh cheeses.

2002—Zingerman's Mail Order and zingermans.com merge to become one business headed by Tom, Toni, Mo, and Jude.

2003—*Inc.* magazine calls us "The Coolest Small Company in America."

Chef Alex Young becomes managing partner and executive chef as **Zingerman's Roadhouse** opens up in the old Bill Knapp's building at the corner of Jackson and Maple Roads on Ann Arbor's far west side.

Zingerman's Coffee Company opens, and roastmaster and managing partner Allen Leibowitz starts selling Zingerman's coffee throughout the Zingerman's Community of Businesses and to wholesale customers across the country.

Zingerman's Guide to Giving Great Service is published and details the steps we take to provide the Zingerman's Experience for our guests, our staff, our vendors, and our community.

Zingerman's Guide to Good Eating by Ari Weinzweig is published and written up in *Fine Cooking, Saveur*, the *Chicago Tribune*, the *New York Times*, and other national publications at the top of their holiday book gift lists!

Zingerman's Creamery packs up their operation in Manchester and moves to Ann Arbor (a scone's throw from Zingerman's Bakehouse!), where we now make our cheeses and sell them in our cheese shop.

2004—Deli retail manager Grace Singleton takes the reins as Deli managing partner.

Zingerman's Roadshow, Ann Arbor's hippest drive-up coffee counter, opens in the parking lot of Zingerman's Roadhouse.

Zingerman's Coffee Company is featured in *Travel + Leisure* as one of the country's top roasters.

2005—The birth of the Zingerman's candy bar. Zzang!® bars coming out of the Bakehouse are quickly named "the ultimate handmade candy bar" by *Chocolatier* magazine.

2006—BAKE!, Ann Arbor's hands-on, teaching bakery and CAKE!, a showroom worthy of the imagination-defying creations from the Bakehouse cake designers, opens at Zingerman's Bakehouse.

For the first time, produce from Alex Young's **Cornman Farms** highlights the Roadhouse's annual Harvest Dinner.

2007—Deli restaurant manager Rick Strutz joins Grace as co-managing partner at the Deli.

On March 15, Zingerman's celebrates our 25th anniversary with a 6,000-person street fair on Detroit Street outside the Deli, featuring guests and friends from our first quarter-century. We sell 3,044 Reubens and 1,241 cappuccinos!

The *New York Times* relaunches their Wednesday Small Business section with a feature on the Zingerman's Community of Businesses, "The Corner Deli That Dared to Break Out of the Neighborhood."

Zingerman's launches our 2020 vision charting the course for the Zingerman's Community of Businesses for the next thirteen years.

Bon Appetit bestows their Lifetime Achievement Award on Ari and Paul (previous winners include such food luminaries as Alice Waters, Jacques Pepin, and Julia Child)!

2008—Zingerman's Coffee Company manager Steve Mangigian joins Allen as co-managing partner of the business.

Zingerman's is featured on Oprah's sandwich episode, and #97 Lisa C.'s Boisterous Brisket is Oprah's favorite, rating an "11" on a scale of 1–5.

The ZCoB nets a long piece on NPR's *Weekend Edition Sunday* detailing our growth from a corner deli into a nationally renowned community of businesses.

Travel + Leisure features the Roadhouse in their November issue.

2009—Zingerman's Candy Manufactory, a wholesale candy maker creating old-fashioned American sweets by hand, opens with Charlie Frank as managing partner.

Zingerman's Guide to Better Bacon, Ari Weinzweig's tome on pork (featuring bacon history, recipes, and lore) is published.

Zingerman's Coffee Company opens its retail and café space.

2010—Zingerman's hosts its inaugural Camp Bacon, bringing together artisanal bacon makers, including Allan Benton and Herb Eckhouse, and pork enthusiasts from around the world for a celebration of porcine poetry, songs, tasting, learning, and more.

Publication of *Zingerman's Guide to Good Leading, Part I: A Lapsed Anarchist's Approach to Building a Great Business*, the first volume in Ari Weinzweig's leadership series.

Rodger Bowser moves from chef to co-managing partner at Zingerman's Delicatessen.

After a four-year . . . dialogue with the Ann Arbor Historic District Commission, Zingerman's Deli is granted permission to begin its long-awaited expansion project!

Alton Brown from the Food Network names the macaroni and cheese at Zingerman's Roadhouse "America's Best Comfort Food."

Inc. magazine hails *A Lapsed Anarchist's Approach to Building a Great Business* as one of the "Best Books for Business Owners."

2011—Jane and Michael Stern, writing in *Saveur*, name Zingerman's Bakehouse rye bread as the "very best" in America!

May 2011—Chef Alex Young wins Best Chef in the Great Lakes Region from the James Beard Foundation.

2012—Publication of *A Lapsed Anarchist's Approach to Being a Better Leader.*

Zingerman's celebrates our 30th anniversary.

Zingerman's Bakehouse celebrates its 20th anniversary.

sara fitzgerald and candy manufactory managing partner
charlie frank making zzang bars

Time to Eat!

Nine Recipes to Cook in Your Own Kitchen

If you've gotten this far in the book you've probably been through a healthy portion of our organizational "recipes"—all those steps and stuff about how we manage energy, provide Servant Leadership, live Anarcho-Capitalism and all that. Putting them to good use is guaranteed to get you better business results and improve the quality of your life. They will—indirectly—put food on your family's table. On the other hand, the next few pages will serve that purpose more directly—the recipes that follow are the kind you can take into the kitchen when you want to start cooking.

Here at Zingerman's, food and business are inseparable—so here's a small taste of Zingerman's food for you to enjoy while you're digesting all the ideas included in the last 300-plus pages. As with Part 1, we've decided to go with one recipe for each Zingerman's business. Again, we've added one for good luck—a really delicious roast Taiwanese-style pork belly that we serve at San Street, the Asian street food cart that's one of our potential, but not yet fully formed, businesses. None of the recipes are hugely difficult, but all are pretty tasty.

Enjoy!

Zingerman's ®
DELICATESSEN

NOODLE KUGEL

We've been making this simple and delicious "noodle pudding" since we opened the Deli back in 1982. It's based on one my grandmother used to make, and probably not unlike what Emma Goldman would have been eating back in her day. Noodle kugel is good hot out of the oven, but also a few hours later when it's cooled down to room temperature. If you're not into raisins you can substitute pretty much any dried fruit, cut into small pieces.

12 ounces fettuccine egg noodles

½ vanilla bean, seeds scraped and reserved

½ cup plus 2 tablespoons granulated sugar

9 large eggs

¾ cup butter, melted

2 cups raisins

1 ½ cups farmer's cheese

1 ½ cups sour cream

1 teaspoon cinnamon

½ teaspoon fine sea salt, plus additional for boiling the noodles

Preheat oven to 350° F.

Bring a large pot of salted water to a boil. Add the noodles and cook, according to the package instructions, until al dente, then drain well.

Meanwhile, combine the vanilla bean seeds and the remaining ingredients in a large bowl and stir until well blended.

Gently stir the noodles into the sauce.

Pour into a 9 x 13 x 2-inch pan and bake for 30 minutes, or until golden on top.

JAMWICH

I've long loved this little sandwich. I'm exceedingly spoiled by—and biased towards—the handmade, no-vegetable-gum-added cream cheese we make at Zingerman's Creamery, but you can certainly use a commercial product as well. It's great with figs and fig preserves, but any full-flavored fresh fruit and the matching preserves work well. Strawberries with strawberry preserves, blueberries with blueberry preserves, raspberries, peaches, plums . . . you name it—just pair pieces of the fresh fruit with preserves made from the same fruit, and you'll be rocking!

1 bagel, sliced and toasted

2 tablespoons cream cheese

4 teaspoons preserves of your choice

Fresh fruit of the same variety as the preserves, sliced thin

Spread each bagel half with 1 tablespoon cream cheese, then with 2 teaspoons preserves. Generously top each half with fresh fruit.

MANDELBREAD

I suppose Mandelbread (or Mandelbrot) could be classed as Jewish biscotti. It is definitely something my grandparents would have dipped in a glass of tea, and the truth is that I probably enjoy it equally well in the same way nearly a century later.

1 cup butter

2 cups granulated sugar

1 teaspoon fine sea salt

2 large eggs

1 tablespoon fresh lemon zest

2 tablespoons fresh orange zest

1 tablespoon plus 1 ½ teaspoons pure vanilla extract

2 ⅓ cups all purpose flour

1 ¾ cups whole almonds

1 cup coarsely chopped almonds

Pre-heat the oven to 325° F.

In a large mixing bowl, combine the butter, 1 cup sugar, and salt. Cream together on medium speed until light and fluffy. Continuing on medium speed, add the eggs one at a time. Cream until the eggs are fully incorporated. Stop the mixer and scrape down the sides and bottom of the bowl if necessary.

Add the lemon zest, orange zest, and vanilla extract to the bowl and beat until combined. On low speed, add the flour a little at a time until the dough is mixed thoroughly. Continuing on low speed, add the whole almonds and mix until just incorporated. Remove the dough from the bowl. Fold the dough to combine fully.

In a medium bowl, combine the chopped almonds and remaining 1 cup sugar. Divide the dough in half and roll each half into a log shape about 10 inches long and about 2 ½ inches thick. Roll each log in the sugar and chopped almond mixture to coat.

Place on a parchment-lined baking sheet with 6 inches between each log. Bake the mandelbread for 35 to 40 minutes. Remove from the oven and cool for 15 to 20 minutes.

With a serrated knife, slice the still-warm (not hot) mandelbread on the bias about ½ inch thick. The sawing motion is key here—be careful not to use too much downward pressure, or your slices will tend to break apart. Place the slices back on a parchment-lined sheet pan and bake for another 25 to 30 minutes.

Remove from the oven and cool. Store in an airtight container for up to 2 months.

Zingerman's
roadhouse

ROADHOUSE MEATLOAF

Meatloaf has been the Wednesday night Blue Plate Special at the Roadhouse and a regular customer favorite for many years now. In honor of Melina Hinton's comments about energy and her suggestion to alter the way we served the meatloaf (see pages 71–73), it seemed fitting to have it in the book. It's easy to make and really quite tasty. I like to take it up a notch by laying strips of good bacon across the top. (Of course, I'm biased since I wrote a whole book on the subject—see *Zingerman's Guide to Better Bacon* for more details on the subtleties of smoked and cured pork belly.)

Meatloaf:

1 tablespoon olive oil (or bacon fat if you have it on hand!)

½ Spanish onion, halved lengthwise then cut into thin slices

2 eggs

2 cloves garlic, minced

1 tablespoon chopped flat-leaf parsley

¼ cup fine bread crumbs

2 teaspoons coarse sea salt

1 ½ teaspoon freshly ground black pepper, preferably Tellicherry

½ teaspoon dried basil

½ teaspoon fresh thyme

1 pound ground beef chuck

1 pound ground pork butt

2 strips bacon (optional)

Gravy:

1 tablespoon extra virgin olive oil

1 cup diced onion

4 tablespoons butter

4 tablespoons flour

2 cups beef stock

Coarse sea salt to taste

Freshly ground black pepper to taste, preferably Tellicherry

Make the meatloaf:

Preheat the oven to 350° F.

In a medium heavy-bottomed skillet, heat the olive oil over medium heat. Add the onion and sauté, stirring occasionally, until it is caramelized and golden brown.

Meanwhile, in a large bowl, mix the eggs, garlic, parsley, bread crumbs, sea salt, pepper, basil, and thyme together. When the onions are ready, stir them into the mixture. Add the ground beef and pork and mix well.

Pack the mixture into a 10-inch loaf pan. If you're using them, lay strips of bacon over the top. Bake, uncovered, for an hour and 10 minutes or until a meat thermometer inserted into the center reaches 155° F. Drain; let stand for 10 minutes before cutting and serving.

When the meatloaf is halfway done, make the gravy:

In a medium skillet (cast iron works well), heat the olive oil over medium heat. Add the diced onion and sauté, stirring occasionally, for 25 to 30 minutes, or until caramelized and golden brown.

When the onions are almost ready, melt the butter in a medium saucepan over medium heat. Add the flour, whisking vigorously. When the mixture is hot and bubbly, reduce the heat slightly. To make a roux, cook until the mixture gets a nutty aroma and looks the color of peanut butter, about 2 minutes more, stirring occasionally.

Slowly stir the beef broth into the roux. Bring to a simmer, stirring to avoid lumps. At this point the onions will be ready to stir into the gravy. Add salt and pepper to taste.

Serve the meatloaf, as Melina says, with the gravy on the side. Enjoy.

Zingerman's.
maiL order.

PIMENTO CHEESE

Although it's almost unknown in the North, pimento cheese is hugely popular in the South. Nearly every family in the South has its own recipe, every party spread will include at least one plate of pimento cheese, and nearly every school child goes to school, at some point, with pimento cheese sandwiches. In the six years that we've been making it here—first at the Roadhouse and then everywhere else—it's become one of the most popular products we make.

½ pound sharp cheddar, coarsely grated (we use the two-year-old raw milk cheddar from Grafton Village)

1 cup mayonnaise

¼ cup diced roasted red peppers

¾ teaspoon olive oil

¼ teaspoon freshly ground Tellicherry black pepper

Scant ¼ teaspoon cayenne pepper, or to taste

Pinch of coarse sea salt

Fold all the ingredients together in a mixing bowl. Mix well. Eat.

Repeat as regularly as you like. It's addictive: as more than one person around here has said more than once, "It's kind of good on pretty much everything, isn't it?"

Serves . . . well, it's hard to say. A real addict could probably consume this entire recipe in a single setting. Being more conservative, let's say it's enough to serve 8 as an appetizer. You'll probably have to test it on your family and friends to see how much they can eat!

san
strEꞱt

RED BRAISED PORK BELLY

As I write, San Street qualifies as our most recent (ad)venture—an Asian street food cart run by longtime Deli staffers Kristen Hogue and Ji Hye Kim. Right now, San Street serves a limited menu of handmade pork buns, but our hope is that it will eventually blossom into a full-fledged Zingerman's business —a sit-down restaurant specializing in Asian street food, with Ji Hye and Kristen as the managing partners. The recipe that follows is for a delicious braised pork belly. We serve it on handmade Chinese buns, but you can easily either buy buns in almost any Asian supermarket, or simply slice it and serve it as is for lunch, dinner, or just about anything else. The quality of the pork is critical to the flavor of the finished dish—if you can get pork from free-running hogs, preferably from heirloom breeds, go for it. It costs a bit more, but it tastes about ten times better!

Overnight marinade:

2 tablespoons kosher salt

2 tablespoons palm sugar

1 pound pork belly, skinned (you can order it this way from your butcher)

Braised pork:

4 cups boiling water

1 ½ ounces dried shiitake mushrooms

2 tablespoons lard

2 tablespoons palm sugar

1 tablespoon Shaoxing cooking wine or dry sherry

¾-inch piece fresh ginger, skin left on and sliced

1 star anise

2 dried red chiles

2 whole cloves

3 Sichuan peppercorns

2-inch strip fresh orange peel, preferably mandarin orange, chopped

1 cinnamon stick

2 scallions, chopped

½ cup light-colored soy sauce to taste (not light-sodium soy sauce, but use Chinese light-colored soy sauce)

Make the marinade:

In a medium bowl, combine the kosher salt and palm sugar. Rub the pork belly on all sides with the rub and marinate the pork belly overnight in the refrigerator.

Make the braised pork:

In a medium heat-proof bowl, pour the boiling water over the dried mushrooms. Soak, covered, for 30 minutes. Strain the mushrooms, reserving the liquid. Rinse and clean the mushrooms. Slice them thinly and set aside.

In a large shallow pot, melt the lard over medium heat. Sprinkle the palm sugar over the hot lard and stir in to melt. Watch this closely so it does not burn. When the sugar has become a caramel-brown color, turn up the heat slightly, add the marinated pork belly, and quickly sear it on both sides. The pork belly will have a reddish-brown gloss. Remove the browned pork belly from the pot and set it aside on a large plate, discarding any excess grease from the pot.

Add the belly back into the same pot along with any juice it collected while being set aside. Splash in the Shaoxing wine and the strained mushroom liquid. Any browned bits on the bottom of the pot will add to the flavor. There should be enough water to just cover the pork belly. (The water doesn't have to cover the belly entirely but should cover it at least ¾ of the way. If short of mushroom water, just add some plain water to cover.)

Add the ginger, star anise, chiles, cloves, peppercorns, orange peel, cinnamon stick, and scallions and mix gently. Add the soy sauce and reserved mushrooms and mix again. The flavor should be fairly intense and may (at this stage) be a bit saltier than you'd normally eat.

Bring the pot to a boil, then turn down the heat to a rapid simmer. Cover the pot and allow to simmer for at least 2 ½ hours. At this point, the pork belly will be ready. If you'd like a thicker sauce to serve with the pork, strain some of the braising sauce into a small pan and reduce over moderately high heat until it's reached the desired consistency.

At the San Street cart, we serve sliced pork belly along with pickled Chinese mustard greens, fresh cilantro and crushed peanuts on steamed Chinese buns. Alternatively you can cut and serve it with rice or vegetables on the side—using the braising liquid as a sauce to spoon over top.

BLC—THE 24-7

Since ZingTrain is where we developed and teach Bottom-Line Change (see page 337), and since BLC stands, in my mind, for "bacon, lettuce, and cheese," I couldn't really resist putting this sandwich into this book. And since the best time to use Bottom-Line Change is pretty much all the time, I figured this 24–7 combo was too perfect to pass up. The numbers in the name come from the bacon we use (Nueske's applewood-smoked bacon that spends 24 hours in the smokehouse) and Tony and Julie Hook's seven-year aged cheddar from Mineral Point, Wisconsin. You can substitute any high-quality bacon or cheddar, though of course, the quality of those two ingredients (along with the bread) is really the key to the sandwich.

2 to 4 slices applewood-smoked bacon

2 slices really good sandwich bread

2 slices well-aged cheddar cheese

2 tablespoons mayonnaise

Handful of good lettuce

Cook the bacon in a frying pan until done. Remove the bacon, reserving the fat in the pan. Return the pan to the heat.

Assemble the sandwich with the cheese, give it a gentle press together with your palm and slide it into the hot bacon fat in the pan. Weigh it down with a bowl and fry until golden brown. Flip, brown the other side, and remove from pan.

Carefully open the sandwich and add the mayonnaise, lettuce, and bacon. Cut the sandwich in half, and eat it while it's hot!

ESPRESSO MOUSSE

This is one of the most popular new desserts we've done at the Roadhouse in a long time. A really light espresso mousse served in a cappuccino cup, topped with a thin layer of dark chocolate and a dollop of real whipped cream. It's really not all that hard to make and it is really delicious. Like an elegant cup of coffee and dessert all in one!

4 shots espresso, plus enough water to bring the volume up to ½ cup

¼ cup cold water

1 ¼ teaspoons powdered gelatin

¼ cup boiling water

2 eggs

6 tablespoons sugar

2 ¼ cups heavy whipping cream

½ vanilla bean, seeds scraped and reserved

6 ounces chocolate (we use a 62 percent cacao)

Combine the espresso and ¼ cup of cold water in a bowl. Sprinkle gelatin slowly onto surface of espresso mix. Stir gently and set aside to let soften for 10–15 minutes.

When the gelatin has softened, add ¼ cup hot water and stir until gelatin has dissolved and you can no longer see granules in the liquid. Put the bowl with the gelatin mixture over an ice bath, whisking occasionally.

Meanwhile, separate egg yolks and whites. Whisk yolks with half of the sugar until pale yellow and fluffy. Whip 1 ¼ cups of the cream with the scraped vanilla bean seeds until you get soft peaks. Whip egg whites with remaining half of the sugar until you get soft peaks.

Fold the egg yolks into the gelatin mixture, then fold in the whipped cream, and finally fold in egg whites. Portion the mousse (about ⅔ cup each) into small dessert or coffee cups and refrigerate overnight or at least 3 hours to allow to set up.

When you are ready to serve the mousse, melt the chocolate over low heat. Whip the remaining cream until you get soft peaks.

Pour about 1 tablespoon of the melted chocolate over each mousse (depending on the size of your dessert cups—you'll want a thin layer of chocolate), tilting the cup so the chocolate covers the entire surface of the mousse. Top with a dollop of whipped cream and serve.

ZZANG BAR

I was struggling to come up with a recipe to put in here for Zingerman's Candy Manufactory when I realized that the answer was, literally, at my fingertips all along. This is the easiest recipe in the book and is guaranteed to be really good every time!

4 Zzang Bars, preferably one each: original Zzang, Cashew Cow, Wowza, and What the Fudge

Carefully consider which of the four bars you want to eat, thoughtfully weighing the contrast in flavors and matching those to your taste.

Gently remove the bar of your choosing from the stack. Holding it in your off hand (so your left hand if you're right-handed, and vice versa if you're not), tear open the box. Remove the foil-wrapped candy bar. Tear the foil, taking care not to crush the bar. Pull the bar at least partially out of the foil. Take a second to appreciate the aroma, then take a nice bite. Notice all the different flavors you get in your mouth as you chew. Pause to reflect. Take another bite. Repeat until you're feeling really good, or until the bar is gone.

"chewy, crunchy, sweet, salty and highly addictive—this luscious handmade candy bar puts the vending machine stuff to shame."

—O, The Oprah Magazine

Zingerman's mission statement

we share the zingerman's experience
selling food that makes you happy
giving service that makes you smile
in passionate pursuit of our mission
showing love and care in all our actions
to enrich as many lives as we possibly can

Appreciations

As you may know—either from working here, coming to a ZingTrain seminar, or from reading the first volume of this series—at Zingerman's we end every meeting with a few minutes of appreciations. It's easy to do—anyone who likes can appreciate anyone who comes to mind. It's become such a big part of the way we work that I decided to include it in any book I do as well. So here, at the end of this one, is a list—incomplete as always—of all the people I appreciate for their help, insight, assistance, patience, and support through this whole process.

I'll start off first with those I've inadvertently forgotten to list here by name. Please know that, even if my memory has, in the moment, failed, my intentions are good. And I know that there are thousands of co-workers, customers, writers, musicians, professors, pets, and poets out in the world who, unbeknownst to them, have left a mark on my mind. I appreciate them for being themselves and for so generously helping me be me.

More directly and to the point, I very much appreciate Paul—without him there would be no Zingerman's. We've been at it for nearly thirty years now—no small thing in the food world, where most businesses go under in twelve months or less, and in which long-lasting, productive partnerships are very few and even farther between. Thanks to all of the now thousands of people who've been a part of Zingerman's over all these years, from Marci Fribourg and Ricky Cohen who worked the first day the Deli was open on Detroit Street, to Mike Vianneva who was the last person hired before this book went to press.

Thanks to everyone who's worked on making this book a book—to Meg Noori for great editing, insight, support, to Jim Reische for additional editing and patient insight, Pete Sickman-Garner for leading all the art work, Nicole Robichaud and Liz Lester for great design, and Ian Nagy and Ryan Stiner for the amazing illustrations. Well-designed appreciation also to Betsy Bruner, Billie Lee, Hannah Metler, and Erica Bertram for all their supportive creativity.

Thanks to all the managing partners at Zingerman's for collaboratively constructing an organization great enough that I could actually write a book about it: Frank Carollo, Amy Emberling, John Loomis, Grace Singleton, Alex Young, Rodger Bowser, Allen Leibowitz, Charlie Frank, Rick Strutz, Steve Mangigian, Mo Frechette, Tom Root, Toni Morell, Stas' Kazmierski, and, last but most definitely not at all least, Maggie Bayless. I'm pretty sure that without ZingTrain very little of what's in here would exist, at least not in such a teachable, explainable, and usable way, and without Maggie there would be no ZingTrain. More thanks go to Ron Maurer, our one and only vice president of administration, whose arrival at Zingerman's in 2000 is certainly one of the best things that's ever happened to us.

Thanks to Richard Kempter and Marge Greene for much of the wisdom that underlies what's in here and for helping me to make my life far more fun and much more rewarding.

Thanks to Anese Cavanaugh for Bootist insight, great energy, daring to engage, and good ideas. Thanks for friendship, advice, insight, and good emails to Molly Stevens, Randolph Hodgson, Heather Porter Engwall, Lex Alexander, Daphne Zepos, Karen Pernick, Marifer Calleja, Michele DeLia. Additional appreciation to Keith Ewing, Wayne Baker, Majid Mahjoub, Dean Tucker, Edgar Schein, Jack Stack, Chip Conley, Robert Greenleaf, Peter Block, Skip LeFauve, John T. Edge, Dan Gillotte, and a fair few other folks whom I'm sure I'm forgetting but can't recall right now. Thanks to Patrick Hoban for all the good leadership dialogue and ongoing elbowing. Thanks to Marcia Labrenz for proofing help. Thanks within Zingerman's to Vanessa Sly, Fionna Gault, Amos Arinda, Lynn Yates, Gauri Thergaonkar, Masha Odinostova, Dana Laidlaw, Mike White, Heather Kendrick, Ann Lofgren, and Ally Hurst for reading essays and offering insights.

Thanks to professors William Rosenberg, Arthur Mendel, Roman Szporluk, and Carl Proffer for teaching me history many years ago. Thanks, too, to Professor Jesse Cohn in Indiana for sharing his work on the anarchists.

A few thousand freely given thanks to all the anarchists who've lent their words, insights, and ideas to the world: Emma Goldman, Alexander Berkman, Mikhail Bakunin, Peter Kropotkin, Voltairine de Cleyre, Nestor Makhno, Rudolf Rocker, Étienne de La Boétie, Murray Bookchin, Paul Avrich, Joseph Ishill, Gustav Landauer, Élie and Élisée Reclus, and all the other insightful anarchists who were writing about this stuff so long ago. Thanks to Julie Herrada at the Labadie Collection for all her help in tracking down relevant anarchist writing. Special appreciation to Bo Burlingham, another modern-day lapsed anarchist, for insight and inspiration. Thanks to Jo Labadie, the peaceful and inspirational Michigan anarchist who donated his archive of books and pamphlets to the University of Michigan in 1911. Thanks to Agnes Inglis, who worked for many years to make the Labadie Collection a living archive that people like me could access.

Many thanks to Jan Longone, whose support, good spirit, and commitment to good food and food history have contributed enormously to Zingerman's over all the years. Like Jo Labadie, she donated her collection to the University. If you spend time in Ann Arbor, consider visiting the Longone and Labadie Collections at the University of Michigan libraries.

Special thanks to Dawna Markova for making time to write the foreword. As I said to Dawna, busy as she always is, "You're Emma Goldman's only niece, I'm the only one who's writing about the anarchists and leadership, you happen to teach leadership to organizations in ways that are very compatible to ours, and this book has more about your Aunt Emma than any other I'm going to do." Fortunately, she agreed. I really appreciate her carving out the time to do so. Thanks, too, to Lawson Drinkard III for putting me and Dawna in touch in the first place.

Super special thanks to Jenny Tubbs for keeping tabs on, and leading, the behind-the-scenes work that has made it possible for you to be holding this book in your hands.

And, again, thanks to you for reading!

COMING NEXT

in the *Zingerman's Guide to Good Leading Series*

ZINGERMAN'S GUIDE TO GIVING GREAT SERVICE

"When it comes to service, few establishments can rival Zingerman's." —Saveur

Eighty percent of complaining customers are unhappier after they complain. Why? How do you deal with tough customers? Or really good ones? Here's our quick guide to treating customers like royalty. It details our recipes for giving great service and for effectively handling customer complaints. There are plenty of usable, teachable tips and tools that are applicable for service providers in organizations of any size, in any industry.

paperback
$16.95

Customer Service Training DVDs
$350/ea. or both for **$500**

ZINGERMAN'S 3 STEPS TO GIVING GREAT SERVICE

e share our core customer service concepts m The Art of Giving Great Service Seminar a fun and memorable lesson that will get ur organization started building great service ills and culture into every single element of ur organizational activity.

ast year, I showed it to my employees at the art of our busy season, and we saw an 18% crease in sales! It's the best tool I've found to courage great service."

DIANE RIEHM, RIEHM FARMS, TIFFIN, OH

ZINGERMAN'S 5 STEPS TO EFFECTIVELY HANDLING A COMPLAINT

Our service recipe will help take the stress out of one of the most challenging encounters in customer service. With practice, and using Zingerman's easy-to-follow recipe, you can start seeing complaints as gifts rather than as trials.

"We recently purchased the 5 Steps to Effectively Handling a Complaint video and have incorporated it immediately into our customer service training for our frontline staff."

—PERRY SPENCER, UNIVERSITY OF MICHIGAN HOSPITAL SECURITY

AVAILABLE AT WWW.ZINGTRAIN.COM

Can you name the one
NATIONALLY RECOGNIZED
LEADERSHIP TRAINING PROGRAM
that
wins rave reviews from:

- Bootstrapping Entrepreneurs
- Corporate CEOs
- Nonprofit Leaders
- Bankers
- Busboys
- Creative Attorneys
- Public School Teachers
- Successful Restaurateurs
- Psychology Professors
- Booksellers
- Food Co-op General Managers
- MBAs
- Nationally Known Business Writers
- Naval Engineers
- Bartenders
- Training Professionals
- Liberal Arts Majors
- Anarchists
- And Food Lovers from all over the world?

Only one that we know of! **Zing**TRAIN

www.zingtrain.com

notes

1999

Led by managing partners tom root and toni morell, zingermans.com goes online.

as demand for zingtrain seminars and workshops continues to grow, stas' kazmierski joins zingtrain as maggie's co-managing partner.

2000

amy emberling, one of the original bakers and founder of the pastry kitchen, returns to zingerman's bakehouse as co-managing partner.

2002

zingerman's mail Order and zingermans.com merge to become one business headed by to toni, mo, and Jude.

2001

zingerman's creamery opens up in manchester, mi and cheesemaker and managing partner john Loomis begins making fresh cheeses.

2007

deli restaurant manager rick strutz joins grace as co-managing partner at the deli.

On march 15, zingerman's celebrates our 25th anniversary with a 6,000-person street fair on detroit street outside the deli, featuring guests and friends from our first quarter century. we sold 3,044 reubens and 1,241 cappuccinos!

zingerman's launches our 2020 vision charting the course for the zingerman's community of businesses for the next 13 years.

"bon appétit" bestows their lifetime achievement award on ari and paul (previous winners include such food luminaries as alice waters, jacques pépin, and Julia child!)

2006

bake!, ann arbor's hands-on teaching bakery and cake!, a showroom worthy of the imagination-defying creations from the bakehouse cake designers, open at zingerman's bakehouse.

for the first time, produce from alex young's cornman farms highlights the roadhouse's annual harvest dinner.

2008

zingerman's coffee company manager steve mangigian joins allen as co-managing partner of the business.

zingerman's is featured on Oprah's sandwich episode and #97 Lisa C.'s boisterous brisket is Oprah's favorite, rating an "11" on a scale of 1-5.

2012

we publish volume 2 of zingerman's guide to good leading: "a Lapsed anarchist's approach to being a better leader."

we celebrate our 30th anniversary.

Zingerman's
celebrating
30
years